University of Pittsburgh
at Greensburg
Millstein Library

STRESS MANAGEMENT FOR THE HEALTHY TYPE A
THEORY AND PRACTICE

STRESS MANAGEMENT
FOR THE HEALTHY TYPE A

THEORY AND PRACTICE

ETHEL ROSKIES

Foreword by Richard S. Lazarus

The Guilford Press
New York   London

© 1987 The Guilford Press
A Division of Guilford Publications, Inc.
200 Park Avenue South, New York, N.Y. 10003

Printed in the United States of America

Last digit is print number: 9   8   7   6   5   4   3   2   1

Library of Congress Cataloging-in-Publication Data
Roskies, Ethel.
    Stress management for the healthy type A.

    Bibliography: p.
    Includes index.
    1. Coronary heart disease—Prevention.   2. Stress
(Psychology)—Prevention.   3. Type A behavior.
I. Title. [DNLM: 1. Stress, Psychological—therapy.
2. Type A Personality. WM 172 R821s]
RC685.C6R68   1987   616.1'205   86-31856
ISBN 0-89862-689-7

TO JOHN

Foreword

It is a great pleasure for me to do a foreword for Ethel Roskies's new book, *Stress Management for the Healthy Type A*. Professor Roskies spent a year with me at Berkeley about 10 years ago soaking up our group's outlook and contributing to our collective thought and research. We did an article together on the teaching of coping skills. At that time she was at an early stage of her involvement with behavioral medicine and her clinical intervention efforts with type A persons. One could see that she would later play an important role in this field, given her thoughtfulness and her ability to sense quickly and accurately how people were managing their lives, and to articulate her insights. The auspicious beginnings have now flowered into an impressive program of stress management and research, portrayed in this clear, instructive, and enjoyable book.

The field of behavioral medicine is, in large part, organized around two interrelated questions: (1) Does the way we live have important short- and long-term effects on mental and physical health? (2) Assuming that it does, can we successfully intervene to prevent or treat harmful effects of recurrent or chronic high stress and inadequate or counter-productive ways of coping with them? These two questions are really what this book is all about, addressed specifically to type A phenomena.

Roskies's answer to the two basic questions is yes. Although she deals with theory and research on type A, by far the larger portion of the book is devoted to a description of the therapeutic program designed to eliminate what is pathogenic in type A without endangering the positive personal and social commitments that type As greatly value. This selectivity is one of Roskies's creative contributions; the program makes no assault on the basic type A values but only addresses tendencies that are presumably harmful. Therefore, the motivation of the type A person to change is not undermined.

Although she reviews research and theory on type A, and has in the past been wary of unsubstantiated claims by protagonists of stress management (Roskies, 1983a), Roskies adopts the only stance possible for one who does intervention: the two articles of faith that certain features of type A are dangerous to one's health and that intervention can help vulnerable people to preserve their lives and health. The evidence, of course, is mixed. The contrary position would be that type A and stress—and perhaps even the current enthusiasms of diet and exercise—are if anything really minor factors in heart disease. I don't fault Roskies for her articles of faith; she has outstanding credentials, more experience with type As than most, and some evidence for her claims.

Professionals wanting to begin or improve their interventions will be delighted with Roskies's down-to-earth description of the clinical problems faced in group stress management programs and how she skillfully handles them. She describes, for example, what should be done with clients who miss sessions, the number of clients that are ideal for a therapy group, and what to expect from those who are overly enthusiastic and those who are unimpressed or resistant. Particularly appealing is her attention to the rationale for each procedure and recommendation. Roskies has an engaging tendency to think out loud about problems and solutions, and to acknowledge her own uncertainties when they crop up. Welcome too, especially to me, is the fact that she embeds her concrete decisions in a coherent theoretical framework of cognitive appraisal and coping skills training. She also frequently relates her recommendations to the clinical wisdom of others, such as Donald Meichenbaum, whose ideas about the cognitive behavior therapist as teacher she has emulated.

What emerges, therefore, is not merely a set of intervention techniques for a limited problem, type A, but a broad and systematic approach to stress management that reflects the most advanced state of the art. She enlivens what she terms "the nuts and bolts of treatment" by colorful visual aids. Each chapter of Part II of the book, which presents the "how to" material, addresses practial issues of treatment such as how to modify and control the physical response to stress, how to modify and control the cognitive response to stress, applying what has been learned to the pressures of living, facilitating pleasure in living, and making what has been learned a lifetime objective.

Stress management programs such as this one cannot, of course, be a panacea for all problems of human adaptation, dysfunction, and distress. One suspects that a high proportion of persons with what used to be referred to as neurotic or existential problems of living, those with hidden or unconscious agendas, deeply in conflict, uncertain about what they want and who they are—in short, the sort of person for whom psychoanalytic and existential treatment always seemed most suited—will probably not benefit much from what Roskies offers. In all likelihood, the kinds of people who will gain the most from the best of such programs are those who already function pretty well, whose lives are reasonably well directed, whose patterns of thought, feeling, and motivation are in fairly good harmony, and whose actions are generally in pretty good correspondence with the social environments in which they operate. Those individuals who can do better in the face of the stresses of living are probably legion and have, until now, not been a constituent of any major therapeutic program.

Richard S. Lazarus

Preface

Compared to other populations for whom stress management programs have been devised, the managerial and professional type As with whom I work do not live in unusually stressful life circumstances; nor do they manifest obvious deficiencies in coping resources. On the contrary, because of the many activities that they undertake and their success in accomplishing them, these men and women can be considered as prototypes of the competent coper. Unfortunately for their health and well-being, however, this competency is achieved at high personal cost; by using their abundant energy indiscriminately and inefficiently, these type As not only increase their vulnerability to future heart disease but also experience unnecessary psychological and physical distress in the present. The aim of the stress program presented in this book is to reduce the "costs of coping" for the healthy type A, by teaching him or her new and better ways of managing the inevitable hassles of everyday life.

This program does not contain any techniques that are particularly new or exotic; in fact, one of its advantages for practitioners is that the individual techniques employed are widely used (e.g., progressive relaxation, problem solving) and likely to be familiar to most clinicians trained in behavioral methods. There are three novel aspects to this program, however: (1) its use of stress theory to achieve greater specificity of diagnosis and treatment goals; (2) the manner in which the individual techniques are organized into a structured and hierarchical learning program; and (3), most important of all, the attention devoted to arousing and sustaining motivation for change in a "hard to reach" target population.

The primary audience for this book would be therapists working, or interested in working, specifically with healthy type As. The therapist's task is further facilitated by the availability of a workbook, *Stress Management for the Healthy Type A: A Skills-Training Program* (The Guilford Press, 1987), designed to be used directly by program participants. The workbook contains the program rationales and the homework assignments.

The book is also likely to be of interest to therapists involved in stress management programs with other populations, for this book is not solely a manual of what to do but also considers why and how it is done. Thus, the therapist who has grasped the general principles of program design can then adapt these techniques and procedures to treatment of other problems and populations.

In writing a treatment book for the professional, I am aware that I am stepping on dangerous ground. Therapists not only come in a variety of theoretical persuasions, but they also vary greatly in experience. The imaginary therapist for whom I wrote this book is one who already possesses basic training, but who is a novice in working with healthy type As, and maybe in conducting stress management programs. Even for more experienced therapists, however, it may be useful to review some of the basic assumptions and procedures of treatment.

My understanding of stress, stress management, and the type A behavior pattern has developed over a long period of time, and I am indebted to many people who contributed to my education. Foremost among them is Richard Lazarus, both because of his major contributions to stress theory and because of the model of intellectual rigor and honesty that he has provided. Ray Rosenman, too, was very helpful in fostering my initial attempts to treat type As and in introducing me to the literature. Much of my work with type As has been conducted with cotherapists and I have learned from all of them; I have also benefited, albeit sometimes reluctantly, from the trenchant questions and critiques of my collaborators (Robert Oseasohn, Pete Seraganian, and Jim Hanley) on the Montreal Type A Intervention Project. Normand Martin, a graduate student, forced me to clarify my thinking in responding to his questions and criticisms; he also contributed concretely to this book by providing the cartoons for the homework assignments. Most of all, however, my understanding of the healthy type A, and how best to treat him or her, comes from the many men and women who have participated in these programs.

The research projects in which this program was developed have been financed over the years mainly by Health and Welfare, Canada. The actual writing of this book was facilitated by a Leave Fellowship from the Social Sciences and Humanities Research Council, Ottawa. I am grateful for their support, both financial and moral.

It is customary at this point for the author to express his or her appreciation for the help, understanding, and support received from family and friends. My husband, John Stonehewer, amply deserves this public expression of gratitude because his support played a vital role in every step of this book's production, from initial conceptualization to final proof reading. Even more important, however, has been his contribution as role model for what I was trying to achieve via this program; it is John who has provided me with a living daily reminder that a quiet manner and a reflective stance can be more effective than indiscriminate, frenzied activity.

Ethel Roskies
November 1986

Contents

PART ONE. THEORY   1

Chapter 1. The Healthy Type A: A New Type of Client   3
Coronary Heart Disease: Incidence and Etiology,   4
Type A: Some General Considerations,   5
Precursors to Type A,   6
The Contribution of Friedman and Rosenman,   7
Subsequent Developments in Type A Research,   10
Conclusions,   26

Chapter 2. Stress Management: A New Approach to
Treatment   27
Conceptions of Stress Problems,   28
The Teaching of Coping Skills,   37
Conclusions,   45

Chapter 3. Development of a Stress Management
Program for Healthy Type As   47
Diagnosis and Prescription,   47
Structuring a Treatment Program,   51

PART TWO. PRACTICE   61

Chapter 4. The Nuts and Bolts of Treatment   63
Practical Considerations in Treatment,   63
Problem Situations,   74
Physician, Heal Thyself,   78

Chapter 5. Introduction to the Program   80
Before the Session,   80
Introductions,   80
Reconceptualizing the Problem,   81
Clarifying the Process of Change,   84
Concluding Comments,   84
Program Facsimiles,   85

Chapter 6. Modifying Physical Responses to Stress   102
Awareness of Variations in Bodily Tension,   103
The Relaxation Exercise,   106
Shorter Relaxation Exercises,   110

Relaxation as a Coping Skill,   111
Concluding Comments,   112
Program Facsimiles,   113

Chapter 7. Controlling Behavioral Responses to Stress   124
Awareness of Behavioral Tension,   125
Rationale for Managing Behavioral Tension,   126
Modifying Behavior in One Specific Situation,   127
Controlling Behavior in Several Situations,   129
Controlling Time-Hurry Behavior,   131
Concluding Comments,   132
Program Facsimiles,   133

Chapter 8. Modifying Cognitive Responses to Stress   146
Awareness of Self-Talk,   147
Rationale for Modifying Self-Talk,   148
Modifying Self-Talk,   149
Modifying Self-Talk and Behavior,   152
The Carrot versus the Whip,   153
Concluding Comments,   154
Program Facsimiles,   155

Chapter 9. Applying Stress Management Skills   167
Awareness of Recurrent Stress Triggers,   167
Rationale for Learning to Plan for Stress,   169
Preparing for One Specific Stress Situation,   170
Stress Preparation as a General Coping Style,   172
Coping with Stress Emergencies,   173
Coping with Frustration,   174
Concluding Comments,   175
Program Facsimiles,   176

Chapter 10. Planning for Pleasure   197
Creating a Psychological Balance Sheet,   198
Rationale for Learning to Program Pleasures,   199
Building Pleasures into the Daily Routine,   200
Stress and Restoration,   203
The Carrot versus the Whip (continued),   204
Concluding Comments,   204
Program Facsimiles,   205

Chapter 11. Stress Management: A Lifelong Objective   219
Accepting Credit for Change,   219
Coping with an Unchanged Environment,   220
Relapse Prevention,   222
Concluding Comments,   227
Program Facsimiles,   228

References   237

Index
    247

STRESS MANAGEMENT FOR THE HEALTHY TYPE A
THEORY AND PRACTICE

PART ONE
THEORY

The intervention presented in this book applies a novel treatment approach (stress management) to a new and atypical psychotherapy clientele (the healthy type A). The first part of the book describes and seeks to clarify the key theoretical constructs (the type A behavior pattern, stress, and stress management) on which the treatment program is based. This attention to theoretical underpinnings reflects my belief that effective intervention is not simply a matter of mechanically administering techniques (even good ones) but, instead, must be based on a clear understanding of both the problem being treated and the remedy proposed. To effectively treat the healthy type A, one must first delineate what requires change in the type A behavior pattern and why, as well as the possibilities and limits of stress management.

Unfortunately for the reader, however, the type A and stress literatures constitute two very different and quite separate research traditions, sharing only the dubious distinction that each is complex and controversial in its own right. To reduce this confusion to manageable proportions, I have treated the two topics sequentially, with Chapter 1 devoted to the type A behavior pattern and Chapter 2 to stress theories and treatment approaches to stress problems. In each case I first examine the confusion and controversy that surround the key concepts, and then focus on the elements in each relevant to the construction of a treatment program. Chapter 3 fits the two separate strands together, showing how stress management treatment, as I have defined it, can be applied to the specific coping problems of the healthy type A. The chapter ends with a general overview of the resulting treatment program.

1. The healthy type A: A new type of client

Most people who seek psychological help do so either because they want to change something in their behavior or situation, or because someone with authority insists that change is required. For obesity, anxiety, or depression, it is usually the client himself or herself who identifies a problem requiring professional help, while for the underachieving schoolchild or the alcoholic employee, the task of identification is assumed by a family member, teacher, or employer. In sharp contrast to the typical client, however, the healthy type As with whom I work generally do not identify themselves as sick or deviant, nor are they so considered by their families, co-workers, or even their doctors. On the contrary, these men and women are so full of energy and activity that they give the impression of being superhealthy.

Even a short interview reveals the mental alertness, emotional expressiveness, and rapid pace of thought and speech of these clients. Their ability to fulfill valued social roles is also noteworthy. All hold responsible positions, and most add to their job demands a host of family obligations and community activities. In spite of these multiple pressures, there are remarkably few complaints of anxiety and depression. Some go so far as to state that they thrive on challenge and tight deadlines—the more the better. Others do feel pressured, but consider external constraints to be necessary spurs for overcoming their perceived "slothfulness" and for maintaining productivity. Even when the type A does experience malaise, be it in the form of tight shoulder muscles or difficulty in falling asleep, the usual tendency is to minimize the degree of discomfort and to accept it as a necessary part of the "stress of modern life."

Seeking to intervene in the lives of men and women as well-functioning as these would be patently irresponsible, unless there was strong evidence of health risk serious enough to outweigh the psychological and social dangers inherent in upsetting an existing equilibrium. The rest of this chapter is devoted to a review of the evidence establishing the type A behavior pattern (TABP) as such a health risk. The data are complex and often contradictory, but I shall attempt to present them as clearly and succinctly as possible.

Coronary heart disease: Incidence and etiology

The two symptomatic forms of coronary heart disease (CHD) are angina pectoris (i.e., severe chest pain) and myocardial infarction (i.e., heart attack). Together they constitute a severe medical and social problem for Western countries. The most serious consequence of heart disease is death, and approximately half a million Americans die from heart disease each year. Approximately one quarter of these deaths occur in persons under age 65, establishing death from CHD as the largest single cause of premature mortality in the United States (National Center for Health Statistics, 1982).

Even for those fortunate enough to survive an initial heart attack, the negative impact is severe for the individual concerned, his or her family, and society in general. Financially, there are the direct costs of the coronary care unit and possibly subsequent surgery, while indirect costs include the inability to work for at least several months and, for some, permanent occupational disability, total or partial. Psychologically, there is likely to be some impairment in quality of life, such as reduced sexual activity and deterioration in family relationships (see Hackett & Cassem, 1975). Finally, there is the realistic fear of a subsequent heart attack; among survivors of an initial episode, more than one in three will suffer a second potentially fatal infarction within 5 years (Goldberg, Szklo, Tonascia, & Kennedy, 1979).

Mortality from CHD appears to be a product of Western civilization in this century. Myocardial infarction, or heart attack, was relatively rare until the beginning of this century, but since the early 1920s the increase in mortality rates due to CHD has far outstripped population increases, and the incidence of CHD reached pandemic proportions in the 1950s and 1960s (Anderson, 1973). In recent years CHD mortality rates have begun to decline in the United States, though it is unclear whether there is an actual decrease in incidence of disease, or simply more survivors due to improved medical treatment (Marx & Kolata, 1978).

Coronary heart disease, by definition, is the result of an inadequate supply of oxygen to the heart. While the reasons for this deficiency are not completely understood (Herd, 1978; Obrist, 1981), a major cause is the narrowing of the coronary arteries by the gradual accumulation of plaque or scaling on their walls. The process of plaque accumulation is a slow one, occurring over a 20- to 40-year period, and multiple risk factors contribute to it.

CHD risk factors can be divided into those that are beyond the control of the individual (e.g., familial history of heart disease, advancing age, male sex, presence of diabetes mellitus) and those that are partially or completely under individual control (e.g., smoking, elevated serum cholesterol, uncontrolled hypertension, obesity, and possibly lack of exercise). Risk factors interact synergistically to multiply the probability of heart disease; according to the data of the Framingham epidemiological study, the presence of two risk factors increases the probability of developing CHD fourfold, and a person with three risk factors, such as a smoker with high blood pressure and elevated cholesterol level, is eight times as likely to develop CHD as a person with no risk factors (Kannel & Gordon, 1968).

The CHD risk factors mentioned so far have achieved wide acceptance among epidemiologists and are generally considered to be the standard risk factors (Stamler, Berkson, & Lindberg, 1972). Collectively, however, they account for less than half of the CHD incidents in middle-aged men, the population at highest risk for premature CHD in the United States (Jenkins, 1971). It is the need to identify and attempt to control the risk factors for the remaining 50% of CHD incidents that has led to exploration of possible behavioral and psychological influences.

Type A: Some general considerations

No risk factor for heart disease is completely beyond controversy, but the debate surrounding the type A concept has been particularly vitriolic. Some of the resistance is understandable on scientific grounds; behavior is much further removed from the disease end point than are the standard risk factors, and the physiological mechanisms linking the two are obscure. But, as a psychologist, it is tempting to speculate on other forces that may also be at work. In part, the resistance may be due to what is perceived as territorial infringement: Behavior comes from the soft, fuzzy science of psychology, rather than from the hard, precise, biomedical sciences, and it is pretentious for this interloper to claim to be as important a risk factor for a major physical disease as hypercholesteremia (elevated serum cholesterol levels) or hypertension (high blood pressure). Possible conflicts over territorial infringement become even likelier, of course, if behavioral modification, rather than conventional medical and surgical techniques, is seen as the treatment of choice for this new type of risk factor.

A second major issue is the personal involvement of most health professionals and scientists with type A behavior. When we speak of diabetes mellitus or smoking, we are speaking of other people, "them," "out there"; but when we talk about type A, in contrast, we are talking about ourselves. The writer of this book is a pronounced type A, and I suspect that a substantial proportion of readers would also fall under this classification. Moreover, there is considerable ambivalence about whether it is really that bad to be type A. Consciously, at least, we know that it is harmful to eat and drink too much, to smoke, to drive instead of walking, and so on. But can we really believe that it is harmful to be energetic, ambitious, hardworking, and achievement oriented? For many of us, these are the virtues learned at our mothers' knees!

This highly charged emotional context may help to illuminate the charges and countercharges that characterize the history to follow. The protagonists in this story are two San Francisco cardiologists, Meyer Friedman and Ray Rosenman. While the study of the role of emotional factors in the etiology of coronary heart disease did not begin or end with them, their contribution marks a watershed in our understanding. For this reason we shall use them as markers, conceptualizing the rest of the story in terms of precursors to and subsequent refinements of their work.

Precursors to type A

Scattered references to the role of emotional factors in the symptomatology of CHD can be found as early as the 18th century (Heberden, 1772), but the first clinical description of specific overt type A behaviors is found at the end of the last century in the work of Osler. As described by Osler (1892), the typical coronary patient is a "keen and ambitious man . . . whose engines are set at full speed ahead." In fact, Osler (1910) claimed that this pattern was sufficiently characteristic that he could make the presumptive diagnosis of angina pectoris in a new patient simply by his appearance and mannerisms as he entered the consulting room!

With the dramatic increase in coronary heart disease in the first half of this century, there was strong impetus for psychiatrists and the new breed of psychosomatic researchers to turn their interest to personality factors in heart disease. The Menningers (1936) studied patients with CHD and emphasized these clients' frequent exhibition of a strongly aggressive personality. Dunbar (1943), one of the pioneers of psychosomatic medicine, went even further, claiming that the hard-driving, goal-directed behavior of CHD patients constituted a coronary personality. Kemple (1945) not only confirmed the perception of the CHD patient as overly ambitious and compulsively striving to achieve goals that incorporate power and prestige, but suggested, as a motivation for this overdependence on external achievement, that it might be a compensation for deficiencies in "introversive experiences of creative thought."

In reading these assorted descriptions of the coronary personality, one is struck by the high degree of agreement between them, as well as their similarity to what later became known as the type A behavior pattern. However, unlike what was to follow, these clinical portraits remained largely outside the mainstream of CHD epidemiology and treatment. For one thing, the methods used to establish association did not conform to those used in the biomedical sciences. To cite but one example, Dunbar's designation of the coronary personality was based on subjective, not easily replicable interviews with a small, nonrepresentative sample of 22 cases, over 50% of whom shared a distinct cultural environment in that they were Jewish (Storment, 1951; Weiss, Dlin, Rollin, Fischer, & Bepler, 1957). Even more important, these reports only identified the coronary personality in individuals already suffering from heart disease. This after-the-fact diagnosis weakened the scientific validity of the finding, raising the possibility that the coronary personality was the result rather than the cause of heart disease. Furthermore, a diagnosis restricted to already-ill individuals was of limited practical value, since identification of the coronary personality could not be used to prevent and control the disease.

The contribution of Friedman and Rosenman

In contrast to the psychiatrists who preceded them, Friedman and Rosenman's primary training was in cardiology. As cardiologists espousing a behavior pattern as a major cause of CHD, they managed to ruffle the feathers of both the medical and the psychiatric establishments.[1] Nevertheless, to them goes the credit not only for the name currently in use, the type A behavior pattern (TABP), but also for making the TABP an essential part of CHD epidemiology and treatment. Their critical advance came in developing a reliable method for diagnosing type A behavior in *apparently healthy individuals*, and in demonstrating that this measure could be used to *predict CHD*. Subsequently, the debate might still continue about the importance of the TABP as a risk factor for CHD (see Report of the Joint Working Party

1. It is significant that neither Friedman nor Rosenman has ever held a major academic appointment in a medical school. The negative reaction of the psychiatric community to the prospect of cardiologists applying for federal grants to study psychological phenomena can be seen in the advice given to them to disarm the expected opposition by adopting the neutral, nonpsychological *type A* label for the behavior in question (Friedman, 1977).

of the Royal College of Physicians of London and the British Cardiac Society, 1976), but after Meyer Friedman and Ray Rosenman the TABP itself could no longer be ignored.

Friedman and Rosenman began their research careers in the 1950s, at the Harold Brunn Institute of Mount Zion Hospital in San Francisco, initially studying the relative cardiovascular risk of persons with elevated blood lipids. Many different reasons have been advanced for their shift to the study of personality factors, but my personal favorite is the apocryphal story of the upholsterer, called in to reupholster the chairs in their waiting room. As he went about his work, the upholsterer noted that only the first 3 inches of the chairs suffered from wear, and questioned Friedman and Rosenman about the line of business which led to a clientele with such peculiar sitting habits.

Whatever the cause for the intuition, Friedman and Rosenman began to reexamine their own coronary patients for common emotional and/or behavioral characteristics. As expected, they did find a distinguishing behavior pattern, one they defined as "an action–emotion complex that can be observed in any person who is aggressively involved in a chronic, incessant struggle to achieve more and more in less and less time, and if required to do so, against the opposing efforts of other things or other persons" (Friedman & Rosenman, 1974, p. 67). This definition of coronary-prone behavior differed from traditional psychiatric definitions of the coronary personality in two ways; first, the term *personality* was replaced by the phrase *an action–emotion complex*, making it closer to the level of observable behavior; and second, environmental influences, in the form of opposing things and persons, were accorded an important role in eliciting the pattern. In themselves, however, these differences were not sufficiently great to herald a major paradigmatic shift. What was new and original was the use made by Friedman and Rosenman of the type A concept.

For the first time, search for the coronary personality turned away from those already suffering from heart disease to apparently healthy individuals. Not only was the TABP identifiable in some persons who did not manifest signs or symptoms of clinical heart disease, but, in a series of studies comparing As versus Bs, Friedman and Rosenman demonstrated that even apparently healthy type A individuals manifested biochemical abnormalities characteristic of CHD. Healthy individuals classified as type A were more likely than non-type As to show elevated serum cholesterol and triglyceride levels and reduced blood clotting time (Friedman, Rosenman, & Carroll, 1958), more frequent and marked arcus senilis (Friedman & Rosenman, 1959), excessive catecholamine secretion during working hours (Friedman, St. George, Byers, & Rosenman, 1960), and marked sludging and capillary ischemia in conjunctival tissue (Friedman, Rosenman, & Byers, 1964). The cumulative findings of these studies provided support for two new and powerful ideas: Coronary behavior could precede the appearance of coronary disease, and biochemical pathways do exist by which behavior can influence susceptibility to CHD.

The time was ripe for a full-scale test of the hypothesis that type A behavior could predict CHD. What was lacking, however, was a short, reliable measure of type A behavior. Up to this point, Friedman and Rosenman had proceeded by furnishing a clinical description of the TABP and asking colleagues to identify individuals in whom the pattern was clearly present or absent. This procedure was adequate for gathering the small samples of extreme cases required for the biochemical studies, but it obviously could not be used in a full scale epidemiological study.

The Structured Interview (SI; Rosenman, 1978) was devised as the instrument for eliciting type A behavior in an economical, reliable fashion. The interview consists of 27 questions concerning daily activities: When you are in your car and the car in front of you is moving too slowly for you, what do you do? What bothers you most about your job and your associates? Has your wife ever asked you to slow down? In conducting this 15- to 20-minute interview, the role of the interviewer is very different from that of a typical clinical interviewer in that he or she is expected to be challenging, rather than sympathetic. The interviewer may deliberately interrupt to see how the respondent reacts, or, alternatively, may ask a question in a deliberately slow manner to see if the respondent jumps in. In fact, subsequent studies have shown that the SI serves as a stress situation for respondents, producing physiological reactions similar to those observed in reaction to other laboratory psychosocial stress tasks (Dembroski, MacDougall, & Lushene, 1979; Krantz et al., 1981).

On the basis of the SI, respondents are classified either as fully developed As (A_1), somewhat A (A_2), midway between A and B (X), or definitely non-A (B).[2] The scoring is based much more on the style of the response (e.g., loud, explosive voice; manifestations of hostility) than on interview content (Blumenthal, O'Toole, & Haney, 1984; Scherwitz, Berton, & Leventhal, 1977; Schuker & Jacobs, 1977). Essentially, the SI can be considered a measure of behavioral reactivity to a standardized psychosocial stress task.

The Western Collaborative Group Study (WCGS), begun in 1960, was the trial devised to assess the capacity of the TABP to predict heart disease. The sample for the study consisted of 3,154 apparently healthy California men, aged 39–59, mainly white, middle- and upper-level executives. Upon entry to the study, the men were classified either as

---

2. Initially there were two B classifications (B_3 and B_4), but probably because of the rarity of extreme Bs, these were later combined.

type A (n = 1,589) or as the more relaxed, easygoing type B (n = 1,565). After 8½ years of follow-up, 257 men had developed CHD; 178 of these were initially categorized as type A and 79 as type B. In short, in a sample of apparently healthy middle-aged men, type As were more than twice as likely to develop heart disease than were their type B counterparts (Rosenman et al., 1975). Moreover, the increased susceptibility of type As to heart disease also extended to significant augmentations in mortality risk (there were 25 CHD deaths during the course of the study and 22 were among type As) and, among survivors of an initial heart attack, the probability of experiencing a subsequent reinfarction.

One obvious objection to these findings is the possibility that the greater incidence of CHD among type As could be attributed, not to the behavior pattern itself, but to the greater prevalence of standard · risk factors among them, that is, the possibility that type As were more likely than type Bs to be smokers or uncontrolled hypertensives. However, further analysis of the data showed that the association between the TABP and CHD still held, even when other risk factors (such as smoking, hypertension, and dietary habits) were held constant through statistical means (Rosenman, Brand, Sholtz, & Friedman, 1976).

No single study, however dramatic its findings, can be accepted as conclusive proof that the TABP is a cause of CHD. Not only are multiple replications necessary, preferably with different types of samples, but much further work is required to refine the sensitivity and specificity of the diagnostic instrument, to clarify the biological mechanisms through which the behavior pattern works, and ultimately, to show that modification of the TABP also leads to changes in CHD morbidity and mortality. Nevertheless, in conducting the WCGS, Friedman and Rosenman had made a major breakthrough in demonstrating psychosomatic relationships: For the first time in medical history, a behavior pattern that was not directly associated with consumatory behaviors or clinical symptoms has successfully predicted the emergence of a major physical disease (Jenkins, 1978).

Subsequent developments in type A research

The publication of the final findings of the WCGS in 1975–1976 led to an explosion of interest in the TABP. While the intrinsic importance of the reports could account for some of this attention, there was also a conjuncture of circumstances that provided a particularly receptive climate. It was during the 1970s that government reports first underlined the importance of behavioral factors in chronic disease (Lalonde, 1974;

U.S. Department of Health and Human Services, 1979), and funds became available to support research in this area. At the same time, health professionals themselves were beginning to create the new interdisciplinary specialty of behavioral medicine (Schwartz & Weiss, 1978). For those eager to demonstrate the importance of biobehavioral relationships in the etiology and treatment of physical disorders, the TABP provided a textbook example.

Not surprisingly, the number of publications concerning the TABP rapidly multiplied. Surveying the type A literature between 1959 and 1979, Price (1982) reported that half of all the studies were published in the final quarter of that period. Based only on studies that I personally have come across, my guess is that the literature at least doubled again in the 1979–1985 period. To what has this outpouring been devoted?

Assessment of the TABP

As used in the WCGS, the SI appeared to have adequate reliability. Judgments by two raters on assignment to four categories (A_1, A_2, X, B) agreed in 64% of cases, while a binary A–B classification produced 84% agreement. The ratings were also stable over time, with 80% of men receiving the same classification after an interval of 12–20 months (Jenkins, Rosenman, & Friedman, 1968). Nevertheless, for the WCGS it was Rosenman himself who served as the final arbiter on type A ratings. If study of the TABP were to be extended to other centers, then means would have to be developed to teach the diagnostic techniques to others.

For a number of years, the Harold Brunn Institute conducted week-long training courses for prospective users of the SI. Interrater reliability between interviewers trained in this or similar fashion has proved satisfactory, ranging from .75 to .87 (Dembroski, MacDougall, Williams, Haney, & Blumenthal, 1985; Rosenman, 1978). However, the SI is expensive to learn and use, and its reliance on behavioral observation ran counter to the prevailing *Zeitgeist* of "objective" psychological testing. The need was for less expensive and less subjective diagnostic instruments.

The major paper-and-pencil test of the TABP, the Jenkins Activity Survey (JAS), was initially developed during the course of the WCGS using subsamples of study participants (Jenkins, 1978; Jenkins, Rosenman, & Friedman, 1967; Jenkins, Zyzanski, & Rosenman, 1971). While the items on it resemble the questions used in the SI, here one is measuring response content rather than style, and self-report rather than observation by another person. There are numerous forms of the test, for employed and nonemployed persons, for college students, and so on; but the original validation, against SI classifications and incidence of CHD, was based on the largely white, middle-class, middle-aged men of the WCGS.

The JAS-Form B contains 54 questions, but only 21 of these questions contribute to the global A score. The reason for this discrepancy is that discriminant function analyses were used to select and weigh items so as to mimic SI assessments; only 21 items were weighed heavily enough to contribute to total JAS scores. The traditional scoring of the test involves multiplying positive answers to each of the 21 key questions by their respective weights and then summing the scores to obtain a global type A score. An alternate, simpler procedure is to ignore the weights and simply sum positive responses to the 21 items. In addition to the global score, three subscores have been derived by factor analysis from the scores of the original validation sample (Zyzanski & Jenkins, 1970): Factor H (Hard-Driving Competitiveness), Factor S (Speed and Impatience), and Factor J (Job Involvement).

In contrast to the four-point classification of the SI, the JAS ranges individuals on a continuum, with high positive scores indicating strong A tendencies; and high negative scores, absence of type A characteristics (i.e., type B). Scores are standardized so that the mean of the A-B scores is zero with a standard deviation of 10. For the global A score, test–retest correlations across 1- to 4-year intervals fall between .60 and .70 (Jenkins, 1978).

In spite of its economy, and ease of administration and scoring, the JAS has not become the hoped-for replacement for the SI. First, and most important, the subscales of the JAS are not predictive of CHD (Jenkins, Rosenman, & Zyzanski, 1974), and even the global type A score is less predictive than the SI categorization (Brand, Rosenman, Jenkins, Sholtz, & Zyzanski, 1978). Second, the SI and the JAS appear to be measuring different aspects of the pattern (Matthews, 1982; Matthews, Krantz, Dembroski, & MacDougall, 1982), and of the two, it is the SI which is more closely related to exaggerated physiological stress reactivity, the presumptive mechanism linking the behavior pattern to CHD (Dembroski, MacDougall, Shields, Pettito, & Lushene, 1978; Krantz, Glass, Schaeffer, & Davia, 1982). Finally, the JAS does not appear to be an adequate measure of the anger–hostility dimension, which is increasingly coming to be seen as the TABP component most predictive of CHD (see subsequent discussion).

The Framingham Type A Scale, like the JAS, is a self-report inventory (Haynes, Levine, Scotch, Feinleib, & Kannel, 1978). It was developed, from a pool of 300 psychosocial questions already administered to participants in the Framingham Heart Study, in an attempt to replicate the findings of the WCGS, using the rich lode of Framingham CHD morbidity/mortality data. A panel of experts, knowledgeable with regard to the TABP, selected the 10 items that, in their opinion, best tapped type A behavior characteristics. When tested with the Framingham data, the scale did successfully predict heart disease, and it appears to bear the same relationship to the JAS and the SI that they bear to each other (Haynes, Feinleib, & Kannel, 1980). As a self-report inventory, it would appear to share both the advantages and the disadvantages of the JAS.

The Bortner Short Rating Scale (Bortner, 1969) is another attempt to assess the TABP via a self-report inventory, this time using 14 items of a semantic differential type. Instead of a simple yes or no, the respondent is asked to locate himself or herself in the space between two opposing extremes. The scale has been little used in North America, but one Belgian study reports 75% concordance with the SI (Rustin *et al.*, 1976) and claims that the scale has been successfully used to predict incidence of CHD (Belgian–French Pooling Project, 1984).

In addition to these formal diagnostic instruments, multiple attempts have been made to assess the TABP using conventional personality tests, such as the MMPI, the Gough Adjective Check List, the California Psychological Inventory, the Thurstone Temperament Schedule, and so on. In general, the correlations between these personality tests and other measures of the TABP have been disappointingly low (Matteson & Ivancevich, 1980).

For health professionals interested in treatment evaluation, none of the self-report inventories is really suitable for assessing treatment effects. The JAS, the Framingham, and the Bortner cannot be used for posttreatment versus pretreatment testing, because no clear interpretation is possible for any changes observed. To use the JAS as an example of the ambiguities, it is possible that an individual scoring higher on the JAS following intervention may have become more type A, but it is also possible that the higher score is simply the result of increased awareness of his or her type A behavioral characteristics. One scoring lower, on the other hand, may have modified his or her behavior, but it is equally possible that the individual concerned simply became more aware of the social desirability of a lowered score.

The SI was more predictive of CHD in the WCGS, it is more closely correlated with physiological hyperreactivity, and as such, it remains the gold standard of type A diagnostic instruments. For intervention evaluations, however, it suffers from the limitation of having only four points. Two recent attempts have been made to develop finer gradations for the interview. The first, by Friedman and his co-workers (Friedman & Powell, 1984), involves videotaping as well as recording the interview and employs a continuous scoring system based on 38 observable behaviors. The second scoring method, developed by Dembroski and his associates (Dembroski & MacDougall, 1983; Dembroski *et al.*, 1978), supplements the habitual global rating of type A behavior with six additional ratings of individual components of the behavior pattern (loudness, explosiveness, rapid/accelerated speech, quick latency of response, potential for hostility, and competitiveness), each on a five-point scale. Unfortunately, neither of these scoring methods has yet been tested for predictive validity, though Friedman's recent report (Friedman et al., 1984) indicates that a lowered score on his version of the SI is significantly correlated with reduced rate of CHD recurrence.

Replications and extensions of the WCGS findings

There are at least two prospective studies that have confirmed the ability of the TABP, as defined by one of the assessment techniques that have been described, to predict incidence of heart disease. On the other hand, there are two other major studies that have yielded negative findings.

The clearest confirmation of the WCGS findings comes from the Framingham Heart Study using the Framingham Type A Scale. Although this study, like the WCGS, was restricted to a U.S. sample, it was located at the opposite end of the country, and it contained women, blue-collar workers, and even the nonemployed, in addition to white-collar men. Using type A scores obtained from a sample of 1,674 men and women initially free from heart disease, researchers were able to verify the ability of these scores to predict CHD over an 8-year period. Type A men, aged 45–64, showed a twofold risk of angina, myocardial infarction, and CHD in general, compared to type B men (Haynes et al., 1980). Furthermore, the increased coronary risk associated with presence of the type A pattern was even stronger in women: Type A women had two times the rate of CHD and three times the rate of angina, compared to type B women (Haynes & Feinleib, 1980).

A second confirmation of WCGS findings was reported in a study that, like the WCGS, was also composed of employed males, though these were Belgian and French men instead of Californians. The instrument used to assess the presence of the TABP was the Bortner Short Rating Scale (Bortner, 1969). According to recently published data, the quarter of the sample scoring lowest on the Bortner (i.e., least type A) had an annual incidence of CHD of 5.4 per 1,000, compared to an annual incidence of 9.2 per 1,000 for the quarter of the sample with the highest type A scores (Belgian–French Pooling Project, 1984).

In contrast to these confirmatory findings, two other prospective studies, using samples of men already manifesting CHD or classified as high risk, reported no relationship between the TABP and increased risk of experiencing or dying from a heart attack. Data from the Multiple Risk Factor Intervention Trial (MRFIT), with a sample of men manifesting at least two of three specified CHD risk factors (smoking, high blood pressure, and high cholesterol), showed that the TABP was unrelated to 7-year incidence of CHD. This lack of relationship was evident regardless of whether the TABP was assessed by the SI or the JAS (Shekelle, Hulley, Neaton, Borhani, Lasser, Mittlemark, & Stamler, 1983). Similarly, data from the Aspirin Myocardial Infarction Study (AMIS) showed that, in a sample of survivors of a first myocardial infarction, type A men were of no greater risk of a second infarction or coronary death than their type B counterparts (Ruberman, Weinblatt, Goldberg, & Chaudbury, 1984).

In addition to these major prospective studies, there is one prospective confirmation of the relationship between behavior and CHD using a nonstandard type A assessment (Theorell, Lind, & Floderus, 1975), and also a host of prevalence studies with largely positive results (Cohen & Reed, 1985; Cohen, Syme, Jenkins, Kagan, & Zyzanski, 1979; Kenigsberg, Zyzanski, Jenkins, & Licciardello, 1974; Kornitzer, Kittel, DeBacker, & Dramaix, 1981; Magnus, Matroos, & Strackee, 1983). Another method of seeking to verify the relationship of the TABP to CHD has been to compare the extent of coronary atherosclerosis in type A and B patients undergoing diagnostic coronary angiography. Here the results have been mixed, with positive and negative findings just about evenly balanced: Positive findings were reported by Blumenthal, Williams, Kong, Schanberg, and Thompson (1978), Frank, Heller, Kornfeld, Sporn, and Weiss (1978), Williams *et al.* (1980), and Zyzanski, Jenkins, Ryan, Flessas, and Everist (1976) versus negative findings reported by Dimsdale, Hackett, Hutter, Block, and Cantanzano (1978, 1979), Krantz *et al.* (1981), and Scherwitz *et al.* (1983).

In the face of these contradictory findings, it largely depends on one's status as a type A believer or nonbeliever which set of data one chooses to explain away. As a type A believer, at least a would-be one, I shall focus on possible reasons why two prospective studies, and some of the reports based on coronary angiography, do not confirm the WCGS findings. None of the negative findings was reported in a sample of the apparently well, and it is possible that in individuals with high-risk status, or clinical signs of heart disease, the effect of the TABP is masked. As Siegel (1984) points out, we do not yet know the extent to which even the traditional risk factors are predictive in such populations. A second possibility is that there may have been subtle shifts over the years in the classification of individuals as type A, thereby reducing the predictive validity of the SI (Matthews, 1985).

In 1978, the (U.S.) National Heart, Lung, and Blood Institute sponsored a major review of the evidence linking type A behavior to heart disease. After reviewing the conflicting data, the panel of medical and behavioral scientists concluded that, for employed middle-age men at least, there was sufficient evidence of the independent association between the TABP and CHD to categorize the behavior pattern as a major risk factor, one of the same magnitude as smoking, elevated cholesterol, and hypertension (Review Panel on Coronary-Prone Behavior and Coronary Heart Disease, 1981).

Increasing the specificity of the TABP

In the WCGS, 1,589 men were classified as type As. Eight and a half years later, 178 of these, or 11% of those initially classified as coronary-prone, had developed heart disease. The incidence of heart disease may have been twice as great in type As as in type Bs, but 89% of those initially categorized as high risk for CHD remained free from the disease.

In a disease where multiple risk factors interact to produce the end state, it is probably inevitable that the diagnosis of risk on the basis of any single factor will result in a large number of false positives. What complicates the situation in the case of the TABP, however, is that over the years there has been a tendency to classify greater and greater percentages of samples as type As. In the WCGS, the split between As and Bs was 50–50, but more recent studies of similar middle-class samples have yielded 75% or more type As, with a corresponding dearth of type Bs (Chesney, Black, Chadwick, & Rosenman, 1981; Howard, Cunningham, & Rechnitzer, 1976; MacDougall, Dembroski, & Musante, 1979; Shekelle, Hulley, Neaton, Borhani, Lasser, Mittlemark, & Stamler, 1983). In fact, Matthews et al. (1982) have complained that it is difficult to recruit a sufficient number of middle-class type Bs even for experimental purposes!

It is, of course, possible that there has been an actual increase in type As. But any classification that grows to include most of the population of North America is not very useful, either for epidemiological or for treatment purposes. Unless it is possible to sift out the specific coronary-prone characteristics from the general type A classification, we shall soon find ourselves in the ridiculous situation of seeking to treat just about everybody. Moreover, most of these treatments will be directed to modifying characteristics that are largely irrelevant to coronary risk (Roskies, 1982).

The most comprehensive review of the attempts to increase the specificity of the TABP is contained in a recent chapter by Thoresen and Ohman (in press), and my discussion of this issue will draw on their work. To isolate the specific components of the TABP that are the best predictors of CHD, Matthews, Glass, Rosenman, and Bortner (1977) selected a subsample of subjects from the WCGS who had suffered a heart attack over a 4-year period, and compared them with a matched subsample of "healthy controls." The total sample was composed of 186 men. Seven items out of 44 significantly differentiated coronary from healthy subjects, all related to anger or hostility. Interestingly, time-urgent behavior did not distinguish the two groups.

Thoresen and Ohman (in press) report that Spielberger has recently reanalyzed these data over an additional 4 years (8½ years in all) and confirmed the predictive validity of the anger–hostility items. Spielberger's reanalysis of the WCGS data, via principal components analysis, revealed one major factor that is best described as the Anger–Hostility factor. Over 65% of the variance was accounted for by this one factor, which included all the significant predictive items found in Matthews *et al.* (1977). Once again, items related to rapid psychomotor movement (e.g., eats rapidly), a high drive level, and job involvement were not predictive.

As used in this context, hostility is defined as "a durable predisposition to evaluate people or events negatively, often in a suspicious, distrustful, cynical and even paranoid fashion. Anger represents an emotional state incorporating feelings ranging from irritation and aggravation to rage and fury" (Thoresen & Ohman, in press). "Potential for hostility," as evaluated on the SI, is a judgment based on both observed and inferred characteristics:

> Responses [suggesting hostility] are argumentative, repeatedly and unnecessarily qualified, pointlessly challenging of the interviewer. The voice characteristics suggest boredom, condescension, or surliness. Subject's answers to specific questions suggest impatience and irritability when faced with obstacles and the tendency to make harsh generalizations. Extreme levels of hostility may be accompanied by obscenity and the use of emotion laden words. (Dembroski, 1978, p. 103)

Other studies confirm the importance of anger and hostility as predictors of CHD, though in some they appear to be independent from, rather than components of, the TABP (Williams, Barefoot, & Shekelle, 1985). Recently Dembroski *et al.* (1985) validated SI-related components of Potential for Hostility and Anger-In via multiple regression to various CHD endpoints, and found significant relationships to the degree of occluded coronary arteries, angina symptoms, and number of myocardial infarctions. Using the Cook–Medley scale from the MMPI, Barefoot, Dahlstrom, and Williams (1983) have reported a predictive relationship between hostility and CHD over a 25-year period in a sample of physicians. Significantly, this relationship was independent of smoking, age, family history of hypertension, and current hypertension. A similar relationship in factory workers over a 20-year period has also been reported (Shekelle, Gayle, Ostfeld, & Paul, 1983).

Based on these findings, one might be tempted to replace the global type A rating by various measures of anger–hostility as more efficient predictors of CHD. But this would ignore the fact that questionnaires, such as the JAS, the Framingham, and the Bortner, have also been shown to be predictive of CHD, even though none taps the anger–hostility dimension. Instead, these questionnaires (as does the content of the SI) focus on what has recently been termed (Thoresen & Ohman, in press) the "pressured drive" component of the TABP, that is, time urgency, perception by self and others of high drive level, perception of excessive demands, and heavy work load. To the degree that the pressured drive component in the TABP serves as an independent predictor of CHD, it must also be considered in diagnostic and treatment efforts.

A very different approach to increasing the specificity of the type A assessment is to identify those life circumstances that increase or decrease coronary risk for susceptible type A individuals. After all, most definitions of the TABP have emphasized that the type A pattern is not to be considered a fixed personality trait but, rather, a set of behaviors "that is elicited from susceptible individuals by an appropriately challenging environment" (Matthews, 1982, p. 293). While there are only a few studies with samples heterogeneous enough to permit the study of differing environments, these do provide support for the hypothesis that life circumstances can influence the relationship between type A predisposition and risk of CHD. In the Framingham Heart Study, for instance, white-collar type A men were found to be at increased risk for CHD, but for blue-collar men there was no prospective relationship between being type A and eventual development of CHD. For type A women, on the other hand, the relative risks for developing CHD were higher among housewives than in working women (Haynes, 1984; Haynes & Feinleib, 1980; Haynes et al., 1980). Life-style was also found to influence coronary risk in type As in a sample of Japanese-American men, with the highest risk of CHD found among those who, in addition to being type A, also sought to discard traditional folkways and adopt a Westernized life-style (Cohen et al., 1979).

Ongoing personal relationships may also be a significant factor in moderating the coronary risk of the type A. In their recent review of the relationship of marriage to coronary risk in type As, Smith and Sanders (1986) report that a reanalysis of data on a subsample from the WCGS indicated that type A men who were married to educated, active, and dominant wives were at significantly increased risk for CHD compared to type A men whose marital partners did not manifest these characteristics. These findings confirm an earlier report from the Framingham Heart Study, also linking higher educational level of wives to increased coronary risk for type A men (Eaker, Haynes, & Feinleib, 1983). The hypothesis here is that active, dominant, and educated wives might provide a continuous source of challenge to their susceptible husbands, leading to more frequent activations of the sympathetic–adrenomedullary system, and thereby increasing coronary risk.

Only these few studies provide a direct test of environmental influences on the development of heart disease in type As. There does exist a body of laboratory research, however, confirming that even for individuals classified as type A, there are situational variations in the manifestation of physiological arousal. For instance, type As at rest do not generally show significantly higher blood pressure levels or catecholamine levels than type Bs, and may not do so even under simple conditions of task performance. When there is some risk of failing in the task, and some incentive to perform well, or if the situation includes aspects of social harassment, however, type As are more likely to manifest elevated reactivity (Krantz & Manuck, 1984; Matthews, 1982). At the other extreme, type As placed in a situation of forced inactivity are also likely to show increased physiological arousal compared to type Bs (Frankenhaeuser, Lundberg, & Forsman, 1980). Since exaggerated physiological reactivity is considered to be the major pathway linking the TABP to CHD (see next section), this might be considered indirect evidence that coronary risk depends on environmental influences as well as personal predispositions.

The role of situational demands in eliciting coronary-prone reactions in susceptible type As has important treatment implications. If coronary risk in type As is increased in specific environmental settings, then the most effective method of reducing this risk might be changing to a more appropriate job, or otherwise removing oneself from a harmful environment. However, the relationship between the objective environment, subjective perception of that environment, and potentially harmful physiological reactions is far more complex than it initially appears. For while type As as a group might show a typical reaction to a specific situation, there are wide individual variations among type As in degree and type of response to the same situation (Dembroski & MacDougall, 1983; Roskies, 1983b), or even in the same individual in response to similar situations on different days (Roskies et al., 1986).

In summary, the search for the type As at greatest coronary risk is not likely to yield a simple response. The anger–hostility component of the pattern is suspected of being particularly important for coronary risk, but there is also evidence supporting the "pressured drive" component. Environments containing challenge and harassment appear to be particularly arousing, and therefore potentially harmful, but so are environments that enforce inactivity. To further complicate matters, there is almost as much variation in perception of challenge and mode of response *within samples of type As*, as differences *between As and Bs*. For treatment purposes, one possible way of assessing coronary risk might be to consider the extent and generality of type A behavior, as well as its intensity. Intuitively, a person who manifested both anger/hostility and pressured drive in a wide variety of situations might be considered at greater coronary risk than one with fewer and/or less frequent manifestations of the TABP (Matthews, 1985; Thoresen & Ohman, in press).

Biological mechanisms linking the TABP to CHD

The identification of the biological mechanisms linking the behavior pattern to the disease endpoint is important for both scientific and clinical reasons. Scientifically, to establish a causal relationship between behavior and disease, one must first demonstrate that this relationship is biologically plausible. Clinically, these biological mechanisms can serve as markers, providing us with relatively quick and economical process measures by which to evaluate the effectiveness of our interventions. Friedman and Rosenman began the work of demonstrating biological plausibility in their studies of biochemical differences between As and Bs, and most of the literature since then has been devoted to extending this work.

The most promising approach to a physiological explanation of the increased risk of CHD in type As comes from a series of laboratory studies comparing the physiological responses to stress of type A and B individuals. Multiple studies report that, in response to certain types of challenge and threat, type As tend to show greater elevations in blood pressure, heart rate, cortisol, epinephrine, and norepinephrine than type Bs (Dembroski et al., 1978; Glass et al., 1980; Manuck, Craft, & Gold, 1978, Williams et al., 1982). Episodic elevations in blood pressure and heart rate are thought to damage the inner layer of the coronary arteries, thereby contributing to atherosclerosis and subsequent CHD. Elevations in circulating catecholamines play a role in cholesterol mobilization, which in turn contributes to the formation of arterial plaque. Should the stress responses of type As in the laboratory be typical of their responses in the natural setting, then these frequent, intense activations of the sympathetic–adrenomedullary system could potentiate arteriosclerosis and, eventually, clinical heart disease (Herd, 1978; Krantz, Glass, Schaeffer, & Davia, 1982; Krantz & Manuck, 1984).

To further strengthen the argument, physiological and behavioral reactivity appear to be related. Individuals who show the strongest behavioral reactions to the SI are also those who manifest the strongest physiological reactions to other laboratory psychosocial stressors (Dembroski et al., 1978; Krantz, Glass, Schaeffer, & Davia, 1982). Conversely, about half the studies using the JAS, which is a measure of content rather than of style, failed to show a correlation between type A classification and physiological response to laboratory stress tasks (Siegel, 1984).

Although the hypothesis of exaggerated physiological reactivity leading to heart disease in type As is a plausible one, it is far from proven. For one, the relationship between reactivity in the laboratory and reactivity in the natural setting has not yet been tested empirically. Even more important, there is only one published study to date providing empirical support for reactivity as a predictor of CHD (Keys et al., 1971), and no empirical data as yet supporting the converse, that is, indicating that a reduction in physiological response to stress reduces risk (Dembroski & MacDougall, 1983; Manuck & Krantz, 1984). Finally, there are still many unresolved problems in the definition and measurement of hyperreactivity (Engel, 1983; Krantz & Manuck, 1984; Roskies et al., 1986). Nevertheless, the hypothesis is a tempting one.

Etiology of the TABP

For the clinician seeking to treat type A individuals, debates concerning the etiology of the TABP are of more than academic interest. To the degree that we can identify the factors causing and maintaining the pattern, this will greatly aid us in knowing what types of intervention are likely to be most effective in changing it, or even to prevent its development.

The most comprehensive psychological explanation for why type As respond to perceived challenge or threat as they do has been provided by Glass (1977). According to his view, type A behavior is essentially a coping response used to counter the threat of actual or potential loss of control. In contrast to individuals who are unable or unwilling to adapt to social norms, type A individuals have internalized all too well Western society's emphasis on the ability to control one's environment. The positive side of this mastery orientation is enhanced self-esteem and increased social reinforcement. The negative side of this adaptive pattern is the threat experienced in any situation in which the individual cannot be sure of complete control. When signs of possible loss of control occur, as inevitably they must, the initial response is an increased effort to regain control, involving greater mental and physical exertion, stepped up pace, heightened competitiveness, and so on (Glass, 1977). Even in situations where control is not attainable, type A subjects tend to avoid recognition of this fact and continue actively struggling. Only when the cues signifying absence of control are virtually inescapable will the type A individual lapse into a state of learned helplessness (Glass, 1977; Krantz, Glass, & Snyder, 1974). Thus, the usual coping style of the type

A person is one of psychosocial and physiological hyperresponsiveness to stress, interspersed with periods of helplessness and hyporesponsiveness.

A second hypothesis relating the behavior pattern and heart disease is that type As are more self-involved than type Bs (Scherwitz, Berton, & Leventhal, 1978; Scherwitz *et al.*, 1983). According to this line of reasoning, self-involvement may promote constant comparisons between the self and ideal self, thus resulting in overt type A behaviors such as achievement striving or impatience. Furthermore, this focus on the self could intensify emotional reactions, which, in turn, could increase physiological reactivity and, eventually, susceptibility to heart disease. While this second hypothesis is less intuitively satisfying than the first, there is some empirical evidence to support it (Scherwitz *et al.*, 1983).

Underlying both Glass's and Scherwitz's explanations of the TABP is the assumption that type A behavior is a learned response, probably acquired in childhood. Supporting this assumption is a growing body of data showing that the constellation of behaviors called type A can be identified in children as young as kindergarten age. Furthermore, children classified as type A appeared to behave and respond physiologically to stress similarly to their type A adult counterparts. In their effort to understand the emergence of type A behavior in the young, Matthews and Siegel (1982) have suggested that it is an adaptation to high but ambiguous performance standards imposed by adults.

The causal chain implicit in the hypotheses discussed up to now is that the psychological characteristics of the type A give rise to excessive physiological reactions that, in turn, predispose the individual to clinical manifestations of heart disease. Recently, however, Krantz and Durel (1983) have suggested that the causal chain may also operate in the other direction. Based on the finding that type As show greater elevations of systolic blood pressure than type Bs even when they are under general anesthesia, and thus free from conscious influences, they hypothesize that there might be a genetic tendency to exaggerated physiological reactivity in type As (Krantz, Arabian, Davia, & Parker, 1982). It is the way the type A perceives and interprets his or her state of physical arousal that leads to the typical type A behavioral characteristics. Further support for the notion of a constitutional predisposition comes from some recent work indicating increased familial resemblance in cardiovascular stress reactivity in twins (Rose, Grim, & Miller, 1984). But regardless of whether the physiological arousal precedes or follows the type A behavioral response to a potentially stressful situation, most observers agree that both elements must be present for the completely developed TABP to manifest itself.

Type A and occupational achievement

The discussion up to now has dealt with the health risks associated with the TABP. But a major reason why type As are so resistant to change is that type A characteristics are also associated, at least in the popular mind, with occupational advancement and achievement. To the degree that this generally held conviction is true, seeking to modify the TABP involves serious potential losses as well as potential gains. If modifying type A behavior improves future physical health but, at the same time, reduces current occupational productivity or success, then how much change can a person be expected to risk, or legitimately be advised to risk? If type A behavior does indeed make the wheels of industry go 'round, then how much intervention can our society afford to support?

Positions among type A researchers on this issue vary from Friedman and Rosenman (1974) at one extreme, who argue that type A characteristics are deleterious to the creativity and acuity of judgment necessary for the highest levels of occupational achievement, to Mettlin (1976), at the other extreme, who categorically states that the type A pattern "is integral to the modern occupational career." Not surprisingly, the empirical evidence available to date supports a position somewhere between these two extremes.

Most studies that have gathered occupational data have found a positive association between occupational level and type A scores. For example, in the WCGS higher occupational levels were associated with increased percentages of men classified as A (Rosenman et al., 1975). In the Chicago Detection in Industry Study (Shekelle, Schoenberger, & Stamler, 1976) type A scores were also positively correlated with occupation. This latter finding is particularly interesting because the sample included blacks as well as whites, women as well as men. Outside the United States, a similar relationship between the TABP and occupational level was reported in a large Belgian sample, composed of both Flemish- and French-speaking individuals (Kittel, Kornitzer, DeBacker, & Dramaix, 1982). Moreover, in a study of white-collar, middle-class males from five different work organizations in Buffalo, Mettlin (1976) found that type As attain their higher status and income at a younger age, suggesting that they are likely to receive faster as well as more promotions. Thus, the popular belief that type As have above average success in the work world is amply supported by the research data.

To counter these data, Friedman and Rosenman might claim that type As succeed occupationally because they do more, not because they do it better. In other words, quantity of work is increased at the expense of quality. To the best of my knowledge, there is only one direct test of the quality versus quantity hypothesis and here, too, the data suggest that "pattern A does not hinder meritorious research. It may actually help" (Matthews, Helmreich, Beane, & Lucker, 1980, p. 966). This study compared the number of publications (quantity) produced by 118 male midcareer social psychologists during a 3-year period with the number of citations (quality) of these works. Using the JAS as the measure of type A behavior, men who were above the median on type A scores had a significantly greater number of citations than those with more type B scores, even though the two groups did not differ in number of publications per se.

To further strengthen the argument for a positive link between type A and achievement, the superior performance of type As is manifest at school, even before they enter the labor market. As a group, type As receive higher marks and, not surprisingly, are more likely to pursue higher levels of education (Mettlin, 1976; Rosenman et al., 1975; Shekelle et al., 1976; Waldron, Zyzanski, Shekelle, Jenkins, & Tannenbaum, 1977). There is no evidence that this superior achievement is the result of higher innate intelligence. Instead, according to the testimony of As themselves, it is primarily work habits and attitudes that distinguish them from Bs.

In two separate Canadian studies, of prison administrators and senior corporate officers, respectively (Burke & Weir, 1980; Howard, Cunningham, & Rechnitzer, 1977), extreme As claimed to put in the longest work weeks, work more discretionary hours per week, travel more days per year, and supervise larger numbers of people. They were keenly aware of the time expended on work, reporting that work encroached substantially on their leisure, their home life, and their relationships. Nevertheless, they perceived their jobs as requiring such effort, describing them in terms of intense competition, heavy work loads, conflicting demands, and multiple responsibilities. To offset these stresses, however, there was the gratification provided by the opportunity to utilize skills and influence the course of events. In fact, Burke and Weir conclude that the psychological gratification and tangible rewards that extreme type A individuals obtain from the work experience far outweigh whatever stress they experience.

For women, the occupational success associated with the TABP may be offset somewhat by that fact that being type A is not related to what would traditionally be considered marital success, that is, being married and having a husband of high occupational status (Waldron, 1978). It is possible, of course, that it is not the fact that a woman is type A, but simply the fact that she has reached a high occupational level, that may limit marital opportunities. Apart from this, type A behavior in women, as in men, is positively related to higher levels of socioeconomic status, occupation, and education. In fact, while random samples in the United States show a smaller percentage of type A women compared to men, the sex difference disappears when socioeconomic differences are controlled (Baker, Dearborn, Hastings, & Hamberger, 1984).

The evidence to this point appears to be overwhelmingly in favor of a strong association between the TABP and occupational achievement and advancement. Two critical questions, however, remain unanswered. Type As as a group may show greater occupational success, but is type A behavior a *necessary condition* for occupational achievement, or at least for certain types of occupations? Is it possible to separate the positive aspects of the TABP from the coronary-prone characteristics?

The evidence is clear that although the TABP may help occupational success, it is not a *necessary condition for it*, regardless of the demands of a specific occupation. The correlation between the TABP and occupational success is significant, but it is not overwhelming: In the Matthews study (Matthews *et al.*, 1980), for example, the correlation between number of citations and type A score was .17, an association that explains less than 4% of the variance. Moreover, no study has found high occupational status to be exclusively reserved for As; even among the most senior officers of the fastest growing of the largest corporations in Canada, fully one third (34%) were classified as clear-cut Bs (Howard *et al.*, 1976). In fact, as president of the United States, Ronald Reagan has provided a prime example of the fact that it is possible to retain type B work habits and attitudes even in the most demanding position!

It is more difficult to answer the question whether the positive and negative aspects of the TABP can be separated. But the possibility does exist that it is not the high drive level of the type A in itself, but the indiscriminate manner in which it is used, that causes harm. For instance, in comparing the *performance* of As and Bs on various laboratory tasks (e.g., mental arithmetic, puzzles), eight studies reported no differences; one reported superior A performance, but only under a high distraction condition; and two actually reported inferior A performance when As were required to delay their responses. Nevertheless, in all these studies the type As showed significantly greater autonomic and/or endocrine arousal than did type Bs (Roskies, 1981). A field study of white-collar workers in a large, Canadian manufacturing organization (Jamal, 1985) corroborates this suggestion that type As may be working harder than Bs for results than are no better, in that supervisors' ratings of quantity of work performed did not show any differences between type As and type Bs, but type A individuals themselves reported significantly more "effort on the job" and more psychosomatic complaints. To the degree that they were expending more energy to achieve the same results, these type As were inefficient workers. Assuming that type As are in the position of oil-rich nations that possess abundant supplies of energy and carelessly squander them, one might seek to improve the health status of type As, while leaving productivity untouched, by focusing on more efficient use of energy.

Conclusions

The data presented in this chapter suggest that the TABP does indeed constitute a serious health risk for coronary heart disease. Thus, therapeutic intervention for the type A, even the apparently healthy one, is ethically justified. However, the correspondence between the behavior pattern and the disease is far from perfect and, unlike other health risks such as smoking and hypertension, the TABP also facilitates valued personal and social objectives. In order to avoid harming rather than helping, therefore, the therapist who seeks to work with this population of apparently healthy and well-functioning type As must face the challenge of devising treatments that will reduce or eliminate coronary risk, while leaving untouched those aspects of the behavior pattern that foster productivity and achievement. In short, the aim is to achieve a maximum reduction in coronary risk at minimum cost for the individuals concerned.

2. Stress management: A new approach to treatment

A recent cartoon strip by Jules Feiffer neatly summarizes the current fad of stress treatments: A rather bedraggled young woman declares that she once had anxiety, but now she has stress. Therefore, she goes to a weekly stress lab where she stress raps, takes stress tests and stress exercises, follows a stress diet and pops stress vitamins, goes out with stress mates, and plays stress games. She even has stress sex. As she triumphantly concludes: "Anxiety was so isolated; thank God for stress."

Like all good cartoons this one caricatures reality, but also reflects it. Stress has become the fashionable disease of our time, and treatment of stress is a popular and profitable activity (see Roskies, 1983a). Moreover, this is an activity in which everyone can participate, since there are no evident restrictions on types of therapists, treatments, or clients. Even if one excludes the obviously fraudulent and bizarre, the list of treatments currently being packaged under the stress management label is wide; massage, exercise, nutrition, progressive relaxation, meditation, biofeedback, social skill training, and stress inoculation training are only a few of the better known ones. The clientele to whom these assorted treatments are being addressed is equally diverse, including top military brass (Gill *et al.*, 1985), corporate workers (Murphy, 1984), the elderly (De Berry & Einstein, 1981), teachers (Forman, 1982), and even the physically handicapped (Garrison, 1978). In fact, the most distinctive characteristic of stress management as a treatment is its universality; there is no one for whom treatment is apparently unneeded or inappropriate.

It is tempting to dismiss this confusing diversity of treatments and clienteles as just another therapeutic fad, a successor to previous fads such as T groups, soon to be succeeded itself by the next fashionable disease and its accompanying treatments. Nevertheless, in spite of the hyperbole surrounding it, stress management is also a novel and fruitful way of treating human distress. However, contrary to popular views, stress management is not a specific treatment technique applied to a specific illness labeled "stress." Rather, stress management is best conceptualized as a general treatment approach to a broad category of

27

adaptational and health problems. The theoretical basis for this treatment approach lies both in conceptions of health and illness provided by stress theorists, and in the self-management therapies developed by the cognitive behavioral practitioners (Roskies & Lazarus, 1980). This chapter traces the twin theoretical roots of stress management and defines the characteristics that distinguish it from other psychotherapeutic approaches.

Conceptions of stress problems

A fundamental prerequisite of any rational intervention is an understanding of the condition being treated: What are stress problems, and who are the people likely to be affected by them? Unfortunately, in spite of its widespread usage, there is no single, precise definition of the term *stress* or, consequently, of *stress problems*. In fact, to try to understand the concept of stress via the writings of stress theorists and researchers is analogous to the old story of a group of blind men seeking to learn about an elephant by feeling different parts of its body. The man who felt the trunk and declared that the elephant was a long tube was partially right, as was he who felt the flank and declared the elephant to be a rough wall. In each case, however, the reality reported was colored by the specific and limited perspective from which the phenomenon was viewed. Similarly, most stress theorists agree that the elephant (i.e., stress) does exist; they might even go so far as to concur that the term describes a disturbance of homeostasis, an interruption in the smooth flow of habit that forces the individual to engage in active efforts to regain the old equilibrium or to attain a new one. How this disturbance is defined and studied, however—stimulus versus response, universal versus individual reactions, physiological versus psychological and social levels — depends on the particular perspective of the specific researcher.

Stress as a physiological response

Selye is popularly considered to be the father of modern stress theory, the man, in fact, who both gave the field its name and provided one of the first systematic descriptions of stress responses (Selye, 1956). As defined by Selye, stress was an orchestrated sequence of hormonal and tissue changes observed in response to any form of noxious stimulus. The stress response occurred when the insult was neither extreme enough to kill the organism immediately nor mild enough to be easily overcome. The physiological changes observed reflected the struggle to overcome this disturbance in equilibrium or, as we would now phrase it, to cope with it. Extreme cold, various toxins, and a physical blow would each produce different specific physiological effects, but in addition there would be the constant or "nonspecific" physiological markers of the struggle to resist the noxious agents.

The genius of Selye's work lies in the recognition that ultimately the effects of struggle against the invader might be more harmful to the organism than the direct effects of the noxious agent itself. Should the resistance phase be prolonged unduly, the animal might even die from sheer exhaustion. Thus, the emphasis in Selye's work is not on the stressor per se, but on the toll exacted by the efforts to cope with it. Disease is no longer defined solely in terms of external agents, but is also considered to be a product of the organism's finite resources and energy in adapting to its environment. This conceptualization and description of the role of the organism, or in epidemiological terms the *host*, marks an important shift in our understanding of the etiology of disease.

Selye's general adaptation syndrome—complete with diagrams depicting the three stages of alarm, defense, and exhaustion—constitutes an obligatory part of most stress management manuals and is commonly used to "explain" stress. But Selye's theory alone cannot provide an adequate blueprint for clinical diagnosis or treatment of stress disorders, because the stress phenomena with which he dealt are very different from those of interest to the clinician. Selye's empirical work was largely based on the study of the *typical, physiological reactions* produced in animals by *physical stressors*, such as cold and toxins. As clinicians, our primary interest is in people, of course, but also in *individual, idiosyncratic behavioral and emotional reactions to psychological threats and challenges*. The general adaptation syndrome may provide an accurate depiction of most rats' sequence of physiological reactions to a toxin, but it does not help us understand why one college student copes with the anticipation of an exam by devising a study schedule, and a second collapses in helpless panic.

In spite of its limitations for clinical purposes, the physiological work of Selye and his successors remains important for the clinician because it provides the needed link between behavior and biology. If excessive environmental demands or inadequate coping resources are believed to have physical illness as a possible outcome, then biological pathways must be found to explain how one could lead to the other. Thus, as we have seen in the previous chapter, the best explanatory hypothesis linking the TABP to CHD is that of exaggerated stress responses, with the conjecture that frequent, excessive innervations of the sympathetic–adrenomedullary system can lead to arteriosclerosis and, eventually, to clinical heart disease.

However, if we as clinicians are to appeal to physiological stress theories as scientific support for our treatments, then it behooves us to keep abreast of developments in this complex and fast-moving area. For even on the physiological level itself, the stress reactions described by Selye present only part of the picture. By focusing on the sympathetic–adrenomedullary system, instead of the pituitary–adrenocortical system, Cannon (1939) described a rather different sequence of physiological reactions, the well-known "fight or flight" syndrome. Subsequently, technical advances in hormonal analysis have made it possible to go beyond these two systems and study a broad spectrum of hormones and endocrine systems, including the pituitary–gonadal, growth hormone, and insulin systems (Mason, 1975; Ursin, Baude, & Levine, 1978). Based on this research, it appears that there is no single "stress hormone," neither corticosteroid nor catecholamine, but that all endocrine systems are responsive to psychological stress. Furthermore, recent work in the new field of psychoimmunology suggests that the immune system, too, is responsive to psychological demands (Ader, 1980). Thus, even the physiological response to stress cannot be described solely in terms of the general adaptation syndrome or the fight-and-flight response but, instead, must be viewed as a complex and interrelated patterning of autonomic, hormonal, and immune systems.

Stress as an external stimulus

When most people speak of being under stress, they are usually referring to external demands impinging on them, such as pressure at work or illness of a family member. The study of stress as a stimulus coincides with the popular view, focusing as it does on the triggers that provoke emotional, behavioral, and physiological reactions. For clinical purposes, it would be desirable to have a ranking of stress triggers, either in terms of type of problem engendered (child beating vs. heart disease) or even in terms of severity of consequences (major vs. minor). No such global rankings exist; instead, once again, there is a variety of classification systems, each providing somewhat different indications concerning outcome.

In the Institute of Medicine report *Stress and Human Health* (Elliott & Eisdorfer, 1982), stressors are classified according to duration: (1) acute, time-limited stressors, such as a job interview or a visit to the dentist; (2) stressor sequences, or series of events that occur over an extended period of time as the result of an initiating stress trigger, such as the multiple residential, financial, job, parental, and social changes that can follow a divorce; (3) chronic intermittent stressors, such as periodic arguments with a spouse or a weekly project meeting; and (4) chronic stressors, such as permanent disabilities and marital strife, which may or may not be initiated by a discrete event and which persist continuously over a long time. Presumably, longer-lasting stressors would have more serious consequences than acute, time-limited ones, although studies on chronic illness and physical handicap (Davis, 1963; Goffman, 1963) suggest that habituation may attenuate the impact of at least some chronic stressors. Thus, duration in itself is not an adequate criterion for predicting the impact of a given stressor.

A second taxonomy of stress triggers is based on the quality of the (2) event, rather than its duration. Lazarus and Cohen (1977) speak of three types of stress triggers: major changes, often cataclysmic and affecting large numbers of persons (e.g., war, earthquake, financial depression); major changes affecting one or a few persons (e.g., bereavement, divorce); and daily hassles. Most of the research literature has focused on major changes, both collective and individual, with the assumption that the most serious adaptational and health consequences are likely to flow from events such as war and bereavement. However, the vast majority of individuals who complain of suffering from stress have not experienced initiating stress triggers of the catastrophic type. Instead, as they describe job and family stresses, there is a multitude of apparently trivial episodes: running out of coffee and an early morning argument about who was supposed to buy it, disagreement about this weekend's plans, an important letter left untyped, a feeling of anxiety concerning the report one is preparing, worrying about the monthly bills, the stubborness of a colleague in refusing to see one's point of view, the malevolence of a computer that goes down when we most need it, and so on ad infinitum. Moreover, instead of representing sharp divergences from normal routine, many of these minor challenges and threats occur repeatedly and frequently.

Until recently, stress researchers paid little attention to this third category of stress trigger, perhaps because these daily hassles are so universal. However, a number of recent empirical studies by Lazarus and his colleagues (DeLongis, Coyne, Dakof, Folkman, & Lazarus, 1982; Kanner, Coyne, Schaefer, & Lazarus, 1981) have provided data suggesting that these daily hassles, perhaps because of their frequency, may be even more important for adaptation and health than the better recognized major catastrophes and changes. This shift in conceptualization of stress triggers, from major catastrophe to minor irritant, has important clinical consequences in that it helps us understand why even "normal" people living in "normal" circumstances may complain of stress. What it cannot do, of course, is explain the differential effect: If presumably everybody experiences daily hassles, why do some people suffer more than others?

A third way of classifying stressors is by quantity, rather than by (3) quality or duration. The life events approach, exemplified by Holmes and Rahe (1967), put forth the view that the negative consequences of stress for health resulted more from the *accumulation of stressors* requiring adjustment, rather than from the damage wrought by any single one. Thus, positive as well as negative changes, if too many occur in too short a period, can tax the adaptive capacity of the organism and lead to increased susceptibility to psychological and physical illness. This theoretical approach had the unusual advantage of being accompanied by a measuring instrument, the Social Readjustment Rating Scale (SRRS), that made it possible to classify individuals in terms of their exposure to change and consequent vulnerability to illness. In fact, this scale has been used to successfully predict both psychological distress and physical illness in a variety of populations (Holmes & Masuda, 1974; Rahe, 1975; Thoits, 1983). Unfortunately, this measure of illness vulnerability is not as simple and clear-cut as it initially appears. In addition to conceptual and methodological concerns about what specifically is being measured and how, there is the practical consideration that the amount of variance explained is low, usually not more than 4–10% (Rabkin & Struening, 1976; Thoits, 1983). Thus, while SRRS has become another staple of stress management manuals and popular articles about stress, there is little scientific basis for using it to predict illness vulnerability in the *individual*.

For the clinician, the wide number and diversity of stress triggers is eventually self-defeating. If the list of stressors includes acute as well as chronic events, daily hassles as well as major catastrophes, positive as well as negative changes, then presumably all of us are stressed. But not all of us show the same severity or type of negative effects. There is a difference between the individual who survives a concentration camp with surprisingly few signs of pathology (Antonovsky, Maoz, Dowty, & Wijsenbeek, 1971) and the one who breaks down under stressors that appear relatively minor, at least to others. There is also a difference between the individual whose inability to handle stress leads to a heart attack and the one whose stress problem takes the form of addictive drinking. Once again, we are confronted with the problem of individual differences in stress perception and response.

The vulnerable organism

One way of overcoming the inability of either the response or the stimulus definition to account for individual variations in stress perception and reaction is to focus directly on differences in individual susceptibility. In this way the stimulus–response (S-R) paradigm is transformed into a stimulus–organism–response (S-O-R) one. For instance, Schmale (1972) hypothesized that individuals who have unresolved infantile conflicts concerning separation and loss are likely to react to analogous situations in adulthood with feelings of helplessness and hopelessness, thereby increasing their vulnerability to illness. Similarly, categorization of persons according to coping styles, such as repression–sensitization (Byrne, 1964; Welsh, 1956) or coping–avoiding (Goldstein, 1959, 1973), presumably should increase our ability to predict which stimuli are likely to be perceived as stressful, as well as the nature of the stress response.

Unfortunately, this type of effort to incorporate the organism within stimulus–response theories of stress has proven unsatisfactory, because it is both limited and static. Classifications based on a single static trait are usually not complete or dynamic enough to take account of the complexity and variability of actual coping efforts in a specific stress situation. Thus, for patients anticipating surgery, Cohen and Lazarus (1973) found no correlation between their global classification as vigilants versus avoiders on the Byrne (1964) scale and the way that the patients actually coped with the specific threat of surgery. Moreover, even if one could accurately categorize coping style in a particular context, such reactions do not remain immutably fixed in time but are subject to change. For instance, in the classic longitudinal study of parental reactions to fatal illness in a child, S. B. Friedman, Chodoff, Mason, and Hamburg (1963) found that parental reactions were not rigidly fixed, but varied according to changes in the external situation and the changing meanings that parents attributed to these events. In short, just as the study of stimuli and responses in isolation is insufficient to understand stress processes and outcomes, so focus on individual typology or pathology is equally insufficient. Personality traits and past experiences may indicate predispositions, but it would indeed indicate an extreme of pathology for an individual to be totally immune to the influence of external events, or even to feedback from the consequences of his or her own responses during the course of a stress episode itself.

Psychological stress as cognitive appraisal

Since no definition of stress has succeeded in capturing the nature of this complex phenomenon, or even in satisfying the majority of stress researchers (Elliott & Eisdorfer, 1982), some researchers have suggested that the term *stress* be abandoned completely. Lazarus (1966), on the other hand, believes that the term should be retained, but that it should be clearly understood that *stress* does not refer to a specific variable but is a general organizing concept for understanding a wide range of phenomena of great importance in human and animal adaptation. Stress is not the domain of a single discipline but is an interdisciplinary field that encompasses both the activities of the anthropologist investigating stress in an entire culture and the biochemist concerned with variations in a single hormone. Furthermore, although social stress may be linked to psychological stress and to physiological stress, phenomena at each of these three levels of analysis are sufficiently independent that one cannot be reduced to another. Therefore, to avoid the confusion resulting from the multiple meanings attached to the same term, it is incumbent on each stress researcher to define the level of analysis that he or she is using (Lazarus & Folkman, 1984).

As a psychologist, Lazarus is clearly interested in stress at the level of the individual person; the specific perspective he uses is that of a thinking, feeling person continuously appraising his or her relationship with the surrounding environment. Stress is the result of a judgment that a disturbance has occurred in the person–environment relationship: The individual perceives challenge/threat/harm, judges that his or her resources may not be sufficient to manage the disruption, and considers the outcome important to his or her well-being. Thus, stress is localized neither in the environmental trigger nor in the physiological response, but in the individual's conscious appraisal of disturbance. Without this appraisal, there is no psychological stress, regardless of the degree of actual danger to the organism (Lazarus, 1966; Lazarus, Averill, & Opton, 1970; Lazarus & Folkman, 1984; Lazarus & Launier, 1978). For instance, rapid technological change may make many types of jobs obsolete, but a specific worker will not experience this social upheaval as psychological stress until he or she becomes aware of a threat to personal well-being. Conversely, individuals may experience acute psychological stress even when the threat or challenge appears minimal to the observer; one has only to remember the social embarrassments of adolescence to be convinced of this fact.

The individual's judgment that a stressful situation exists, whether it appears reasonable or unreasonable to the observer, initiates a complex process. Immediately, there is an effort to reduce the feelings of disturbance, by seeking to change either the situation, the person's reactions to it, or both. This coping effort and its consequences will itself change the person's appraisal of the situation, which, in turn, will alter the subsequent response, and so on. Thus, stress is not a fixed person–environment relationship but an evolving process, involving multiple appraisals and reappraisals.

Lazarus's theory of stress can also be viewed as a theory of coping, for the individual's continuous appraisal of coping resources and strategies is as fundamental to the process as the appraisal of challenge/threat/harm itself. What is initially judged to be stressful depends not only on the taxing qualities of the environment as appraised but also, and equally as important, on the appraised strength and suitability of the available resources to meet these demands. For example, the same traffic that produces strong emotional and physical reactions in the beginning driver may hardly be noticed by the experienced and confident one. Furthermore, during the course of the stress episode itself, the person is continuously making judgments about how well his or her coping efforts are succeeding, and these appraisals will affect, in turn, the initial evaluation of the stressor. For instance, the beginning driver may see the traffic as less threatening or more threatening depending on his or her perceived success in handling it. Finally, after the dust of battle has settled, it is the individual's evaluation of the way he or she handled the situation, as much as the results themselves, that will determine whether the person emerges feeling strengthened or diminished.

In contrast to previous stress models, Lazarus's is less concerned with isolating common characteristics of stressed people or stressful situations than with exploring the range of behavior manifested by specific individuals in specific situations. Many elements contribute to the individual's stress appraisal (e.g., perception of external environment, perception of coping resources, pattern of commitments, values and beliefs that increase or decrease vulnerability to specific types of threats or challenges, etc.); therefore, we can expect not only that individuals will vary in their appraisal of stressors, but also that the same individual will make quite different appraisals of the same stress trigger at different times or in different contexts.

Coping, too, is viewed as context-bound, an effort to manage a particular stressor, rather than as a universal manner of handling all stressors. Thus, the individual who handles a work conflict regarding division of responsibility as an exercise in negotiation and problem solving may react with anger and denial to a spouse's apparently similar request for reconsideration of household responsibilities. Furthermore, coping strategies not only vary from situation to situation, but they also change during the course of the specific stress episode itself. Even for an acute time-limited stressor, such as an examination, the person may seek to manage the situation by intensive studying and active search for social support before the exam, but may rely more on emotional detachment and wishful thinking during the period of waiting for the results (Folkman & Lazarus, 1985).

Lazarus's stress model obviously differs from those previously described in a number of important respects. For clinical pruposes, however, the most important difference is the predominant role assigned to the individual in the perception and management of disturbance. Rather than being the passive victim of environmental forces, or his or her own body, the individual is seen as a thinking, feeling being actively monitoring his or her relationship with the surrounding environment and seeking to maintain or improve it. Furthermore, because both the person and the environment are changeable, the individual is not necessarily the victim of his or her past but can change cognitions and behavior from one stress episode to another, and even within a single stress episode. This, of course, is very close to the clinician's view of the world, with its double emphasis on both the power and the perfectibility of the individual. It is not surprising, therefore, that this theoretical model of stress and coping has proved particularly attractive to clinicians seeking to develop a conceptualization of stress problems that could be treated by psychological means; in fact, Meichenbaum and Jaremko's (1983) volume, *Stress Reduction and Prevention*, is dedicated to Richard Lazarus.

Differentiating clinically treatable stress problems from stress in general

In spite of the many differences between them, the various stress models that have been described are linked by a common belief: Challenges and/or threats that tax or exceed the individual's capacity to handle them can have important consequences for physical and mental well-being. This view of malfunctioning as a demand–resource imbalance is heuristically powerful for it enables us to group a wide variety of apparently disparate phenomena within a single conceptual framework. However, it also makes it essential to distinguish from the large universe of possible stress problems those that legitimately lie within the province of the clinician. In some cases the distinction is obvious: Both the angry father who beats his crying child and the South African black who hits out at the arresting policeman may be suffering from an insufficiency of resources to meet the demands of the situation, but the first clearly qualifies as a clinical stress problem, while it would be ridiculous to view or attempt to treat the second in those terms. In other cases, however, the lines are less clear-cut or more controversial. For instance, the high alcoholism rate observed in a specific group of workers can be seen either as a deficiency of individual coping abilities requiring clinical treatment (the probable management view) or as a deficiency in working conditions requiring environmental restructuring (the probable union view).

From the clinician's point of view, *the most important criterion for diagnosing a given complaint as a clinical stress problem is the judgment that it is amenable to improvement by changing the way the person perceives and manages his or her transactions with the immediate environment.* Essentially, the diagnosis of a clinical stress problem has less to do with the etiology or severity of the problem itself than with the prediction of its responsiveness to the teaching of coping skills. Thus, we treat the nausea of the cancer patient undergoing chemotherapy by stress inoculation training, not because we consider his or her lack of coping resources to be the root of the problem, but because this is the most effective way we currently have of reducing the distress. Similarly, we may choose to treat the unhappy employee rather than the employing organization, not because of attributions concerning the source of the problem, but because the individual is more motivated for change than is the corporate structure.

The distinction between problems best treated via improving the individual's coping skills—versus those best handled via political action, improvement in drug treatment, or other means—is a judgment, and it will obviously be influenced by the specific values and beliefs of the person or persons making the judgment. Sometimes the diagnosis of a deficiency in coping skills will already have been made by the client himself or herself even before approaching the therapist, as in the case of the panic-stricken college freshman seeking help in coping with the stress of an oncoming examination. At other times, however, as in the case of the chronic-pain patient, it may take all the skill of the therapist to convince a potential client to focus on coping abilities, rather than to continue the search for the magical remedy that will eliminate the pain itself. But unless therapist and client can agree on a conceptualization of the problem that involves learning new coping skills, or using existing ones more effectively, there is no basis for clinical stress treatment. This development of a conceptual consensus constitutes a major challenge for therapists seeking to work with healthy type As or similar populations.

The teaching of coping skills

All psychotherapies seek to help the person feel more comfortable, both within his or her own skin and in relations with others. The distinguishing characteristic of the cognitive behavioral approach to therapy,[1] however, is that it approaches this goal via improving the person's *competency in managing important aspects of the environment.* The basic assumption here is that the individual's well-being depends in large measure upon the relationship with the external world; to feel good about oneself, the person must be able to manage environmental demands in a manner satisfactory to himself or herself and significant others. Effective management, in turn, depends both on possessing the necessary cognitive and behavioral skills to confront a given stressor, and on being able to mobilize these skills whenever necessary. Because of this emphasis on actually teaching coping skills, in contrast to viewing improved ability to handle environmental demands as a natural con-

---

1. The number of therapists identifying themselves as cognitive behaviorists is growing rapidly, and it is impossible to name them all. Some of the major contributors to the development of this treatment approach are Beck (1976), Goldfried (1977, 1979), Mahoney (1980), Meichenbaum (1977, 1985), and, of course, their predecessor, Ellis (1962).

sequence of the resolution of internal conflict, there are important differences between cognitive behavioral and other therapies in defining the goals and methods of treatment, as well as the nature of the therapist–client relationship.

The goals of treatment

The criterion of successful treatment for the cognitive behavior therapist is not necessarily the person's ability to change a troublesome situation, or even to eliminate all painful feelings concerning it. Rather, cognitive behavior therapy defines success in terms of the individual's ability to function adequately *in spite of some distress*. Thus, the ideal model is not the exam-anxious student who takes the exam without experiencing any anxiety whatsoever, but the one who can control anxiety, and even harness it to improve performance. Similarly, the aim of treatment is not to eradicate completely the food binger's yearnings for chocolate cake, but to enable him or her to manage thoughts and behavior so as to reduce the likelihood of succumbing. In short, the successfully treated individual is not "cured" of the presenting problem but is able to cope with it better via improved self-management.

Underlying this focus on effective self-management is the assumption that environmental challenges and threats are an integral and inevitable part of human existence. Even successful treatment is unlikely to prevent the appearance of new problems, and perhaps not even the reappearance of the old one. But the person who has overcome a difficulty in managing one situation should be able to face the next inevitable hurdle both with additional coping skills and with increased confidence in his or her ability to use them (Bandura, 1977a, 1977b). Or, to put it in simpler terms, functional coping is that which permits the individual to emerge from a given stress episode in better shape to cope again another day.

While all cognitive behavioral therapy is destined to increase coping skills, for most stress problems there is no single outcome that can be used as the a priori definition of competent coping. In fact, many stress problems have a range of possible "good" outcomes: The college student can handle exam panic by increasing his ability to manage anxiety, or by lowering his goals of the grade desired, or, alternatively, by learning how to withdraw with honor from a too difficult course; the overweight person can change eating and exercise habits or, alternatively, change her image of what constitutes ideal weight. Which choice will be made in these or similar situations is a question not only of health and illness, or right and wrong, but also of the values and beliefs of both therapist and client. Sometimes, the outcome toward which coping is directed is implicitly agreed to by therapist and client even before their initial encounter, as in the therapist who advertises a weight loss group, or the client who consults for help in overcoming a flying phobia. In other cases, however, specification of the desired outcome may constitute an essential part of the treatment process itself, as in the case of the client with marital problems hesitating between "learning to live with it" and ending this relationship and seeking a better one.

The methods of treatment

The teaching of coping skills borrows from both educational and psychotherapeutic methods. The influence of educational methods is evident in the step-by-step process used to teach a given skill, such as relaxation or problem solving; as in the learning of any complex skill, the task is divided into graded steps, with the individual repeatedly practicing a given step in a variety of contexts until it is integrated within his or her repertoire. The influence of psychotherapeutic methods is evident in the attention paid to the affective component of learning, for example, motivation for and fears concerning change, resistance to a given technique or goal, relationship with the teacher/therapist, handling of successful and unsuccessful practices, expectations concerning extent and rate of change, attributions concerning sources of change, and so on.

Meichenbaum (1985) provides a prototype for cognitive behavioral treatment methods with his division of the treatment process into three main phases: conceptualization of the problem and goals of treatment; skill acquisition and rehearsal phase; application and follow through. Although I define the content of the latter two stages somewhat differently than he does, this division is useful for describing the treatment process.

The first phase is one of mutual education of therapist and client. The therapist will engage the client in a data-gathering process, concerning both the characteristics of the presenting problem (e.g., nature, severity, generality from one situation to another, consequences, reasons for seeking change) and the manner in which the potential client is currently attempting to handle it. At the same time, the therapist is providing information about the process of treatment itself. A number of the assumptions and methods of the cognitive behavioral treatment approach will become apparent in this stage: the importance of person-environment relationships; the active role of the individual in shaping these relationships; the focus on current interactions instead of seeking initial causes; the emphasis on specific behaviors and thoughts in particular situations, rather than fixed, global personality traits. Should therapist and client reach an agreement concerning how the presenting problem is to be conceptualized, the outcome or outcomes considered desirable, and the methods of seeking these outcomes, then therapist and client will have a viable treatment contract and a basis for proceeding further. However, this stage is not simply a preparation for the real work of therapy; on the contrary, often the most significant change occurring in treatment will be a new way of looking at an old problem.

The second phase in treatment is the actual acquisition and rehearsal of specific coping skills. This is probably the most controversial part of the treatment process, since much of the scientific as well as the popular literature has been devoted to fierce battles over the relative merits of specific treatment techniques. For instance, Meichenbaum has termed relaxation to be the aspirin of cognitive behavioral therapy, but the number of "brands" under which this useful "drug" is packaged appears endless (classic Jacobsonian progressive muscular relaxation, modified progressive muscular relaxation, the relaxation response, meditation, autogenic training, multiple forms of biofeedback, etc., etc.), and the wars waged by the devotees of a particular variant bear an uneasy resemblance to the brand wars of television commercials. However, as Meichenbaum (1985, pp. 53–54) points out, while component analysis studies of stress inoculation training have indicated that the skills acquisition phase is critical for treatment outcome, currently at least, there are no research-based guidelines for which techniques to use with each type of patient, nor in what order. Instead, each therapist now constructs his or her own treatment package or packages.

The range of possible techniques is wide. Lazarus and Launier (1978) have divided coping techniques into two general categories: instrumental (problem focused) and palliative (focused on regulating emotional distress). Included under instrumental coping are such techniques as information gathering, problem solving, communication and social skills training, time management, mobilizing supports, and direct efforts to change the environment or to remove oneself from it. The palliative techniques include denial, diverting attention, searching for meaning, emotional distancing, expressing affect, cognitive relabeling, and relaxation training. Which ones a therapist actually chooses should ideally be a decision based on the therapist's assessment of client needs; in practice, it is also likely to be based on the range of techniques with which a particular therapist is familiar and feels comfortable.

Current practice would encourage the use of multiple techniques on the grounds that "having a particular weapon in one's arsenal is less important than having a variety of weapons" (Pearlin & Schooler, 1978). Thus, individuals who complain of shyness in social situations might be helped by direct training in communication and social skills, but also by learning to regulate their physical and emotional reactions via relaxation and cognitive relabeling of stressful social situations. For individuals facing a stressful situation that can neither be avoided or altered (e.g., victimization, serious illness), the primary emphasis might be on regulation of emotional distress, but even here instrumental techniques, such as problem solving and mobilizing support, can be included. The major danger with multimodal therapies is that the client will be overwhelmed by an indigestible smorgasbord of techniques; it is important both to limit the number of techniques used and to develop a rationale explaining how each contributes to the goals of treatment.

The actual learning of techniques may involve a number of steps of graded difficulty. For instance, relaxation training can proceed from a 20-minute practice exercise following live instructions, to the same exercise using taped instructions, to a shorter version of the same exercise also with taped instructions, to self-instruction relaxation exercises, to the use of self-instructed relaxation when feeling tense, and so on. As in any skill training, simple description or demonstration does not in itself lead to learning the skill; for true skill acquisition, the person must also engage in repeated practices with corrective feedback on successes and failures. Depending on the skill to be learned, and the stage of learning, practice sessions can take place both within the confines of the therapist's office and in the natural environment. To enable the client and therapist to monitor in vivo practices, the client is often asked to keep a record of the event for discussion in the subsequent session.

While some of the coping techniques taught are new to the client, often it will become apparent during this stage of therapy that the client already possesses the necessary skills but is not using them appropriately. For instance, the shy teenager who consults because of inability to converse with members of the opposite sex may know, from avid reading of advice-to-the-lovelorn columns, exactly what to say to open a conversation at a party, but be too anxious to implement this knowledge at the social gathering itself. Here the focus of therapy will change from the teaching of social skills to the management of inhibiting anxiety. Similarly, the business person who complains of lack of communication with a spouse may have considerable theoretical knowledge of communication skills, gained in multiple seminars and workshops, but may have never considered these skills relevant to the management of marital difficulties. The task here may be more one of reconceptualizing the marital problem than of learning a new skill.

The third stage in treatment marks a shift in emphasis from techniques to situations. Rather than practicing a single coping skill or coping formula, the person will concentrate instead on applying his or her coping skills to meet the needs of different situations. This involves both the ability to combine skills when necessary and sufficient flexibility to vary coping strategies according to the needs of the specific situation.

Thus, the typical coping strategem for handling the irritation produced by a tardy employee might involve the combination of three skills: relaxation, cognitive relabeling to reduce the supervisor's level of arousal, and communications skills to transmit the supervisor's wish for increased promptness to the employee. Depending on the specific circumstances, however, the most appropriate coping strategy might range from overlooking the tardiness completely to outright firing of the employee. A second characteristic of this application phase is the client's growing independence from the therapist in providing his or her own corrective feedback and reinforcement. Ideally, this stage should also include some preparation for self-management after the end of treatment, particularly anticipation of possible relapses and development of methods for handling them.

Like all models, this one is only a prototype, and actual practice is likely to see some variation in the sequence and content of stages. For instance, the sequence described here is based on an individual therapist–client relationship, where the therapist has maximum flexibility regarding length, content, and pacing of treatment phases. However, much of cognitive behavior therapy, at least that which is reported in the literature, employs a group format, thereby imposing a priori structures on form and content of treatment. For example, when socially inhibited individuals are treated in a group, the therapist will usually decide in advance on the conceptualization of the problem, the general manner in which it is to be treated, and the length of treatment. Here clinical skill is demonstrated via the ability to select appropriate clients and to adapt to individual needs within the confines of the group structure.

The therapist–client relationship

Behavior therapy has traditionally been technique oriented, ignoring the affective relationship between therapist and client. In recent years, however, there has been a rapprochement with psychodynamic psychotherapy in recognizing that the therapeutic relationship is fundamental in mediating behavioral change. As described by Waterhouse and Strupp (1984), the therapist's ability to build rapport and to establish a collaborative working relationship early in therapy is an important predictor of treatment outcome. Nevertheless, even though cognitive behavioral therapists may agree with therapists of other persuasions on the importance of the therapeutic alliance, there are some differences in the way this alliance is defined.

The teaching of coping skills is an educational as well as a psychotherapeutic enterprise, and, reflecting this dual orientation, the therapist in cognitive behavior therapy is also a teacher. In fact, in his recent book on stress inoculation training, Meichenbaum (1985) consistently refers to the therapist as a *trainer*. Thus, rather than serving as a shadowy focus for transference wishes, the therapist plays the active role of coach, explaining, demonstrating, and encouraging. Furthermore, the teacher does not present himself or herself as someone who is immune to the problems manifested by the client, or even as someone who has mastered them completely. Instead, the model presented by the teacher is of someone who must also struggle with some of the same problems confronting the client—all individuals, regardless of their specific life situation, experience pressures and anxieties in some form or other—but who is able to cope with them without feeling overwhelmed or engaging in destructive behaviors. To further strengthen the model of the teacher as a fellow coper, *selected* self-disclosure of the therapist's own coping problems is a useful therapeutic technique.

In this teacher–student relationship, the client is not a passive recipient but an active collaborator. The ultimate goal of therapy is to make clients better problem solvers in handling future stressful events as they arise, and to fulfill this aim the client must learn enough of the therapist's "magic" to be able to use it himself or herself. Thus, from the outset of treatment the therapist seeks to make the therapeutic process as transparent and comprehensible as possible. If a client is asked to gather observations on the frequency of certain behaviors, or asked to practice certain skills at home, he or she must understand not only what to do but also how this self-monitoring and skill rehearsal will contribute to the desired outcome. Similarly, as the treatment progresses, the client should become increasingly familiar with the general process of behavior change, from the initial clarification of the problem to posttreatment handling of relapses.

Cognitive behavior therapy emphasizes the role of the therapist as teacher, but good teaching involves far more than proficiency in the techniques to be taught, or even a warm, accepting manner. Instead, the distinguishing characteristic of the skilled professional, in cognitive behavior therapy as in other forms of psychotherapy, is the ability to adapt general principles and techniques to the specific needs of individual clients. Most clients who seek help present not a single, well-circumscribed complaint, but a constellation of person–environment difficulties. It is part of the skill of the teacher to select those that are most amenable to change, and to choose the coping skills most likely to change them. Even more important is the therapist's ability to arouse and sustain the client's wish for improvement, in spite of the difficulties inherent in changing any established behavior pattern. In fact, because many of the dysfunctional coping patterns brought to the therapist have been overlearned over years, the skill of the therapist may lie more in mobilizing and sustaining the wish for change, rather than in teaching specific coping skills.

In sustaining client motivation, the therapist's sensitivity to language is particularly crucial. Words, or the lack of them, are the manner in which an individual expresses his or her manner of looking at the world. The good therapist listens carefully to the client's language and presents his or her own comments in a manner that facilitates assimilation to the client's existing schemata. The ultimate aim of therapy is to produce change, but the competent therapist reduces the fear of the unfamiliar by couching new thoughts in familiar language.

The range of problems treated

Up to now we have been discussing the teaching of coping skills as a form of psychotherapy. This treatment is offered to clients who, in sociological terminology, have accepted or been thrust into the sick role; the distinguishing characteristic of these individuals is that they or others have identified dysfunctional emotional states and/or behaviors (e.g., abusing children, excessive drinking, frequent headaches, anxiety attacks, performance anxieties, etc.) resulting from their inability to manage important aspects of the environment, and the aim of treatment is to reduce or eliminate the problem emotional states and behaviors. The range of problems treated under this heading is broad; in a recent summary of published studies, Meichenbaum (1985) identifies at least 20 distinct coping problems to which stress inoculation training or closely related stress management procedures have been applied, ranging from adolescents with anger-control problems to adults experiencing dental fear and pain.

However, stress management can also be used to prevent pathology in individuals who are currently well but who are considered to be "at risk." The usual reason for labeling a person "at risk" is exposure to stressful environmental circumstances that are likely to disrupt the individual's habitual way of looking at and dealing with the world. Rape victims, cardiac patients awaiting open heart surgery, and elementary school children making the transition to high school could all be grouped in this category. The aim here would be to reduce emotional distress, and head off deterioration in functioning, by increasing participants' awareness of potential stress reactions and by teaching them coping skills appropriate to the situation they are confronting. A second use of "at risk" stress management programs is directed to individuals in occupations considered particularly stressful, such as nurses, teachers, and police officers.

Stress management for healthy type As also constitutes treatment of an "at risk" population, albeit of a different kind. Here it is not environmental factors per se that place the individual under strain, but rather his or her way of reacting to the environment. Nevertheless, the healthy type A is classified as being at risk, rather than sick, because, until or unless he or she develops clinical heart disease, neither the individual nor society is likely to view this coping pattern as dysfunctional.

For the clinician, treatment of individuals in this "at risk" category poses some difficult challenges. These individuals do fulfill two of the essential requirements of treatment: They need help, and they appear likely to benefit from the type of help offered by stress management training. However, in order to be truly helpful, the clinician must be able to treat them in a manner befitting their nonpatient status. A working policeman, whose functioning and well-being can be improved by training in handling some of the stresses inherent in the job, is very different from a client with acknowledged symptoms, and it would be counterproductive to expect him to assume the sick role as a condition of treatment. Similar, though perhaps less obvious, is the distinction between the healthy type A and the one who has already suffered a heart attack. The first may be at increased risk for coronary illness, but he or she is not yet sick, and to be acceptable and relevant to the healthy type A, stress management programs destined for this population must acknowledge the difference.

Conclusions

Stress theory and research has provided both a novel way of conceptualizing a broad range of human adaptational problems in terms of demand–resource imbalance and a wealth of data concerning the negative consequences of inappropriate or ineffectual attempts to redress this imbalance. Stress management, the effort to prevent or alleviate stress-related problems, is based on this theoretical viewpoint and, consequently, differs from conventional psychotherapeutic approaches by emphasizing person–environment interactions in preference to intrapersonal conflicts: The goal of treatment is to improve, via the teaching of coping skills, the person's ability to manage his or her environment. Other novel features of this treatment approach are the goal of improved coping instead of total cure, the combination of educational and psychotherapeutic methods, and the collaborative therapist–client relationship.

Like stress theory itself, however, stress management has suffered from the confusion engendered by the use of the same label for quite different treatment programs directed to different clienteles. Both stress as a socially acceptable problem and stress management as a fashionable treatment can be considered victims of their own popularity, in that the rubrics are now applied as if they were self-explanatory when, in fact, they mean different things to different people. In fact, there is no all-purpose stress management program that will serve as a universal panacea for all stress ills. Instead, deciding that a given stress problem might be profitably treated by stress management techniques is only the first step in program development. It must be followed by a detailed appraisal of client needs, delineation of specific treatment goals, and selection of appropriate treatment methods. These are the tasks that will concern us in the next chapter.

3. Development of a stress management program for healthy type As

The purpose of stress management training for healthy type As is to provide them with new and better ways of coping with the hassles of everyday life. The first step in achieving this goal is a clear understanding both of what specifically is undesirable in current coping patterns and of how the proposed intervention will remedy these deficiencies. However, therapist understanding is insufficient in itself; it is also imperative that this diagnosis and prescription be couched in terms that are understood and accepted by the prospective client. For, as discussed in the previous chapter, the mutual agreement of therapist and client on conceptualization of the problem to be treated is a necessary and important element in the treatment process itself. In fact, Meichenbaum (1985) has suggested that the critical element in the reconceptualization of a stress problem that is offered to clients is "not its scientific validity *per se*, but its credibility and plausibility to clients and its heuristic value in suggesting specific avenues of intervention" (p. 48).

Diagnosis and prescription

Defining the problem

In contrast to other populations for whom stress management programs have been used, type As as a group neither live in extraordinarily stressful life circumstances, nor do they manifest obvious deficiencies in coping resources for managing the stresses they do encounter. Unlike the posttraumatic stress disorder of Vietnam veterans, or the reactive depression of bereaved spouses, the stress problems of type As cannot be defined by reference to unusually numerous or severe environmental pressures. In fact, while type As may describe their jobs as extremely demanding and pressured, the managerial and professional jobs in which type As are most commonly found are less likely than blue-collar jobs to be directly linked to physical and mental problems (Kasl, 1978).

Conversely, it would be be patently ridiculous to define type As as inadequate in managing important aspects of their environment; on the contrary, as we have seen, type As appear to be unusually competent performers, rating higher then Bs in both effort expended and results obtained. When confronted by obstacles, the type A simply tries harder. Furthermore, he or she is likely to persist in coping efforts long after others would give up, ignoring both fatigue and symptoms in the effort to master his or her world (Carver, Coleman, & Glass, 1976; Matthews & Carra, 1982; Schlegel, Wellwood, Copps, Gruchow, & Sharratt, 1980).

Nevertheless, coping competency can be evaluated not only according to the effectiveness with which a task is accomplished but also, and equally as important, by the cost of this effectiveness to the individual (Silber et al., 1961a, 1961b). And the available evidence suggests that the type A may expend energy unnecessarily and/or ineffectively in coping with the inevitable hassles of daily life. Compared to less reactive individuals, type As are more likely both to evaluate even minor challenges or annoyances as stressful and to react to these minor crises as intensely as to major ones. Furthermore, because of their insensitivity to bodily signs of fatigue and illness, they are also more likely to proceed from one stressful situation to the next without allowing for rest and recuperation. Thus, instead of monitoring and controlling energy expenditures, the type A spends his or her abundant energy profligately, mobilizing resources indiscriminately to win a game of tennis, to solve a difficult and crucial work problem, or simply to fume at a too slow elevator.

Eventually, the cumulative impact of perceiving too many situations as stressful, and reacting too intensely and for too long, may lead the organism to literally wear itself out, as demonstrated by the appearance of CHD. Even in the short run, however, most apparently healthy type As manifest signs of battle fatigue. Often, this fatigue is experienced as physical malaise: tense muscles, churning stomach, raging headache, and sleep disturbances. Emotionally, too, almost all experience frequent bursts of irritation and anger, and many periodically fell drained and somewhat depressed. Furthermore, this state of chronic tension helps to explain why "increased drinking frequency appears to be a concomitant of the Type A Behavior Pattern" (Folsom et al., 1985, p. 228), a method of dissolving tension that in itself can create further distress.

However, few type As see any connection between their own thoughts and actions and these states of emotional and physical malaise. Instead, the tendency is to blame the malaise on an environment that is both too demanding and insufficiently supportive; a superior makes unreasonable demands, a subordinate is not conscientious, a spouse does not understand work demands, machines stubbornly refuse to function when needed, other drivers impede our ability to get where we are going, and so on in an endless list. Sometimes it is fun to match wits with these obstacles, both animate and inanimate, but all too frequently the individual feels more driven than driving. In either case, however, the good soldier goes on marching, dismissing mental and physical malaises as the inevitable cost of an active, productive life-style.

Thus, there are two distinct problems in the type A coping style. The first is the excessive reactivity to the minor challenges and irritants of daily living. The second, and more difficult problem, is the firmly held belief that this hyperreactivity constitutes a necessary condition for achievement and productivity. The only way to break into this closed circle is to deal with the second aspect first, that is, to demonstrate that the habitual type A coping pattern is not only harmful to health and well-being, but also can be improved upon in the search for efficiency and productivity. For while type As are certainly correct in considering stress—particularly in the form of daily hassles—as an inevitable part of their life-style, and indeed all life-styles, one can question whether the responses to these hassles are as inevitable as they would have us believe.

Even in the same environment, individuals can and do differ, not only in their task accomplishments, but also in the "coping costs" incurred. The TABP represents an inefficient use of personal resources in that demands varying greatly in urgency and importance are responded to in the same automatic, undifferentiated "all or none" fashion. In contrast, a more efficient use of energy could be obtained by greater differentiation in stress appraisals and by increased variety and flexibility in stress responses. The ability to be aware of and exert effective control over thoughts, behavior, and physical reactions allows the individual to increase coping efficiency by responding to challenge or threat in a manner that maximizes impact and minimizes strain.

The proposed remedy

The aim of treatment for the healthy type A, therefore, is simply to reduce "coping costs" by increasing the individual's awareness and control of stress perceptions and reactions. Healthy type As have demonstrated their ability to manage the environment, but the new challenge is to improve management of personal resources. Instead of responding indiscriminately and automatically to all the inevitable challenges and threats of daily living, the individual will ideally become both more selective in choosing his or her battles and more skilled in pursuing goals at minimum cost in personal upset and disturbed relations with others.

To do this, however, involves more than learning specific coping techniques, be it relaxation or time management. Instead, the individual must also redefine the criteria of competent coping to include the goal of effective self-management. For, contrary to what the typical behavior of the type A might indicate, human energy is not inexhaustible but, instead, constitutes a precious and limited resource. Consequently, viewed from the perspective of a lifetime, satisfaction and achievement are more likely to be gained by the person who can effectively manage the purposes to which his or her energy is directed, and the manner in which it is used, than by the puppet who automatically responds in a stereotyped fashion to every passing challenge.

Acceptability of conceptualization to healthy type As

This conceptualization of coping deficiencies, with the consequent goals of treatment, is likely to be acceptable to healthy type As for a number of reasons. First, and perhaps most important, this model is as much a recognition of health as a diagnosis of illness; in emphasizing the task accomplishments of type As, this model makes a clear distinction between the healthy type A, whose general mastery of the environment is demonstrated by the ability to fulfill multiple and complex social roles, and "sick" individuals unable to manage basic environmental demands. This recognition of functioning adequacy is an essential prerequisite to any attempt at intervention because type As strongly value their ability "to get the job done" and, consequently, will strongly reject being cast in a sick role that is incongruent with their own perceptions of themselves. Social pressure provides an additional incentive for healthy type As to avoid any treatment based on acceptance of the sick role; at least one of the companies in which this program was tested explicitly listed "ability to handle stress" among the criteria for promotion. The model used here avoids the pitfall of associating type A behavior with illness; rather than seeking to cure bad coping skills, it stresses the improvement of already good ones. In fact, one reason for believing that a short-term program is likely to be effective in changing deeply ingrained habits is that healthy type As have already amply demonstrated their ability to meet other difficult challenges!

A second advantage of this model is that it does not threaten cherished goals but simply seeks to improve the methods used to reach these goals. Stress management for healthy type As is not an attempt to reconstruct the individual in the image of the "healthy personality," or even to refashion him or her according to the tastes and preferences of the therapist. For instance, if a given type A values occupational achievement more than personal relationships, then the purpose of the intervention is not to alter that preference in favor of closer family ties. Similarly, one would not seek to change a life-style based on serial sexual conquests into one committed to monogamy, or to advocate quiet walks in the woods to a devotee of gambling at Las Vegas. Instead, the scope of treatment is limited to showing individuals how to use resources more efficiently in pursuing existing goals and commitments.

The third major advantage of this model is that it leads to an intervention focused on active acquisition of new skills, rather than one stressing rest and inactivity. Given the barrage of publicity that the TABP and its negative consequences have received in North America in recent years, it would indeed be the unusual type A who was not somewhat aware of and uneasy about his or her stress reactions. However, many type As are caught in the dilemma of seeing no acceptable alternative to what they are currently doing; they are continuously advised to "take it easy," but life in the rocking chair is not particularly appealing to active men and women. In fact, many type A individuals who have tried to "slow down" at the behest of physicians or spouses have found these attempts at enforced relaxation even more stressful than their usual routines. The model presented here does not require the type A to become less active but, instead, emphasizes active pursuit of a new challenge, that of self-management.

Structuring a treatment program

Up to now, the coping deficiencies of the healthy type A and the goals of treatment have been described in general, fairly abstract terms. This section marks a transition from the general to the specific, from the abstract to the concrete. In it I describe, first, what it is the type A has to learn and, second, how the program was organized to facilitate this learning.

What has to be learned

The basic premise of this program is that there is no way to identify in advance all the situations in which hyperreactivity to stress is likely to occur, nor all the forms that it is likely to take. Even within an apparently homogeneous group of healthy type A managers, life situations are too varied, possible stress responses too numerous, and individual differences too great, to be able to provide the individual with a prepackaged coping formula, or even several of them. Instead, to effect any real and lasting change in habitual stress responses, the individual must learn to function independently as a behavioral engineer, capable both of *discriminating* between "good" and "bad" stress perceptions and responses, and of *devising and implementing coping strategies* for transforming the latter into the former.

One obvious prerequisite for developing appropriate coping strategies is that the individual possess a sufficiently large repertoire of coping skills; maneuverability in coping, as in other spheres of life, is facilitated by having ample resources on which to draw. While type As cannot be characterized as generally impoverished in coping skills, they do tend to manifest some lack of skills in certain areas, such as reducing physical tension. Thus, one of the goals of this program is to increase the range of available skills by teaching specific techniques, including progressive muscular relaxation, controlling behavior via delay and focusing on incompatible behaviors, communication skills, cognitive restructuring, and problem solving.

But effective coping depends on more than the possession of a multitude of coping techniques; one must also know when and how to use them. And it is precisely in this area that the coping deficiencies of the type A are most evident. In fact, type A managers are likely to be familiar with some of the techniques we teach (e.g., problem solving, time management, and communication skills) from a host of previous training seminars but they are not likely to use these skills to manage daily hassles because they: (1) lack awareness of what they are actually feeling, thinking, and doing during a stress episode and of how these reactions adversely affect mental and physical well-being; (2) do not see the relevance of a given technique to a stress situation or reaction; and (3) lack practice in using the coping technique, especially while emotionally aroused. The goal, therefore, is not only to teach new coping techniques, but also to facilitate the effective use of existing ones.

In operational terms, the objectives of this program can be summarized in four points:

1. Increased *awareness* of the many levels—physiological, behavioral, emotional, and cognitive—and of the many situations in which dysfunctional responses are occurring.
2. *Acquisition* of multiple new coping strategies—via learning of new coping techniques and mobilization of existing ones—for evaluating and responding to potential stressors.
3. Ability to *evaluate* the effect of different coping strategies on mental and physical well-being.
4. Repeated *practice* of new coping patterns in an ever widening variety of situations until these new patterns themselves become habitual.

The learning process

The program presented here is designed for 20 sessions. This length was selected as the maximum that healthy type As are likely to tolerate. I have also used abbreviated versions of 10 and 12 sessions, and suggestions for structuring these shorter versions are contained in the next chapter.

As in the learning of any complex skill, the acquisition of coping skills can be facilitated by dividing the matter to be learned into a series of graded steps. By dividing the final goal into multiple subgoals, the individual will taste success sooner and more frequently, and will be more motivated to continue learning. It is also easier to focus on one clearly defined task at a time, especially when the subject matter is unfamiliar and new methods of learning as well as new content are involved.

The program is divided into eight modules (see Table 3-1). The first serves as a general program introduction while the next three are devoted to basic skill building, teaching the individual to monitor and modulate physical, behavioral, and cognitive responses to stress. The next two modules build on these basic skills by teaching participants how to combine them and apply them, first, to anticipating and planning for predictable stress triggers (i.e., trouble shooting) and, second, to regaining control when suddenly confronted by unpredictable and un-

TABLE 3-1. Program structure

Modules	Skills taught
1. *Introduction to the program*	General overview
2. *Relax:* Learning to control physical stress responses	Self-monitoring of physical and emotional tension signs; progressive muscular relaxation (Bernstein & Borkovec, 1973; Goldfried, 1977)
3. *Control yourself:* Learning to control behavioral stress responses	Self-monitoring of behavioral signs of tension; incompatible behaviors, delay, communication skills (Stuart, 1974)
4. *Think productively:* Learning to control cognitive stress responses	Self-monitoring of self-talk; cognitive restructuring (Beck, 1976; Goldfried, 1977; Meichenbaum, 1985)
5. *Be prepared:* Learning to anticipate and plan for predictable stress situations	Identification of recurrent stress triggers; stress inoculation training (Meichenbaum, 1985)
6. *Cool it:* Learning emergency braking in unpredictable stress situations	Identification of signs of heightened tension; application of physical, behavioral, and cognitive controls; anger control (Novaco, 1975)
7. *Building stress resistance:* Learning to plan for rest and recuperation	Identification of pleasurable activities; problem solving (D'Zurilla & Nezu, 1982; Goldfried & Davison, 1976)
8. *Protect your investment:* Stress management as a lifelong investment	Relapse prevention (Marlatt & Gordon, 1985)

expected stress emergencies. The seventh module extends the scope of self-management to the realm of pleasures; the aim here is to teach the individual how to attain needed rest and recuperation by planning for them. The eighth and final module focuses on relapse prevention, awareness of possible reversions to old habits, and methods for managing these lapses.

For impatient type As, however, the step method can be difficult to accept unless they can clearly see the relationship between what they are doing today and their ultimate goals. The challenge then is to divide the matter into steps that are small enough to be manageable, but also to provide a map of the entire path so that the relevance of each part to the whole is clearly visible. To guide individuals through the program, a written manual made up of eight "road maps," or rationales is provided to participants. The first rationale constitutes a general introduction to and overview of the program, defining the problem(s) to be treated, listing the goals of treatment, and summarizing program content and methods. The remaining seven rationales serve as introductions to specific modules, defining what is to be learned in that module and why, and the steps involved in learning it. During the course of the program this written manual helps the participant place the present task in the context both of past learning and of future goals. After the program, the manual can be used as a refresher course.

After the general introduction, the same basic sequence is used in the remaining seven modules: problem identification, learning of remedial techniques, application to a specific situation and evaluation of effects, and generalization to other situations. To use the module on modification of behavioral stress responses as an example, the person first learns to monitor behavioral signs of tension (e.g., shouting, interrupting, grimacing, gulping of food, aggressive driving, etc.) and to identify the negative consequences of uncontrolled displays of tense behavior (e.g., churning stomach, angry secretary, etc.). The next step is to select targets for change and identify existing coping techniques, or learn new ones, that could be used to change the behavior. For instance, a person who wanted to reduce the barking quality of his or her voice on the telephone at work could engage in both incompatible behaviors (pausing to relax before making a call or answering one, speaking slowly, listening carefully to the other person) and delay (10-second time-out when the person perceives that he or she is barking). After deciding which techniques to use, and where and when (e.g., "tomorrow morning at the office," "every time I answer the phone"), the person would engage in a trial practice, monitoring both success in using the techniques and the effect of any changes in voice quality on feelings about himself or herself, relationship to the person with whom he or she is speaking, content of telephone call, etc. Once the basic process of modifying a specific behavior in a specific situation was familiar, the person would gradually extend the range and complexity of target behaviors, developing, implementing, and evaluating coping strategies as needed. The same learning sequence, from initial awareness to final generalization, is repeated in each of the other modules.

Distinctive program characteristics

A noteworthy departure from usual cognitive behavioral procedures is the blending of the assessment and treatment phases in this program; instead of completing an exhaustive inventory of the type A's coping problems before beginning intervention, the procedure used here is to alternate problem identification with remedial action, proceeding from module to module. This sequence was adopted to solve a common conundrum faced by therapists working with type As: To change behavior the individual must become aware of what is dysfunctional in his or her current actions, but most type As are unaware of what they are actually experiencing and doing in stress situations and, even more important, are unwilling to become aware of dysfunctional stress responses because they are convinced that there is nothing that can be done about these characteristics. Here we seek to build confidence in the therapeutic process by beginning with minimal disclosure (e.g., recordkeeping of variations in physical tension) and immediately instituting effective remedial action (e.g., relaxation training). As type As become increasingly confident of their ability to change dysfunctional responses, they also become more willing to recognize their existence.

A second distinctive characteristic of this program is the emphasis on behavioral assignments or "homework." Each session has its accompanying homework assignment (see Table 3-2), and, in fact, therapist–client meetings are designed mainly as a preparation for and as follow-up to the in vivo practices provided by the homework assignments. This focus on behavioral assignments reflects my belief that coping skills, like any other skill, can be learned only through repeated practice and corrective feedback. One does not learn to play tennis or speak French without multiple trial-and-error sessions, and the same principle holds true for relaxation or problem solving. Furthermore, it is important that these skills be practiced under the conditions and in the environment in which they are to be used; learning to cope better with daily hassles is best done while one is actually experiencing them.

Convincing time-pressured type As to add still another demand to an overburdened day is far from an easy task, but a number of techniques have enabled me to reach a compliance rate of 75–90% with the homework assignments. I shall discuss these techniques in greater detail in subsequent chapters, but is it worth noting here that one important aid to adherence is the physical format in which these homework assignments are presented. Each is a finished product, numbered, titled, and

TABLE 3-2. Division of program by session

Session	Materials	Content
1	R1; H1	Introductions; program overview (R1); physical tension stress diary (H1)
2	R2; H2; relaxation tapes	Follow-up of H1; Relax (R2); relaxation group practice; relaxation homework (H2)
3	H3	Follow-up of H2; awareness of behavioral tension (H3)
4	R3; H4	Follow-up of H3; Control yourself (R3); modifying behavior in one situation (H4)
5	H5	Follow-up of H4; modifying behavior in several situations (H5)
6	H6	Follow-up of H5; time-hurry behavior (H6)
7	H7	Follow-up of H6; self-talk diary (H7)
8	R4; H8	Follow-up of H7; Think productively (R4); changing self-talk (H8)
9	H9	Follow-up of H8; combining behavior and self-talk modification (H9); introduction of short relaxation (H9)
10	H10	Follow-up of H9; awareness of stress triggers (H10)
11	R5; H11; ranking of triggers (sheet)	Follow-up of H10; Be prepared (R5); ranking of stress triggers; preparing one stress situation (H11)
12	H12	Follow-up of H11; application of stress preparation skills (H12)
13	R6; H13	Follow-up of H12; Cool it (R6); coping with stress emergencies (H13)
14	H14	Follow-up of H13; coping with frustration (H14); introduction of one-step relaxation (H14)
15	H15	Follow-up of H14; creating a psychological balance sheet (H15)
16	R7; H16	Follow-up of H15; Building stress resistance (R7); making a wish list (H16)
17	H17; scoring of wishes (sheet)	Follow-up of H16; scoring of wishes; making wishes happen (H17)
18	R8; H18	Follow-up of H17; Protect your investment (R8); relapse prevention (H18)
19		Follow-up of H18; changed behavior in an unchanged world
20		Summary and good-bye

Note. R refers to rationale; H refers to homework assignment.

prepackaged, indicating that behavioral assignments are not simply afterthoughts but occupy a central role in the program. Furthermore, the task to be done is clearly described; the title page of each assignment indicates the topic, what is to be done, and for what purpose. Of even greater value in making the assignment understandable is the example sheet that is included in each one; here participants can see concretely how a completed assignment might look. Finally, to minimize response costs, participants are furnished with prepared response sheets requiring only a minimum of writing on their parts.

A third novel characteristic of the program is its highly structured nature; not only the general outline is determined in advance, but also the content of each session, with its accompanying homework assignment (see Table 3-2). This unusual degree of preplanning was originally a by-product of the research program in which the program was developed: Since more than one treatment group was involved, it was necessary to introduce structure so as to make the product consistent across groups. As we proceeded, however, it soon became obvious that this structured format helped to make the program acceptable to the clientele for which it was designed. Most of the healthy type A managers with whom we worked were unfamiliar with psychological treatments in general and were quite anxious about psychological "mumbo jumbo." They were, however, both familiar and comfortable with training seminars and professional development workshops, since these appear to be a standard feature of corporate life in North America. By casting the intervention program in this familiar form, complete with outlines, bibliography, and assignments, we had succeeded, albeit inadvertently, in using a format that was extremely useful in alleviating initial anxieties. Furthermore, a structured program did not necessarily inhibit the individual skills of the therapist; within these structures there remained considerable scope for therapist ingenuity and flexibility.

The final distinguishing characteristic of this program is its specificity. Rather than seeking to serve as an all-purpose stress cure, it is custom designed for the specific population (healthy, adult type As, probably managers and professionals) to whom it is directed. Format, language, and examples are all selected with this population in mind. This specificity may make modifications necessary for other populations, but it increases the power to reach our target population.

Empirical support for program effectiveness

The program presented here was developed and tested during 10 years of work with healthy type A managers and professionals. Some of this experience is purely clinical, as in stress management groups run for corporations, but I have also conducted three formal research programs in which various interventions for healthy type As were compared (see Roskies, 1983b; Roskies & Avard, 1982; Roskies, Spevack, Surkis, Cohen, & Gilman, 1978; Roskies et al., 1979, 1986).

The specific version of the program described in this book was developed for the Montreal Type A Intervention Project, a clinical trial comparing the efficacy of three short-term treatments (this program, aerobic exercise, and weight training) in modifying the putative mechanisms for coronary heart disease in a sample of healthy, type A male managers (Roskies et al., 1986). Participants were screened for absence of heart disease, presence of type A, and presence of exaggerated physiological reactivity to laboratory psychosocial stress situations. One hundred and eighteen men were randomly assigned to the three treatment groups, and 107 of them completed the treatment and posttesting. Treatment effects were evaluated by comparing changes (pre- to posttreatment) in behavioral reactivity (the Structured Interview scored by the Dembroski protocol) and physiological reactivity (heart rate and systolic and diastolic blood pressure).

For behavioral measures the results were clear and consistent: This program was substantially superior to the other two (aerobic exercise and weight training) in effecting behavioral changes on the Structured Interview, as regards both global type A rating and the components rated in the Dembroski protocol (voice loudness, explosiveness, rapidity, quick latency of response, potential for hostility, and competitiveness). Participants in this program demonstrated reductions of 13–23% in ratings on these characteristics, compared to no change for the aerobic group and smaller and less consistent change for participants in the weight-training program. Furthermore, these changes were consistent across treatment groups; there were three treatment groups using this program, and all obtained virtually identical results.

The behavioral changes we observed were corroborated by program participants. While participants in the three treatments gave their respective programs equivalently high general rankings (over 80% of the total sample rated the program received as "very worthwhile"), participants in this program reported substantially greater behavioral changes than did those in the other two groups (45% vs. 28% and 27% for the aerobic and weight-training groups, respectively), and a substantially greater number of them reported that spouses, co-workers, and friends had also noticed and remarked on positive behavioral changes.

This finding is of potential clinical importance because Friedman et al. (1984) recently reported that, in a sample of postinfarct patients, changes of this magnitude on the Structured Interview were associated with reduced recurrence of heart disease. We do not yet know whether the same effect holds in a sample of nonpatients, since no one has yet tested this or any other intervention against a disease endpoint in the population of healthy type As.

Another unknown element is the ability of behavioral treatments to affect key physiological mechanisms. In testing the effects of the three treatments on cardiovascular reactivity to laboratory stressors, no meaningful changes attributable to intervention were observed in any of the treatment groups. It may be that measuring techniques currently available are not sufficiently sensitive to track changes that are produced or, alternatively, that behavioral treatments in general are incapable of modifying physiological reactivity. The latter possibility raises the more fundamental question of whether changes in physiological reactivity, particularly as measured by laboratory stressors, constitutes a relevant outcome measure for treatment of type As. Before deciding whether the problem here lies with the measurement process, the treatment approach, or the outcome criterion, further work is required both to improve measurement procedures and to clarify the relationship between the TABP, physiological reactivity, and heart disease (Roskies et al., 1986).

For the time being, therefore, we are left with the ability of this stress management program to significantly reduce behavioral reactivity, as measured by the SI in healthy type A managers. Based on this evidence, the program cannot be touted as a miracle cure, but for the population of healthy type As, it is the program with the strongest empirical support of efficacy available to date.

Equally as important, neither in this program nor in previous ones has there been any case of negative effects resulting resulting from the intervention. I feel strongly that this program is best suited for well-functioning individuals not in acute life crisis (see Chapter 4 for a fuller discussion of this issue), but even our treatment failures do not appear to have left individuals worse off than they were initially. From the clinical standpoint, this is an important and reassuring program characteristic.

In working with healthy type As, clinically as well as in research programs, I share with them both the extent and limits of our current knowledge concerning intervention effects. Far from reducing credibility, the modestness of our therapeutic claims appears to increase it. Most participants are sufficiently wary of "miracle cures" that they appreciate a treatment that does not pretend to be one. Even more important, most participants have claimed to derive sufficient short-term benefits to make participation worthwhile on that basis alone.

PART TWO
PRACTICE

This part of the book describes the treatment process itself. Chapter 4 is a general discussion of some of the practical aspects of treatment, while Chapters 5–11 are devoted to a detailed examination of the individual program modules.

To facilitate cross-references between text and program, the relevant rationale and homework assignments are indicated on the first page of each chapter. In addition, facsimiles of materials from these program components are placed at the end of the chapter in which they are discussed. A complete treatment program, suitable for use by clients, is bound separately (see *Stress Management for the Healthy Type A: A Skills-Training Program*).

4. The nuts and bolts of treatment

As the title indicates, this chapter focuses on some of the practical considerations involved in treatment, such as the comparative virtues of individual versus group treatment, recruitment and constitution of a treatment group, and the frequency and structuring of sessions. It also deals with some of the problems likely to be encountered by the therapist, including nonmotivated and overeager clients, missed sessions, and control of self-exposure. Obviously, some of the topics to be covered in this section will already be familiar to experienced therapists, particularly those who have worked with groups. However, the healthy type A is very much an atypical client, and consequently even familiar topics may require a new approach.

Practical considerations in treatment

Individual versus group treatment

Although I have treated a few healthy type As individually, most of my experience is with groups and my personal preference in working with this population is definitely for group treatment. In terms of dollars and cents, group treatment is much more economical for clients, and possibly more remunerative for therapists. But economic considerations are not the prime reason for choosing group treatment for healthy type As; the group format also makes therapeutic sense. As we have seen, healthy type As are extremely reluctant, and probably justifiably so, to assume the sick role. Individual treatment by a "shrink" connotes illness, while group treatment, particularly if it is held on company premises, can be viewed as just one more skills-training course. This latter conception is very helpful in making the intervention socially acceptable, hence lessening resistance.

A second advantage, particularly for men, is that the group provides a new type of interaction with peers. While this may change with evolving social norms, I am continually surprised by how few male clients ever share feelings or experiences with their colleagues or friends. Thus, for many men one of the most beneficial aspects of this program is to discover that others experience the same irritations and frustrations that they do. It is also instructive to discover that it is possible to admit to weakness, be it in the form of a churning stomach or anxiety about a forthcoming sales presentation, without others necessarily pouncing on this vulnerability. The program seeks to convey the message that relations between individuals need not always be competitive, and the relationship between participants within the group serves as a concrete illustration of this principle.

As with so many other aspects of this program, the novelty and importance of noncompetitive sharing of feelings and experiences for type As was not one of my initial considerations, but was brought to my attention by clients. In the very first type A group with which I worked, I was rather surprised to discover that reputedly busy, over-worked, and time-pressured small businessmen were arriving a half hour early for the scheduled sessions and sitting there "idly" chatting with neighbors. Only in the final program evaluation did I discover the reason for this obvious discrepancy between type A reputation and actual behavior: Participants rated the relationship with other group members as one of the major benefits of treatment. In fact, over half the members rated other group members as the best friends they had ever made!

For the therapist, the group structure also helps to diminish resistance to change. Many participants enter the program convinced that, given the circumstances of their lives, no change is possible. The usual refrain of the first few sessions is "If you had my job, boss, spouse, etc." The therapist may try to convince the group participant intellectually that even in these circumstances alternate action is possible, but the best motivator is the concrete example of a fellow group member who has tried a new coping strategy and is all too eager to share his or her success with group members. Fortunately for the therapist, a good type A remains sufficiently competitive that he or she is not likely to stay behind the group if others embark on change. Thus, once the therapist has won over one or two members, he or she has a good chance of winning over the group.

As the program proceeds, group members also play an increasingly active role in evaluating fellow members' efforts and suggesting alternate actions. This is a useful intermediate step in gradually transferring initiative and responsibility from therapist to client. One of the basic objectives of this program is to help participants become independent behavioral engineers, capable of initiating and evaluating coping strategies on their own, and the advice and support provided by the group facilitates the transition from reliance on the therapist to autonomous action.

No format is without its drawbacks, and the group format obviously makes it more difficult to tailor the program to the personal needs of a specific individual. Some of the treatment failures and/or dropouts of group treatment might be helped via individual treatment. Here, as elsewhere, the good therapist does not rigidly adopt a fixed policy, but adapts his or her treatment strategy to the specific circumstances in which he or she is working. On the whole, however, the benefits of group treatment for healthy type As would appear to outweigh the disadvantages.

One versus two therapists

In clinical groups I usually work alone, except when I am training a new therapist. In research groups, on the other hand, concern about adhering to a tight schedule in the event of therapist illness has led us to adopt a system of cotherapists. To date, I have not observed any clear advantages of one mode over the other. The team approach reduces the strain somewhat on the therapist in that there is someone else to help carry the ball during fast-moving sessions. On the other hand, working with a cotherapist requires additional time and effort in joint planning to ensure effective team work. It is also more expensive for clients in that there are two therapists to be paid.

Recruitment of a treatment group

The groups with which I have worked have been recruited in a variety of ways. In some cases, the medical or personnel director of a company would decide to sponsor the program, and it would then be open to volunteers meeting certain criteria. In other cases, a company would decide on the program and then conscript members from selected management levels; for instance, one president chose to have a stress management program and then enrolled his entire senior management team! Other groups have been recruited by a physician specializing in corporate health screenings who would suggest the program to appropriate patients and then contact me when he had sufficient enrollees. And one of the earliest groups was formed by a newspaper story describing my interest in recruiting healthy type As.

Depending on how the group is recruited, the individual may pay directly for the program, or the company may assume part or all of the cost. For the research programs there was a third alternative, with programs being funded by research grants. Regardless of who is ultimately responsible for payment, I think it is important that individuals have a personal financial stake in the outcome (e.g., payment of a deposit refundable upon successful completion of program), or else that the sponsoring company clearly shows its interest in employee attendance (e.g., program held on company time). These external motivational aids are insufficient to keep the participant in a program that he or she does not find useful, but they are very helpful in assuring that participants assign sufficient priority to program attendance, particularly in early sessions. In the long run, the program will have to win people over by its intrinsic merits, but one must be present in order to be amenable to seduction.

Screening prospective participants

In some cases, such as our research groups, participants have undergone elaborate screening batteries (SI, measurement of autonomic and endocrine reactivity to laboratory psychosocial stressors) before being admitted to a group. In other cases, the screening has been relatively informal and conducted by the referring source. Thus, the referring physician uses mainly clinical interviews to decide on the suitability of prospective clients. In the latter case, there are three main stipulations that I make for group constitution: absence of major life crises, absence of overt psychopathology or heart disease, and social homogeneity.

The first stipulation, absence of major life crises, is based on the consideration that this program is essentially a skills-training course; therefore, to benefit from it an individual must be psychologically open to this type of learning. Someone who is in the acute stages of marital separation, or coping with the loss of a loved one, needs help with his or her immediate problem rather than general skills training. Essentially, this course is based on changing idiosyncratic, inappropriate reactions to an "average expectable environment," and it is therefore inappropriate for individuals who are dealing with truly unfavorable life circumstances. On the other hand, individuals who have passed through the period of acute crisis and are beginning to reconstitute their lives have proven particularly receptive to this form of skills training.

The second screening criterion, that of apparent mental health and absence of cardiovascular disease, is based on the consideration that this is a program designed for *healthy* type As. Throughout the program, the basic message is that the intervention will serve to make already healthy people healthier. The presence of individuals with obvious psychopathology would obviously negate this message for other group members. Similarly, individuals with a history of cardiac disease would obviously be excluded from this health category and therefore be a hindrance to the cohesiveness of the group. I think the program can be adapted to cardiac rehabilitation, but it would be better to treat coronary patients in separate groups.

The third criterion, that of social homogeneity, refers primarily to occupational status. One obvious reason for this criterion is to promote a comfortable relationship between group members; if company executives and secretaries do not usually attend workshops together, then they are unlikely to feel comfortable in the group together. In fact, the presence of superiors or subordinates may serve as an inhibiting factor on group members. But occupational homogeneity also serves the therapeutic purpose of focusing attention on idiosyncratic responses to the same or similar stress triggers. As we have seen, one of the basic excuses of the type A for his or her frenetic coping style is that it is the inevitable product of environmental stressors, particularly job demands. This rationalization becomes increasingly difficult to maintain, however, when other people with similar occupational demands start to behave differently.

I have worked with groups where members had relationships outside group sessions (all from the same company, for instance) and those where members previously did not know each other. The former is more difficult for the therapist because he or she comes as an outsider into an already-formed group. It also complicates discussion within the group somewhat in that some of the stress situations described may involve actual group members. In one group, for instance, a major complaint of a participant was the too frequent and too long executive meetings; the person responsible for the meetings was sitting next to the complainant! Even when the stress situation discussed does not involve other group members directly, the existence of extra group contacts requires the therapist to exercise considerable control over the degree of self-disclosure, so that group members are not embarrassed when they meet their colleagues the next day. Counterbalancing these disadvantages, however, is the substantial advantage of the ability of several members working in the same department or section to impact on their immediate work environment, thereby facilitating and helping to maintain individual change. Groups constituted of co-workers are also likely to have greater control over individual members and, consequently, can be quite powerful in promoting change in resistant participants.

Interestingly enough, age, marital status, and even sex appear to be less important in group formation. In tapping given management levels, I have recruited men and women ranging from their 20s to their 60s. Marital and parental status, too, has been quite varied, covering the single, married, separated, widowed, and divorced, as well as childless and parents of children of all ages. Similarly, groups have been constituted of men only or both sexes. (Unfortunately, I have not yet had the opportunity to work with women alone.) For type As anyhow, these "extracurricular" differences appear much less relevant than variations in occupational status. If anything, variations in marital and parental status among group members have been very useful in emphasizing the message that stress is inevitable regardless of life circumstances; what is essential is how we deal with it. Thus, it has been instructive for a group member struggling with the problem of competing family demands at Thanksgiving to discover that absence of family ties also creates problems. Similarly, the single person who deplores his or her lack of a marital partner is both entertained and enlightened by the woes of married group members.

Based on this description of the criteria for group constitution, the reader may be concerned about the absence of formal screening for the TABP. Obviously, such screening is important in a research program, but for clinical purposes I would be much less concerned about eliminating the occasional type B who might come into a program. There is nothing in this treatment that is likely to be harmful to the type B, and there are some elements that may even be helpful. Thus, if an individual volunteered for one of these programs who did not strike me as type A, I should probably rely on his or her self-perception of need as the prevailing criterion.

The final consideration is the size of the group. I usually prefer to work with groups of 10–14 members. Beyond 14 or so, I have difficulty in interacting with each person individually during a session. On the other hand, I prefer not to have groups with fewer than 10 members, because there will inevitably be absences from a session and a group that is too small does not achieve the interaction that is an essential element of the program. Group members, too, can feel threatened when group size diminishes beyond a certain point, experiencing the focus on the individual as too intense.

Frequency and timing of sessions

Ideally, this 20-session program should be delivered in a 10-week period with sessions held twice a week. One needs a few days between sessions for individuals to work on the homework assignments, but by having sessions twice a week no individual gets too far off the track before corrective feedback and renewed motivation are provided via another group meeting. In my experience one of the major reasons for dropout is that an individual misses one or more sessions, or simply fails to do a few homework assignments, and then feels there is no more point in continuing. By scheduling sessions close together, the therapist has fairly continuous contact with the group and can pick up danger signals before the damage is done.

However, no aspect of this program is graven in stone, and depending on the specific needs of a group, the therapist may wish to vary this schedule. One possibility is to have the first few sessions on a twice a week basis and then switch to a once a week schedule. Less desirable, but also possible, is 20 weekly sessions. In fact, the only limitations are allowing sufficient time between sessions to permit homework assignments to be done (hence, daily sessions would be contraindicated) and having sessions sufficiently frequent to maintain motivation (hence, a minimum of one weekly, at least at the beginning).

In scheduling group sessions for type As, the primary aim is to minimize response costs for participants. Thus, the ideal situation is the therapist who makes "house calls," holding sessions in a company meeting room. Failing a cooperative company with an available meeting room, the next best alternative would be a centrally located office building or hotel. An additional advantage of using company space, or a neutral space such as a hotel room, is that these are the usual locales of training seminars, unlike hospital or clinical settings, which are associated with sick people. However, what is desirable is not essential, and I have conducted some groups without too much damage in the unpropitious surroundings of a psychiatry outpatient department.

As far as time is concerned, I personally prefer 1-hour sessions. Shorter sessions for groups of this size make it difficult for each individual member to report on the homework assignment. Longer sessions, on the other hand, can become too dragged-out for impatient type As; I have experimented with 1½-hour sessions and discovered that we worked more efficiently in the shorter time period. As far as time of day is concerned, my preference is for the beginning of the working day, 7:30 or 8:00 a.m. By capturing participants before they arrive at their desks (or at least most of them!), we minimize the absences caused by "emergencies," "too much work," or prolonged meetings. I have worked successfully with groups at other times of day, however, and here, too, there is no time that cannot be used if it is convenient to group members.

Season of year is also a consideration in planning group sessions. In the city in which I work, Montreal, the business and professional communities recognize two distinct holiday periods in which people frequently plan vacations or are preoccupied with social engagements: the Christmas season, running from the middle of December till at least the second week of January, and the summer months of July and August. Once again, in the interest of minimizing response costs and maximizing participation, I should be very reluctant to plan group sessions during these periods. Similarly, many professions or businesses have a specific rush period (such as income tax filing for accountants, the Christmas selling rush for retailers), and it is not wise to expect individuals to engage in new learning when they are overburdened by other obligations.

Paying attention to holiday and rush periods, however, does not mean waiting for the mythical time when the type A hopes to be less busy than he or she currently is. On the contrary, I point out to reluctant enrollees, the best time to follow this program is when feeling swamped by competing obligations, because then one has immediate, practical application for the new skills learned. Much as participants might prefer it otherwise, stress management skills are best learned, not in the isolation of a stress retreat, but in the actual environment in which the stressors are occurring.

Shortening the program

For a variety of reasons, it may not be possible to use a 20-session program. Table 4-1 presents a modified version of the program, one designed for 12 sessions. I have used this version clinically, as well as in a pilot study for one of the research programs. In this pilot study, we did evaluate changes in the Structured Interview; interestingly, there was a clear dose–response effect, with participants in the 12-session

TABLE 4-1. Session program

Session	Materials	Content
1	R1; H1	Introductions; program overview (R1); physical tension stress diary (H1)
2	R2; H2; relaxation tapes	Follow-up of H1; Relax (R2); relaxation group practice; relaxation homework (H2)
3	H3	Follow-up of H2; awareness of behavioral tension (H3)
4	R3; H4	Follow-up of H3; Control yourself (R3); modifying behavior in one situation (H4)
5	H5	Follow-up of H4; modifying behavior in several situations (H5)
6	H7	Follow-up of H5; self-talk diary (H7)
7	R4; H8	Follow-up of H7; Think productively (R4); changing self-talk (H8)
8	H9 (relaxation); H10	Follow-up of H8; awareness of stress triggers (H10); introduction of short relaxation (H9)
9	R5; H11; ranking of triggers (sheet)	Follow-up of H10; Be prepared (R5); ranking of stress triggers; preparing one stress situation (H11)
10	H12	Follow-up of H11; Application of stress preparation skills (H12)
11	R6; H13; H14	Follow-up of H12; Cool it (R6); Coping with stress emergencies (H13); introduction of one-step relaxation (H14)
12		Follow-up of H13 and H14; summary and good-bye

Note. R refers to rationale; H refers to homework assignment.

program manifesting changes that were 60% of the magnitude observed in participants in the full program.

Structuring of sessions

The sequence of events in individual sessions is discussed in the chapters describing these specific program modules; this section, therefore, is a collection of more general observations.

The usual physical locale of a session is a conventionally furnished meeting room, with participants sitting around a table. The circle facilitates interchange between members, while the table provides a surface for placing materials, such as homework assignments. It is a nice touch to have a lighting system that can be dimmed during the relaxation practice, but not essential. Except for a tape recorder for the relaxation cassette, no other equipment is necessary.

To concentrate on the essentials, I try to routinize the details as much as possible. Before each session, any handouts for that session (e.g., bibliographic selections) are placed in the center of the table and members help themselves to this material as they enter. An attendance record sheet is also placed there, and members also sign it as they enter.

There are no fixed places at the table. In fact, I try to vary my seat regularly so as to shift the center of the group to some of the shyer and less verbal members. To facilitate quick contact between members in groups where individuals do not know each other (and to overcome the therapist's handicap in groups where they do!), cards with the participants' names are prepared, and each participant puts the appropriate name card in front of him or her when seated. My usual practice, with the group's permission, is to use first names.

The purpose of these sessions is to change participants' inappropriate coping responses, rather than to recast business and professional type As in a new image. To reinforce this message, I consider it important to conform to the norms of the business and professional communities whenever possible. Thus, contrary to usual academic practice, sessions begin and end exactly on time. Similarly, I and anyone working with me wear conventional business dress (suit, tie for men) at sessions. Once again, this is behavior that has been positively reinforced by participants in previous groups who have commented favorably on this in their program evaluations.

At least the first half of each session is devoted to discussion of the homework assignment for that session. It is one of my basic beliefs that if therapists want clients to do their homework, then they must structure the treatment session in a way that reinforces the desired behavior. Thus, the opening comment of a session usually begins with a question about the homework: "What did you learn about yourself?" or "How did the —— go?" To further emphasize the importance of these assignments, I ask participants to read directly from their homework assignments, rather than responding in broad, general terms.

As an additional aid to compliance with homework assignments, most of my time and attention, particularly in early sessions, is focused on those who have done the assignment. Professional and business type As are very sensitive to group expectations, and it is important early in the program to establish a group norm of compliance. Fortunately, in all beginning groups there are some individuals who will have completed the homework and initially it is on these that I concentrate. Only after the compliers have reported do I turn my attention to the problems. It may smack of the kindergarten to see high-powered type As bursting with the desire to talk, and being excluded from the discussion because of the absence of a written homework record. However, control of who talks is one of the most effective techniques I have found for motivating individuals to comply with written homework assignments. Obviously, the success of this maneuver, as of any other therapeutic technique, depends not only on what is done but on the skill and warmth with which it is done.

Depending on the complexity of that session's homework assignment, the new material of a session can occupy anywhere from 15 minutes to half an hour. I think it is important that the therapist not lecture group participants, or read from the manual. Instead, I very much prefer the principle of Socratic discussion, using questions and answers to elicit the desired points. It is not of fundamental importance that all points be covered in the discussion. Members do have the written material available and all can read. What is essential is that the coverage of new material include specific discussion of the homework assignment. In some cases (e.g., diary of physical tension, relaxation exercise) it is possible to begin the homework assignment within the session itself. In other cases (planning for a stress situation, planning for pleasure), I go around the circle asking individual members to describe their intentions. This gives the therapist an opportunity to provide preventive correction, for instance, to suggest an alternative to an inappropriate target situation. The essential point here is that homework is not simply an afterthought to the main business of a session; on the contrary, the main purpose of the session is to prepare participants for the subsequent homework assignments. Thus, group participants should be thoroughly familiar with the requirements of the homework assignment before they leave the session.

Although the sessions may look spontaneous and free flowing to the casual observer, they are far from being so. One of the obvious dangers of this type of group is to be derailed into a prolonged gripe session. It is, of course, far easier to complain about the stresses one is experiencing than to change one's manner of coping with them. Thus, it is the role of the therapist to keep the group on target. Fortunately, the egos of healthy type As are not that fragile, and it is possible to interrupt a participant, or to treat a complaint with humor, without permanent damage.

This pragmatic, matter of fact attitude to participants' difficulties is not incompatible with therapist warmth. On the contrary, the therapist's warm acceptance of type As as equals, matching and perhaps surpassing him or her in intelligence and competence, should be obvious. Nevertheless, it is precisely because I consider these type A clients to be competent adults that I treat them as such. In fact, most would soon begin to resent any false pampering.

Evaluation of treatment effects

As we have seen in the theoretical discussion of the type A behavior pattern (see Chapter 1), there is no simple, valid measure of treatment effects for healthy type As. Self-report measures, such as the Jenkins Activity Survey or the Framingham Type A Scale, suffer from problems of interpretation, in that many type As are relatively unaware of their behavior before intervention and very sensitive to considerations of social desirability posttreatment. To add to the problem, conventional questionnaires of general psychological distress, such as the Hopkins Symptom Checklist (Derogatis, Lipman, Rickels, Uhlenhuth, & Covi, 1974) or the Langner Scale (Langner & Michael, 1963), are not acceptable substitutes, since many type As tend to deny or underreport psychological symptoms.

In research programs we try to overcome the problems of questionnaires by obtaining samples of behavior, such as pre- and posttreatment administrations of the SI. In clinical settings, I would tend to rely on three criteria to judge program effectiveness: observable behavior during sessions, reports of behavior in stress diaries and homework assignments, and reports from significant others in the participant's environment, either directly or as transmitted by the participant. Obviously, there is the danger of selective perception here, too, both in what the client presents and in what the therapist chooses to see, but it may be preferable to accept the imprecision of our measures, rather than to strive for pseudoprecision. Thus, if the client claims that he or she is handling stress situations more appropriately, and can document this claim with specific examples, I would consider this to be a legitimate measure of treatment effects. Subsidiary measures would be changes in general well-being, also with specific examples (e.g., reduced consumption of aspirin, sleeping better), and comments by others on changes in behavior (e.g., "You are yelling less at the children.").

Problem situations

The reluctant client

Many group participants begin as professed nonbelievers, claiming that they have been propelled into the program by the entreaties of someone else (e.g., wife, physician) or that they enrolled simply out of curiosity. They either don't see their present behavior as requiring improvement (e.g., "I thrive on challenge and competition.") or else they don't see any viable alternatives to present coping patterns (e.g., "I can't get anything done without deadlines."). My tendency is to not to seek to convert the unbelievers, but instead to treat this initial skepticism as understandable and perhaps even desirable. Why should the consumer not be skeptical about the claims of yet another course?

In handling the reluctant client, I tend to focus on what the client is doing rather than what he or she is saying. The client who does not believe in the benefits of intervention must be present at sessions in order to voice his or her disbelief, and for the purposes of treatment an atheist who attends sessions is far preferable to a fervent believer who does not. Consequently, there is little to be gained by debating the merits of stress management in general terms, or even in making the client aware of the contradiction between his or her continued attendance in spite of disparagement of the program. Instead, my preference is to avoid the issue of resistance completely with these clients, and to focus instead on positive reinforcement for a partially completed homework assignment or any evidence of altered coping patterns.

One of the most frustrating clients I have ever dealt with was a young man who claimed to have no stress triggers in his life. "Mr. Cool," as I soon labeled him, claimed to have no difficulties on his job, in his relationships with family or friends, or even with inanimate objects. Apparently nothing bothered him. In fact, as he clearly proclaimed at each session, the major stressors of his life were attending stress management sessions and trying to find suitable target situations for the homework assignments! I was tempted to write off my unflappable client as a treatment failure, except for the fact that he never missed a session. Fortunately for my learning, Mr. Cool was in a research program with an extensive posttreatment evaluation. And, contrary to my expectations, he was one of the participants who, as evaluated by others as well as himself, had changed most during the program. Moreover, he reported himself as extremely satisfied with the intervention, explaining to one of the technicians that he was particularly impressed with our ability to deal with problems that were bothering him before he mentioned them, making it unnecessary for him to raise issues!

More difficult, of course, is the client who expresses resistance by nonattendance. A number of techniques are possible for handling this problem, but my preference is for pointing out openly that the person is wasting time and money (personal or company) by being enrolled in a program without attending it. I should try to contract with the reluctant client for a 2-week "suspension of disbelief" in which, in the interest of fairness, the program is given a chance. Furthermore, I should try to shape behavior by positively reinforcing attendance when it does occur.

No therapeutic strategies, however, can win over all clients, and the client who is determined to prove treatment ineffectiveness by non-attendance will do so. Thus, when someone persists in missing sessions without a good reason, I am prepared to concede defeat. At this point, occasional presences of the nonattender are likely to be more disruptive to the group than helpful to the individual, and it is more profitable to focus on those who wish to be helped. Sometimes I might suggest a switch into individual treatment for this type of reluctant client, so that we might discuss his or her doubts more extensively, but at other times I must accept, as gracefully as I can, the client's right not to change. Surprisingly enough, I can recall only about a dozen such cases in the hundreds of healthy type As with whom I have worked.

The overeager client

Paradoxically, the client who enters treatment convinced of its miraculous possibilities is likely to pose more of a challenge to the therapist than the initially skeptical one. For changing well-established habits is slow and hard work, and the beginning enthusiasm can just as quickly be replaced by disillusionment. One sign of client overeagerness is a report of sudden cure, especially in the early sessions. Asked to chart variations in physical tension for a homework assignment, or to practice a relaxation exercise, the client will return reporting dramatic changes in physical tension levels; he or she no longer gets upset at all. Tempting as it may be to the therapist to seize on these claims of powerful program benefits, my tendency is to pass over them in silence and focus, instead, on the content of the immediate homework assignment. Unfortunately for both therapist and client, substantial and permanent changes in coping patterns do not occur via sudden, global conversions; indeed, flight into cure is a well-known resistance for avoiding real change. The prudent therapist should take reports of dramatic, general change with a grain of salt; usually, simply failing to positively reinforce them will lead to their disappearance.

Another common example of overeagerness is the client who uses enrollment in a stress management program as a signal to improve his or her life generally and decides, at the same time, to lose an unwanted 20 pounds, to stop smoking, to cut down on alcohol, to embark on a regular exercise program, etc. It is perhaps typical of the type A that once convinced of the desirability of putting one's personal life into shape, he or she is likely to attempt to overcome 20 years of neglect in 10 weeks! Here, again, the therapist can provide some general guidance about the process of behavior change. I warn beginning participants about the temptations of instant reform, and point out to them that New Year's resolutions typically have a very short life. This time, however, they are embarked on a program of permanent behavior change, and this is best accomplished one step at time. Behavior change is hard work, and it is important to maximize chances for success by focusing on one attainable objective before proceeding to the next one. Accordingly, I ask participants to make no other changes in personal habits for the duration of this program. I do promise them, however, that skills learned in this program can then be transferred to other objectives; the person who has learned to control his or her stress reactions is also better able to manage eating, smoking, and exercise behavior.

Missed sessions

The problem of missed sessions is one of the major problems encountered in scheduling group sessions for business and professional type As. On the one hand, the individual who misses multiple sessions is unlikely to benefit much from the group and will probably be disruptive to group functioning. On the other hand, it is unrealistic to expect participants to be present at all sessions; even the most highly motivated participant is, in the course of a 10-week period, likely to have at least one out-of-town trip or an all-day seminar.

I try to handle this problem in two ways: screening out any prospective participants whose anticipated absences are expected to be sufficiently prolonged or frequent to make treatment unfeasible, and making special provisions for enabling other participants to keep up with the group in spite of occasional missed sessions. Thus, in discussing enrollment with prospective participants, the schedule of proposed sessions is presented, and individuals are asked about possible obstacles to regular attendance. Those who plan an absence of longer than a week, or who have conflicting obligations making it impossible to attend at least 80% of sessions, are considered unsuitable for the group. It may be difficult for the therapist to turn down would-be participants, but it is unhelpful to the individual to be placed in a situation where failure can be predicted, and it is bad for the morale of the therapist as well as the group to experience multiple treatment failures. A secondary benefit of this discussion of proposed attendance prior to enrollment is that it becomes part of the treatment contract; those who enroll have committed themselves to regular attendance.

Not all individuals eliminated from a specific group need be excluded from treatment entirely. Sometimes, as in the case of an individual planning a holiday, the problem can be solved by postponing enrollment to a subsequent group. In other cases, such as a group of salesmen who were regularly on the road, I have managed to run a group by scheduling sessions for the one day of the week, Friday, that they were likely to be in head office. There are times, however, when the individual's scheduled out-of-town trips are so frequent and/or irregular as to make group treatment unfeasible, and individual treatment, with its greater flexibility of scheduling, is then the best available alternative.

Even after screening out individuals unable to meet the attendance requirements, the therapist is still confronted by the problem of occasional absences of those enrolled. I have attempted a number of ways of overcoming this problem, some more effective than others. The most effective solution has been to schedule an additional weekly session, where individuals who had missed a session, or anticipated a forthcoming absence, could meet with the therapist. Unfortunately, this is also the most expensive solution in terms of therapist time, and not all groups are prepared to absorb the supplementary cost. A second possibility is to have the therapist arrive 15 minutes before the scheduled session and invite participants who have missed a session, or anticipate missing one, to use this as makeup time. This is probably the most feasible solution for most groups. One attempted solution that did not work was to pair members in teams and make one partner responsible for the other; this provided no way of dealing with instances where both partners missed the same session.

Control of self-exposure

Most type As who enter a program such as this are concerned about the degree of self-exposure that will be required of them. I share that concern and I expend considerable effort during the sessions toward shaping the degree and type of self-exposure.

The primary reason for seeking to limit self-exposure is that revelation of personal tragedies and sorrows is unnecessary, and probably counterproductive to the aims of the intervention. For the purposes of becoming aware of dysfunctional coping responses and correcting them, the ordinary, mundane hassles of everyday life are far more useful practice situations than the truly tragic or difficult stress episodes. It is much easier to show someone that his or her reaction is idiosyncratic and inappropriate when dealing with an interrupting telephone than when hearing the news of the fatal illness of a loved one. Similarly, the novice practitioner of relaxation techniques is likely to achieve much greater success if these fledgling skills are first applied during an ordinary project meeting rather than during a job termination interview.

A second reason for avoiding the tragic and pathological is that such disclosure may be harmful to the client, in that the program is not designed to deal with this type of problem. It will not take long for the experienced therapist to realize that some of the marital interactions described are the expression of seriously disturbed relationships, or that some job stresses described reveal important vocational difficulties. It is useless and probably harmful, however, to work at uncovering these difficulties unless the therapist is prepared to follow through on the material revealed. And this program is not the appropriate forum for doing so.

This does not mean that individuals with "real problems" cannot benefit from the intervention. Often increased self-control in dealing with daily hassles can be a useful first step in tackling more serious problems. Occasionally I have even had someone in a group who was simultaneously undergoing marital counseling or psychotherapy, with training in coping skills serving as an adjunctive treatment. For the purposes of this intervention, however, the focus is on "socially acceptable" hassles, the kind that can happen to anyone. Fortunately for our purposes, the supply of these is more than sufficient!

A number of techniques can be used to shape self-exposure. One of the most useful is the example sheet accompanying each homework assignment. Type A managers and professionals are extremely sensitive to group norms and they are quick to respond to clues of what is desired. The illustrations used in the example sheets provide such clues; for instance, the example sheet used in preparing for predictable stress triggers discusses waiting in the doctor's office, rather than coping with the drinking bouts of an alcoholic spouse. Even when a participant delves into a complex or sticky situation in presenting his or her homework assignment, the therapist can focus on how the individual reacted, rather than on the details of the situation itself.

Physician, heal thyself

One of the problems in conducting treatment programs for type As is that most of the professionals qualified to do so are likely to be type As themselves. How does one seek to change in others that which is evident in oneself? Fortunately, the cognitive behavioral literature suggests that the therapist who presents a model of coping with a problem is more effective than the one who presents a "mastery" model (Meichenbaum, 1977). Thus, for purposes of treatment it is sufficient that the type A therapist demonstrate how he or she controls innate tendencies.

For instance, I devote considerable effort and advance planning to assuring that I do project an aura of calm and self-control during sessions. To avoid the flurry of last-minute searches for needed material, I prepare papers needed for a given session well in advance and keep them in a separate briefcase. Since I usually travel to meet group participants, rather than vice versa, I allow sufficient extra time to arrive at least 20 minutes before a scheduled session. This extra time is used to switch off other concerns and mentally prepare myself for the forthcoming session. It also permits me to be ready to chat with early arrivals. This modeling of appropriate preparatory behavior is a very useful example in later discussions of planning to reduce stress (see Chapter 9). Ever so often, of course, my well-laid plans go awry and then I am in the position of giving a practical demonstration of how to cope with frustration!

A second problem likely to be encountered by the type A therapist working with type A clients is their common perfectionism. One of the major reasons for client discouragement and dropout is the inability of an individual to meet his or her personal standards for compliance with program requirements and behavioral improvement. For instance, the individual who has only partially completed homework requirements is likely to term this as failure and conclude that she is unable to follow the course. Similarly, the individual who loses his temper in a family discussion, in spite of his plans to the contrary, may be quick to conclude that there is nothing to be done about his type A behavior; he was born to be this way. It is important that the therapist, who may have similar high expectations about his or her own performance, not fall into this trap of unrealistic perfectionism. It is not enough to tell our clients that there are many gradations of performance between absolute success and absolute failure; we must also demonstrate it in our behavior and in our reactions to their efforts. Thus, instead of focusing on the glass that is half empty, the effective therapist is both sufficiently perceptive to detect even faint signs of improvement and patient enough to shape these behaviors to desired levels.

A final point concerns the problem of pacing—the allowance of sufficient rest and recuperation between periods of intense activity. While I very much enjoy leading groups of healthy type As, the expenditure of energy involved is simply too great to make this a viable full-time activity. Sessions with this clientele are extremely fast moving, and the therapist must be continuously alert and responsive. At the end of such a session I usually feel drained, a sentiment shared by my various cotherapist over the years, and even by casual observers at our sessions. Thus, in conformity with our advice to clients, I think it important that the therapist limit this form of hyperactivity. My personal limit is one session, or at the most two, a day.

5. Introduction to the program

Program reference: Rationale 1, "Introduction"

This chapter is a very short one because the material covered in it occupies barely half a session. Nevertheless, it is important; the manner of introducing participants to the program sets the tone for that which is to follow.

Before the session

In preparation for this session, I put copies of the manual, an attendance sheet, and cards with participants' names in the center of the table. I also place a card with my name in front of me. As each participant arrives, I greet them, introduce myself if we have not met before, and check off the name on the attendance sheet. I also invite the new client to take a manual and the appropriate name card, suggesting that he or she read the introductory rationale in the manual while waiting for the others to arrive.

An alternate procedure is to mail or otherwise distribute copies of the manual to participants before the first session, asking them to read the introductory rationale in preparation for it. While this latter procedure appears more efficient, it has the serious disadvantage that a fair number of participants are likely to forget to bring the manual to the session with them. Thus, unless one is prepared to furnish second copies of the manual to those who forget the first one, one should not risk it.

Introductions

The first session begins with my welcoming participants to the program and stating briefly who I am and my relevant training for and experience in conducting programs of this type. Most participants in these groups are quite anxious about what is involved, and it reduces anxiety considerably for the therapist to take the initiative in self-exposure.

Far more important than who I am, however, is the question of how and why group members were selected for participation. Particularly in corporate settings, participants are likely to be concerned, and understandably so, that their invitation to join the group indicates a perceived weakness on their part. Being told that this program is being offered to all managers at a given level, or whatever the basis for selection actually is, provides considerable reassurance. Even when group members are selected because of individual coping problems, as in the research program, it is still possible to couch the selection criteria in terms acceptable to participants. There, for instance, we congratulated groups members on the "good news" (i.e., absence of heart disease, competence in handling complex environmental demands as evidenced by their managerial status) before communicating the "bad news" (i.e., presence of behavioral and physiological hyperreactivity to stress).

I try not to let this part of the session drag on too long but turn, instead, to having individual participants introduce themselves to the group. In this introduction I ask participants to tell us their names, where they work and what they do, and what they hope to gain by participating in the program. Names and job descriptions are used because this is a form of identification with which participants are familiar and comfortable, while the goal descriptions orient individuals toward the personal benefits anticipated from attendance in the program. Some participants will spell out fairly specific goals (e.g., get rid of my stomach upset every time I have to submit a report), while most will speak in more general terms of "learning how to deal with stress better." In both cases, however, the therapist is made aware of client goals and can later use this knowledge of desired benefits to help motivate group participants.

Reconceptualizing the problem

After participants have finished introducing themselves, I take a few minutes to repeat the various goals expressed, classifying the specific examples given into a few general categories (e.g., the desire to handle stress better is an example of the wish for increased control, reduction of stomach upset is an example of the wish for reduced physical signs of tension, etc.). For most participants a stress management group is a very ambiguous situation and they are initially diffident about talking, fearful that they might say the wrong thing. This feedback concerning individual goals is designed to reassure them that their answers were appropriate, as well as to highlight similarities in the problems and goals of group members. Just as it is reassuring for corporate type As to learn that many others have preceded them in this type of skills training, so is it comforting to learn that other group members, too, sometimes feel overwhelmed by stress.

In describing their individual goals, participants repeatedly use the word *stress*. I remark that this is a commonly used word and suggest that it is important that we understand what we mean by the term. I ask group members, therefore, to define the term as they understand it, listing their answers on a chalkboard or flipsheet. The answers received can usually be grouped according to precipitating situation (e.g., an unreliable supplier) or resulting negative effects (e.g., feelings of frustration). In recapitulating their answers, I point out that both views of stress are correct, but that still leaves us with the fact that not all people perceive an unreliable supplier in the same way (e.g., nuisance vs. disaster), and not all react to the frustration in the same way (change suppliers, scream, reason with supplier, stomach ache vs. headache, etc.). Thus while it is impossible for the individual to avoid stress completely, there is the possibility of *increased control* via better management of perceptions and reactions.

At this point I usually take care to reassure professional and managerial type As that by most criteria they already manage stress effectively: Regardless of the threat or challenge, they get the job done. Where they are wasteful is in their use of themselves: by responding in an indiscriminate, undifferentiated fashion to a variety of potential stress triggers, they exact an unnecessarily heavy toll from themselves, and they increase their immediate discomfort, as well as long-range vulnerability to disease. The analogy here is with a furnace that has a defective thermostat and continues to heat even when the desired room temperature has been attained. The furnace is performing its task of heating in that the room remains warm, but the energy bill at the end of the month is much too high for the service received. One can attain greater comfort at lower cost by repairing the thermostat to more accurately and sensitively respond to the ambient room temperature. In the same way, this stress management course is designed to help participants achieve greater control and lower personal coping costs by increasing the range and flexibility of their responses to the inevitable stressors of daily life.

Almost inevitably, some participants will break into this sales pitch and voice objections to what I have said. In the exceptional case where group participants are too diffident to voice their objections, I assume the role of devil's advocate and express some of the common reservations myself. Objections and reservations can be expressed in a number of ways, but most are variants of a few basic themes: "Type A behavior has worked for me up to now; why should I change it?" "It's my basic nature." "I don't want to turn into someone else; it will remove my freedom of action." Before seeking to answer these reservations, it is important that the therapist reassure group members that these voiced doubts—and other, unexpressed ones—are a natural reaction to a new and untried program. Members in previous groups have also expressed them initially. While the therapist will try to reassure them about some of their concerns, the best proof of the program's worth will be their own experience with it.

In answer to the objection that type A behavior has been functional for the individual up to now, and therefore should not be changed, I point out that it is normal practice to change management style as one proceeds up the career ladder. The skills that make one a good employee at one level are not necessarily those most useful at a higher level; a good salesperson, for instance, is likely to be active, energetic, and quick moving, while a vice-president functions better in a more deliberate, reflexive manner. Thus, at this level of their professional development it may be appropriate to learn a different way of doing things. I also point out that most of us begin our working lives treating work as a sprint race, one best served by short-term, total effort. As we proceed, however, we discover that an occupational career is more like a marathon race, one best won by the person who can manage resources over the long haul. Therefore, it is precisely as individuals finish the first few years of work experience that a change in tactics is called for.

I counter the argument of "being born that way" be remarking that many of our behavioral habits feel that way because they have served us so long and so well. But even habits that feel part of us were initially learned, and can be unlearned. Granted that learning new ways of doing things is not easy, but these men and women have not gotten where they are now by choosing the easy path. They have faced other challenges successfully; why not this one?

The third major reservation concerns the individual's fear of becoming a stranger to oneself and losing freedom of action. Here it is possible to reassure the person that even should we wish it, psychological treatment is not very powerful in effecting global personality transformations: No type A need fear becoming a laid-back type B! Moreover, turning the person into a controlled puppet is far from the goal of the program; on the contrary, its purpose is to increase the person's freedom by increasing the variety and flexibility of coping strategies. Furthermore, in learning new habits, old ones need not be abandoned completely; the hard worker will continue to work with enthusiasm but may be better able to modulate his or her efforts to suit the needs and importance of the task in hand.

Clarifying the process of change

In spite of the detail in which I have dealt with common objections to the program and possible replies, the discussion of the merits and disadvantages of stress management for the healthy type A should be limited in time. The only really convincing argument for the participant is personal experience of benefits, and for this to occur one must move on into the program itself.

Nevertheless, before proceeding to the first homework assignment one important task still remains to be done, that of establishing an initial understanding on how change is to be achieved. For this purpose, I quickly summarize the program modules and describe how the sessions will proceed. In describing the program, the emphasis is on stress management as a skills-learning process. I underline that I do not have a magical potion to eliminate stress, but that participants will learn how to manage it better via their improved coping skills. However, like all skill learning, repeated practice is required to achieve proficiency; hence, there are behavioral assignments attached to each session.

While homework may seem like another imposition on an already overcrowded day, every effort possible has been made to minimize response cost. None of the assignments takes longer than 20 minutes, and all are relevant to the individual's daily situation. Furthermore, group participants have already proved in the course of their careers their ability to learn a host of varied skills. Isn't their personal health and well-being worth 20 minutes a day?

Passing quickly from the philosophical to the practical, I find this an opportune moment to obtain group agreement about starting and ending times for sessions, possible displacement of sessions because of holidays, etc. It is also a good time to establish procedures for recording attendance, use of first names, and for making up missed sessions.

Concluding comments

This chapter had described one possible script for handling the initiation into the program. It is obviously not the only one; other therapists may choose to proceed somewhat differently. Whatever the specific procedures used, however, it is important that this session begin to build participants' trust in the program. This is accomplished by showing that the therapist understands their concerns about the process of change but also is confident that they can succeed in it, and that the necessary skills will be taught in a manner to facilitate learning. I try to keep the atmosphere in this session matter of fact and businesslike, asking a minimum of exposure or commitment from participants.

One potential difficulty with this session, as well as the subsequent one on relaxation (see Chapter 6), is the management of time, for these are the two most crowded sessions in the entire program. In this first session it is important to keep the group atmosphere relaxed, to allow ample time for participants' comments and questions, and yet also to reserve sufficient time at the end for adequate discussion of the first homework assignment. In budgeting this session, I allow 15–20 minutes for the homework assignment and another 15–20 minutes at the beginning for the introductions. The middle part of the session, the part devoted to the general discussion of stress and stress management, is the most flexible and can be condensed or enlarged as time allows. I should not worry unduly about covering all the material in the introductory rationale; most of the issues raised there will resurface many times in the course of the program, and the therapist will have many subsequent opportunities to deal with them.

Program facsimiles

Rationale 1

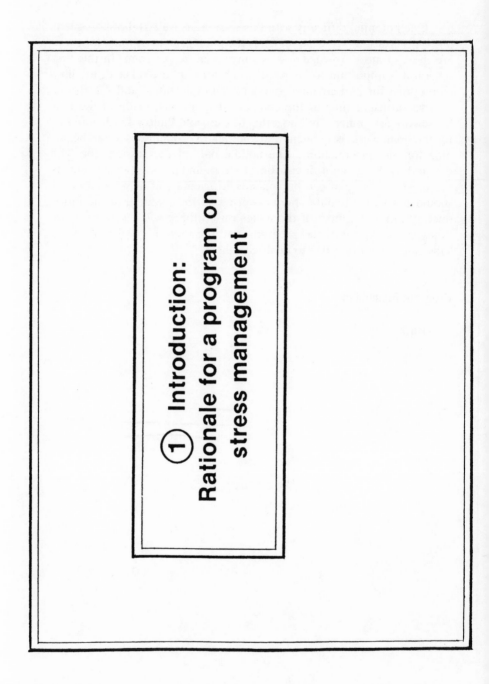

① Introduction:
Rationale for a program on
stress management

What is stress?

Stress is a state that you experience when you are facing an important challenge (e.g., when you are making a presentation to your superiors) or threat (e.g., someone questions your competence) and there is a *possible imbalance between demands and resources.*

Stress arises, therefore, in a specific kind of *interaction* between you and environment:

1. You *perceive* a situation of *challenge, threat, or harm.*

2. You *consider* the outcome *important* to your welfare.

3. You *are uncertain* whether you *will be able* to successfully meet the challenge or avoid the threat.

[handwritten margin notes:]
or previously activated (memories) of reality

or is it conflict between feeling you can + can't
→ internal feeling of anxiety or failure

to acknowledge anxiety, doubt

Who experiences stress?

All of us inevitably encounter challenge or threat in the course of daily living, and in this sense stress is universal. What varies from individual to individual are:

1. The situations to which we are *exposed*. The potential triggers may be quite different for the junior executive compared to the company president.

2. The events *perceived* as stressful. Both past experiences (cultural and personal) and present circumstances (place, time, life situation, and mood) influence the way we evaluate situations.

3. The way stress is *experienced*—physical, emotional, cognitive, and behavioral signs.

4. The way we *cope* with it.

What produces stress?

Almost any event will trigger stress for somebody.

External stress triggers

Many stress triggers come from *outside:*

Unsatisfactory person–environment fit (responsibility without authority, job ambiguity, unpleasant colleague); change (new superior, new project, change in business conditions).

Or simply:

Daily hassles (the line at the bank, the car that won't start, the person who hogs the phone when you have to make an urgent call, etc., etc.).

Internal stress triggers

Some triggers come from *inside* ourselves (e.g., unrealistic self-expectations):

I can't afford to make a mistake.

I ought to be further in my job level than I am.

What happens during a stress episode?—A first look

Before	The trigger	Mobilization	Recuperation
Before the trigger: The mental and physical *set* with which you approach a potential stress trigger.	Traffic light, broken shoelace. New task to master. "That same old routine is get-ting me down." "Now that I'm 40, it's now or never." Change in job, family circumstances.	*Dealing with the trigger:* A state of war in which all resources—thoughts, feel-ings, and physical responses—focus on meeting the challenge or threat.	*After the battle:* Time for relaxation. Closure on what is passed. Energy replenishment. Ready for the next challenge or threat.

What happens during a stress episode?— A second look

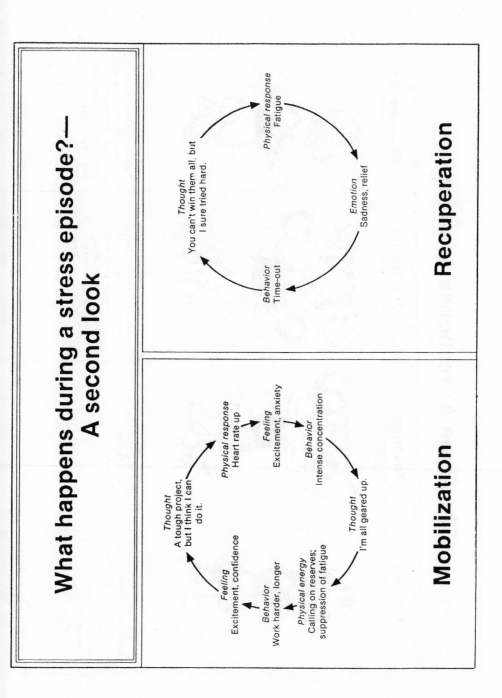

Mobilization

Thought
A tough project, but I think I can do it.

Physical response
Heart rate up

Feeling
Excitement, anxiety

Behavior
Intense concentration

Thought
I'm all geared up.

Physical energy
Calling on reserves; suppression of fatigue

Behavior
Work harder, longer

Feeling
Excitement, confidence

Recuperation

Thought
You can't win them all, but I sure tried hard.

Physical response
Fatigue

Emotion
Sadness, relief

Behavior
Time-out

91

The "type A" response to stress

Before	The trigger	Mobilization	Recuperation

Before the trigger:
Type A is highly vulnerable to threat/challenge because of his or her mental and physical set:
a. Mental—expectations of self and others.
b. Physical—constitutional hyperreactivity.

Anything and everything:
Type A treats even minor obstacles as major provocations.

All wars are nuclear wars!
Type A has no brakes to modulate the response. Therefore, arousal is too strong, too long lasting. Strong arousal may even interfere with performance.

What's that?
Type A is unable to enjoy recuperation. He or she rests only when exhausted. No sooner is one battle over than the process begins again.

Why type A is ineffective

Too quick on the trigger.
Indiscriminately strong mobilization.
Too slow to recuperate.

Result: You get the job done, but with a too high, wasteful use of energy.

Goals
of this program:
"Effective use of energy"

1. *Learning* to be more *selective* in choosing *which triggers* to respond to.

2. *Learning to modulate* the *degree* of your response to any stress trigger.

3. *Minimizing* the duration of your mobilization.

4. *Maximizing* the benefits of your recuperation.

How are these goals achieved?

- By *learning to become more aware* of your physical tension level, your thoughts, and your behavior.

- By *learning skills to control* your physical tension level, your thoughts, and your behavior.

- By *practicing* these skills until they become a part of your life.

- By *using* these skills:

  In *preparing* for stressful situations.

  In *meeting* unexpected stresses.

- By *increasing* stress resistance:

  In *learning* to balance threat and challenge with pleasure and tension release breaks.

How is the program structured?

Learning new skills—whether the skill is playing tennis or stress management—takes time, effort, and practice. To facilitate learning in this program, we have made it a step-by-step process. There are eight modules;

1. *Introduction* to the program.
2. *Relax:* Learning to control physical stress responses.
3. *Control yourself:* Learning to control *behavioral* stress responses.
4. *Think productively:* Learning to control cognitive stress responses.
5. *Be prepared:* Learning to anticipate and *plan* for predictable stress situations.
6. *Cool it:* Learning emergency *braking* in unpredictable stress situations.
7. *Building stress resistance:* Learning to plan for rest and recuperation.
8. *Protect your investment:* Stress managements as a *lifelong investment.*

Format of program

When?

Where?

What happens if I miss a session?

What happens if I must be away for a whole week?

The first four modules are devoted to introducing the program and learning basic stress management skills: How to control *physical*, *behavioral*, and *mental* signs of stress.

In each case the format is the same:

A. *Self-awareness*—What do you have to *know about yourself* to institute change?

B. *Developing new skills*—What do you have to *do* to institute change?

C. *Applying new skills*—How do you *apply* the new skills to daily life?

Once you have learned the ABCs of stress management, the next two modules (5 and 6) are devoted to showing how to *combine* and *apply* them in order to play the stress management game. This involves:

Learning how to *anticipate* and *plan for* potentially stressful situations.
Learning to maintain or regain your cool even in the face of *unexpected stress.*

Module 7 deals with increasing your general *resistance to stress.* The emphasis is on learning how to increase your stress tolerance by scheduling "pleasure breaks" into your daily routine.

The final module is devoted to *protecting your investment,* learning strategies that will make stress management a lifelong habit.

You can't always control the world *outside,* but you can learn to *control the way you respond to it.*

The importance of homework

To systematize and guide this practice, we have developed a series of homework assignments. Everyone knows that homework is a drag and that trying to find time to do it only adds to your stress! We agree!

But homework is also essential for learning. We have kept the homework assignments:
● Short and snappy (no more than 20 minutes a day).
● Relevant to your daily routine.

Aren't you worth spending 20 minutes a day on yourself?

6. Modifying physical responses to stress

Program references: Rationale 2, "Relax";
Homework 1–13

The response to stress occurs on multiple levels—physical, behavioral, cognitive, affective—and, logically, intervention could begin on any level. I have placed modification of physical responses first in this program because the techniques used to reduce physical tension provide the quickest therapeutic benefits. Although real proficiency in relaxation can take weeks to achieve, most people will feel some beneficial change after even just one experience. For impatient, doubting type As, this almost instantaneous reinforcement provides a powerful motivation for continuing to persevere.

A second reason for beginning the program at the level of physical tension reduction is that this coincides with the popular view of the harmful effects of stress. When we come to modification of behavior or thoughts, many type As are quite resistant to change since they consider their characteristic manner of proceeding necessary for getting things done. Even a type A, however, is unwilling to defend a sleepless night or a splitting headache as integral to his or her productivity. Thus, we begin at the level where our clients are most amenable to change.

Because relaxation training occurs at the beginning of the program, it also serves as the vehicle for establishing what this program is really about. This clarification of roles and expectations will occur through many specific interactions, including how punctually the sessions begin and end, the therapist's reaction to expressed doubts or undone homework, the group's reactions to a member's self-disclosure via homework, and how the therapist interprets modest or no improvement following the initial relaxation practice. During these initial sessions the therapist and program are on trial, and what takes place is the real job of selling the program and specifying what exactly is being sold. For this reason, I shall describe some of the possible interactions in these initial sessions in considerable detail.

Awareness of variations in bodily tension

A key tenet of this intervention approach is that bodily tension first occurs and can be detected at levels far below the actual eruption of symptoms. For most type As, however, a state of high arousal is so habitual that they are completely oblivious to the process of tension buildup. Conceptually, too, they have difficulty in envisioning the possibility of mental alertness without physical tension. Being physically relaxed, in their view, is reserved for flopping in front of the TV set or for sleep. Thus, before we can provide a remedy for reducing physical tension in the course of daily activities, it is first necessary to establish a consensus that a problem exists and to develop a common language for describing that problem.

The process of increasing awareness of variations in physical tension begins with the development of a measuring instrument, the *tension thermometer*. In the last quarter hour or so of the initial session, I might simply remark that the first area we shall work on is reducing bodily tension, and that it would be convenient to have a measuring scale for describing variations in this tension. The analogy of a thermometer is used, but this is a different type of thermometer in that each person establishes his or her own personal anchoring points. Group members are asked to remember situations where they felt most relaxed and situations at the opposite extreme of maximum tension, to recall the sensations experienced at each of these times, and to label these sensations as "low" and "high," respectively. I then go around the table, asking participants to situate their current level of tension, using a personal scale with numbers from 1 (low) to 9 (high). I reassure participants that it does not matter if one participant's "4" is another's "6"; the purpose here is not to compare individuals, but to develop a method for describing each person's variations in tension over time.

At this point, the novice type A therapist may encounter a rude shock. Around a table crackling with tension, where people are fidgeting, finger tapping, and coughing, no one admits to a tension level above "2." This is likely to be the first confrontation in the program and the manner of handling it is important. My basic rule is not to directly dispute what the client is saying, since I have never yet won an argument with a type A (or any other client, for that matter). Instead, my inclination is to accept these reports of low tension as valid perceptions, but also to point out that almost all beginners in the program tend to report low levels of tension initially. Since up to now there was very little group members could do about managing tension, it made sense to screen it out. As they learn new techniques for reducing tension, however, they will also become more proficient in recognizing it. Sometimes, this can be an appropriate moment for self-disclosure, with the therapist remarking that his or her current tension level is "5," since embarking with a new group is always somewhat stressful. The message we are trying to communicate is that experiencing bodily tension is not necessarily a sign of weakness or sickness.

This discussion of the tension thermometer leads to presentation of Homework 1 (Stress Diary). This assignment is relatively straightforward, but a number of possibilities for confusion do exist. It is important to clarify that we want individuals to record every hour, even if they are not experiencing any particular signs of tension. Second, clients should not try to recall the whole hour, but should simply write down what they are experiencing at the moment of recording. Since memory can be misleading, the aim is not to record a whole day's tension levels at bedtime, but to record each on the hour, as it happens. Thus, the daily record sheets can be separated and a single sheet carried in a pocket or purse. Should it be impossible to record at one period (e.g., middle of a meeting), one might try to make a note on a scrap of paper, or simply skip that recording period.

Since this is the first homework assignment, it is worth spending a few minutes preparing participants for what is involved. On the one hand, we can reassure them that this type of hourly recording will last only a short time. Once they have achieved proficiency in noting hourly variations, we shall go on to other things. But the general requirement of a homework assignment for each session cannot be glossed over. Since stress occurs in the real world, the basic work of observing and changing it must also take place there.

The first half of the second session is devoted to discussion of this initial homework assignment. To focus the discussion, I usually begin with a question such as "What have you learned about yourself from this homework assignment?" This question can be thrown out to the group at large, but if no one responds, it will be repeated addressing a specific individual. Group members should be encouraged not to respond in general terms, but to illustrate their responses by reading directly from the homework sheets.

A number of possible difficulties are likely to occur here. One arises because most individuals find it easier to describe stress in terms of the situation eliciting it, rather than in terms of the person's response to it. Thus, a participant may launch into a vivid description of the incompetent serviceman at the garage, completely ignoring his or her own emotional and physical reactions to that serviceman. To get the participant started, one might allow a brief description of the situation; the homework assignment itself, in recognition of this tendency, puts the "situation" heading first. But in the discussion the therapist then would seek to shape the desired response by questions on how the person *reacted* to that provocation, in terms of feelings and bodily sensations.

A second common difficulty is that a participant will respond that he or she experienced no high tension levels over the recording period. This is particularly likely to happen when the recording period has covered a weekend or holiday since, initially anyhow, stress is likely to be perceived as the product only of the work situation. Once again, my inclination is not to argue, but simply to ask the participant to describe a period of low tension. "When did you experience the lowest tension level and what did it feel like?" can be as useful a question as the reverse one. Our aim here is simply to increase awareness of *variations* in tension level, and any change from neutral can be grist for the mill.

Inevitably, in any group there will be at least one person who "did \ot have time" to do the assignment. At this point in the program, my tendency would be to pass over it quickly, turning to someone who has done the homework. The aim here is to establish a positive atmosphere of group conformity, hoping that the desire to be part of the group will motivate the recalcitrant individual. More common are individuals who have done the homework, in whole or part, but who complain that the assignment is time consuming and that it is difficult to find words with which to describe bodily sensations. Here reassurance is in order. It is a normal reaction to find the homework assignment stressful; in fact, it is even possible that for the first 2 weeks or so participants may experience increased rather than decreased stress, since they will have the homework assignments added to the usual demands of the daily routine. We can assure them, however, that if they can take the program on faith for about 2 weeks, almost all participants will experience increasing benefits by then. It is also understandable that participants will lack an adequate vocabulary for describing bodily sensations; vocabularies develop according to perceived need, and since up to now there was little to be done about signs of physical tension, it made sense to ignore them.

The rotation around the table, with each person describing moments at high and low tension, provides a convenient opportunity to introduce the concept of *stress signatures*. Often individuals will describe the same stomach churning or shoulder pains in a number of high tension situations. For this particular individual, it is the stomach or shoulders that are most vulnerable to stress and, therefore, constitute the best signals of a high tension state. The identification of stress signatures has an additional purpose. Often the first real moment of shared fellowship in a group comes when two "stomachs" or "shoulders" discover each other!

In completing these homework assignments, participants often have difficulty in distinguishing between emotional and physical states. Words like "rushed" or "tired" are sometimes used for one, sometimes for the other. This is not an issue I would dwell on; our aim is not to train scientists, but simply to increase awareness that something is happening. More important are the beginning connections between the two, as when a participant recognizes that anger is accompanied by a pounding heart. Paradoxically, the lack of connection between physical state and perceived emotion can be even more significant; for example, the individual did not feel angry, but his or her heart was pounding. In these cases, the physical sign can serve as a signal of the unrecognized feeling.

At the end of this session, and all other sessions, the individual homework assignments are collected. The ostensible purpose of this collection is to permit the therapist to look them over and track individual progress and problems. In doing so, however, we also reinforce the message that these homework assignments are important.

The therapist can use these initial homework assignments to make a collective, group list of all the words used to describe emotions and bodily sensations. The presentations of copies of this list to participants at the next session serves a number of purposes. It demonstrates that even though individuals may lack an adequate vocabulary with which to describe feelings and bodily states, the group as a whole has considerable resources. On another level, this feedback reassures participants that the therapist has taken the time and trouble to read the homework. Finally, the pleasure in identifying one's own contribution to the group production serves as still another motivation for conformity with the homework assignments.

The relaxation exercise

Group participants are likely to easily understand and accept the desirability of reducing excess bodily tension (Rationale 2). What does arouse considerable questioning is the specific procedure (i.e., progressive muscular relaxation) used for modifying these states. Participants want to know why relaxation is used rather than physical exercise, biofeedback, meditation, and a host of other treatments. They also question the possibility of finding the time necessary to practice relaxation.

It is not particularly profitable for the therapist to engage in a lengthy discussion of the comparative merits of various treatments, or to disparage alternative methods of reducing physical tension. It is usually sufficient to indicate that the literature reports more similarities than differences between the various techniques (see Hillenberg & Collins, 1982; Holmes, 1984; Lehrer, Woolfolk, Rooney, McCann, & Carrington, 1983; Silver & Blanchard, 1978), and that just about any method will be useful for someone. The great advantage of relaxation for our purposes, however, is that it is portable. It is not realistic to jog, meditate, or even to practice relaxation at 7 a.m., and to expect this single exercise to act as a charm, warding off excess physical tension throughout a long, harried day. Instead, to truly modulate tension levels, one requires a technique that can be called upon throughout the day. And while it is not socially acceptable to get up and jog around the conference table during a tense business meeting, it is almost imperceptible, and therefore acceptable, to take a deep breath and relax. Thus, in contrast to most other methods of tension reduction, relaxation can be used as a coping technique on the daily battleground, where stress is actually occurring (Goldfried, 1977).

The difficulty in finding the time necessary to practice relaxation twice daily is accepted as a legitimate one. Many participants do have very crowded schedules and, in any case, I have not found it useful to argue the point. Instead, the emphasis is on the temporary nature of this requirement, only until proficiency in relaxation is acquired. These men and women have already acquired a host of occupational and athletic skills, and they are aware that a certain investment of time and energy is required before the benefits of that skill can be enjoyed. The eventual benefit of the time invested to acquire relaxation proficiency will be the ability to monitor and modulate tension levels during the course of daily activities.

Although this is usually not dwelt on during the group sessions, there are three other considerations that led me to choose progressive muscular relaxation as the tension reduction technique of choice. The first is simple economy; unlike biofeedback, for instance, no machines are required. A second is that this is the tension reduction technique placing the most emphasis on *discriminating* tension from relaxation, a prime necessity for type A clients who have difficulty in detecting and labeling tension states. Finally, relaxation appears to be the least anxiety-provoking tension reduction technique for type As, perhaps because of the activity involved in tensing and relaxing muscles.

The issues that have been discussed will not come up all at once during the introduction of the relaxation technique. But it is important that the therapist recognize their existence and be prepared to deal with them. Moreover, to the degree that participants feel free to question what is happening, it is a positive sign of their increasing involvement in the process. For me, the danger signal would be a lack of questions or doubts. In that case, I should be tempted to play devil's advocate and voice some of these doubts myself, thereby communicating the message that questions about the program are acceptable.

For training in progressive muscular relaxation, I use the procedures described by Bernstein and Borkovec (1973). I make my own relaxation tape, so that there will be continuity between the therapist voice in the sessions and that heard during the homework, but there would be no serious disadvantage to using one of the many commercial tapes available. Before beginning the first exercise, I briefly review the various muscle groups and the procedures used to tense and relax them. Then I ask participants to turn to the first relaxation homework (Homework 2) and note the day, the time, and their current tension levels. The relaxation exercise to follow during the session will serve as the first practice for that day. Finally, I caution participants that relaxation is a learned skill; the first practice of relaxation is unlikely to produce major changes in tension level, but greater changes can be expected with increasing proficiency.

Prior to beginning the exercise, I ask members to loosen tight clothing and sit comfortably in their chairs. Depending on personal preference, the eyes can be closed or focused on a specific spot. If possible, the lights are dimmed. I try to make the room quiet and comfortable, but it is not necessary to have recliner chairs or soundproofing, since eventually we want these relaxation skills to be used while sitting up in a normal work environment.

My usual practice is to use the tape for this first run-through of the relaxation exercise. This prepares the participants for what they will hear at home and frees the therapist to observe participants' reactions during the exercise. My experience has been that group members vary considerably in their reaction to the initial exercise. A few may appear to almost fall asleep during the course of the exercise, the majority will achieve some degree of relaxation, and a few will look obviously fidgety and uncomfortable.

. Following the exercise, it is advisable to go around the room asking group members to note their current tension levels and the change from the prerelaxation level. Not accidentally, I tend to start with those who appear to have benefited most and to reinforce the tension reduction attained. It is also important to reinforce those who have small changes to report (e.g., a "4" to a "3"), emphasizing once again that even small changes in tension level, if repeated frequently during a day, can lead to significant changes in well-being. Finally, it is important to ask if anyone found the exercise uncomfortable, and to accept this as a common and normal reaction. For most people, being relaxed while alert is an unusual state and may be initially anxiety provoking (see Heide & Borkovec, 1984). Usually, this anxiety will diminish with repeated practice.

This second session is a crowded one, but it is essential to spend a few minutes on preparation for the homework assignment, asking participants when they might schedule their twice daily practices. At this point a number of problems are likely to surface. Inevitably, there is one group member who announces during the distribution of the homework tapes that he or she does not have a tape recorder. Assuming that participants in this program are all employed and have reasonable salaries, this is not an objection that must be taken seriously. A simple remark such as "Aren't you lucky, you're about to buy yourself a present" and the name of a local discount house selling low-cost recorders are usually sufficient to handle this pseudoproblem. Some other group members might announce that they expect to be out of town, or to experience other disruptions of normal routine, during the following days. Rather than seek to provide a ready-made solution—to which they can then find new objections—I prefer to ask the participants themselves to problem solve and suggest their own methods of overcoming these difficulties. For the rest of the group, I simply reassure them that the relaxation exercise can be done at any time of day, though it is preferable not to do it while trying to digest a heavy meal.

The third session begins with a discussion of the relaxation homework. In questioning group members about the relaxation practice, I go into considerable detail about how, where, and when the practice was conducted, as well as its perceived benefits. Invariably, at least one of these type As will report abandoning the tape. When questioned about the length of the exercise, he or she will shamefacedly admit that it was possible to complete it in less than 5 minutes. Here the therapist promises that it will soon be possible to do the exercise in 5 minutes without a tape but also points out that for the initial learning it is better to pace oneself with the tape. The client who, for whatever reason, absolutely cannot use the tape could be advised to repeat the exercise two or three times until 15–20 minutes have elapsed.

Most of the participants will report some modest success with relaxation, claiming that they slept better after a practice or that they felt better able to handle the morning's challenges. These should be strongly reinforced, both as encouragement to those who attained these changes and as motivation for the rest of the group. The message the therapist is trying to communicate is that learning to cope with stress is not an instantaneous transformation but proceeds by slow, gradual steps. As important as inducing change, is learning to recognize and appreciate even small benefits.

One common fear concerning the effects of relaxation is that it will make the person too sleepy or too limp to be effective during the course of the day. For most group participants the notion that one can be mentally alert while physically relaxed is difficult to accept. Perhaps the best method of overcoming this fear is the testimonial of a group member. With a little bit of luck, every group will contain at least one member who practiced relaxation at the beginning or during the day and then functioned even more effectively than usual. This link between the reduction of excess physical tension and increased effectiveness is obviously one that will be heavily underlined by the therapist.

Some participants will report failure because they were unable to restore a state of calm by trying to relax when very upset. The analogy invoked by the therapist here is that one does not usually learn to swim by tackling deep, turbulent water. Transforming a "9" tension state to a "1" is a difficult and probably unrealistic goal; it is far more profitable to strive and achieve change when the initial tension level is not at an extreme high. This is the same answer given to those who eliminated relaxation practice on a given day because they were "already relaxed."

For others, the failure is the result of the inability to do two relaxation periods every day. To avoid the sequence of perceived failure leading to withdrawal from the group, the therapist might concentrate on the half of the cup that is full, and focus on the practice sessions that did occur. Then the help of the group might be invoked in problem solving to overcome obstacles and schedule additional sessions. This procedure has many desirable benefits. For the group, it is the first active involvement of the members in solving each other's problems, thereby promoting group cohesion. It also introduces the fundamental notion that individuals are entitled to time for themselves, and that the environment can be shaped or negotiated with to obtain this time. I am continuously amazed at how new this notion is to program participants, most of whom perceive their days as totally dominated by external pressures and demands.

In working with type As, one can expect at least one member to announce a complete cure by this third session. He or she practiced relaxation a few times and now is no longer stressed by any type of event. This is one of the times when the wise therapist will say nothing.

A good part of the third session is devoted to discussing the relaxation homework. Nevertheless, even as we seek to *change* tension states, we continue the work of increasing *awareness* of variations in tension levels. Part of Homework 2 is a diary of emotional and physical signs of tension, and some time is spent in having participants report on lows and highs, and what they have learned about their daily and weekly rhythms. Similarly, even when the focus shifts to other levels of change in subsequent sessions, a few minutes are always reserved for discussion of the relaxation practice.

Shorter relaxation exercises

A shorter, 5-minute, relaxation exercise is introduced in Session 9 (Homework 9). By then, assuming twice weekly group sessions, participants will have had 4 weeks' practice in the longer relaxation exercise and most will be reasonably proficient in it. The exercise is shortened by three changes: First, muscles are combined into 7 instead of 14 groups; second, each muscle group is exercised once instead of twice; and third, the preliminary tensing of the muscle is eliminated, focusing instead on achieving a deeper relaxation state. For convenience sake, the shorter relaxation exercise is recorded on the reverse side of the original tape.

The introduction of this shortened version is generally welcomed by group members. In addition to reducing the time required for homework assignments, it serves as a sign of progress toward the eventual goal of applying relaxation skills in daily life. Occasionally, however, a participant will complain that he or she does not achieve as deep a relaxation state with the shorter exercise. Here we may suggest that the client alternate the two forms, using a different one at each of the two daily practice sessions. Each homework assignment continues to include daily record sheets for the relaxation practices.

At the 13th session, one-step relaxation is introduced. The procedure for this is very simple (Homework 13). By then, group members are usually able to identify those muscle groups in which they characteristically feel tension, that is, their personal stress signatures. The individual is asked to take a deep breath and focus on relaxing that particular body part. Depending on the circumstances and personal preference, the eyes may be open or closed. This is the promised portable relaxation technique, one that can be used at virtually any time and in any place to modulate tension levels.

With the introduction of one-step relaxation, participants are no longer asked to record daily practice of the longer versions. The elimination of these formal relaxation periods does not occur because of their lack of clinical benefits. On the contrary, it would be very desirable to have participants continue daily relaxation practice. However, it is very unlikely that many of our participants would comply with such a demand, and it would weaken the credibility of the rest of the program to ask for what we know in advance will not be forthcoming. Like the wise parent of teenagers, the type A therapist is advised to "choose your battles," restricting demands to those for which there is a reasonable chance of compliance. Accordingly, we suggest only that it might be useful to return to the relaxation tape a few times a week, or during periods of high tension, and many participants report doing so.

Relaxation as a coping skill

There are three main ways in which relaxation can be used as a coping skill: to monitor and modulate physical tension levels during the course of the day, to prepare for potentially stressful situations, and as the first step in regaining self-control during a high tension state. Of these, the first is the least dramatic but probably the most useful.

I have tried a number of "gimmicks" to serve as signals for monitoring and modulating tension. Thus, in earlier versions of this program I distributed red stars, asking participants to paste them on objects associated with regularly occurring tension (e.g., watch, telephone, steering wheel of car) and to relax every time they saw a red star. This usually elicited considerable laughter in the group, with suggestions of pasting one on a superior's forehead, on the front door of the house, etc. It was also well received on the lecture circuit. In fact, the only thing wrong with this procedure is that it didn't work very well in practice. Within a short time, the stars fell off, the novelty diminished, and members stopped practicing these relaxation breaks.

More useful, albeit more difficult, is to ask each member to develop personal signals for tension monitoring, based on his or her individual habits. Thus, one program participant who habitually used a pencil in his work developed the habit of stopping for a relaxation break every time he had to erase something. Many participants have used the telephone ring as a tension-monitoring and relaxation signal, while others have found that a trip to the bathroom can serve as the stimulus for relaxation. I ask participants to develop a number of signals, in a variety of situations, so that relaxation breaks can be taken at work, at home, and even while traveling.

There is no prescription as to the ideal number of relaxation breaks per day. Since each one will take about half a minute, even 30 in the course of a day will involve the expenditure of only a quarter of an hour. Once again, the purpose of these relaxation breaks is not to eliminate physical tension, but simply to reduce it. Changing a "5" to a "3" may not appear a dramatic change, but doing so repeatedly will result in much less cumulative tension and fatigue at the end of the day. It will also serve the purpose of preventing, or at least slowing, the escalation of the "5" into a "9."

A second major use of one-step relaxation is as preparation for a potentially stressful situation. Just before beginning a difficult conversation or before making a presentation, a moment's relaxation can help the individual attain greater calmness and self-control, thereby increasing the chances for effective performance. The degree of physical tension a person is experiencing affects behavior (e.g., tone of voice) and hence how one appears to others. The person who can reduce extraneous tension is likely to appear more in command of himself or herself and the situation.

The third major use of one-step relaxation is as a method of regaining self-control in high stress situations. This application will be discussed in the section on handling stress emergencies (Chapter 9).

Concluding comments

This chapter has described training in management of physical tension by developing proficiency in the use and application of relaxation techniques. In focusing exclusively on relaxation here, the aim is not to imply that relaxation is the whole of stress management. On the contrary, I consider it a serious tactical error to promote relaxation, or any other single technique, as a stress cure-all. As a participant in one of the early programs graphically expressed it: "I practiced relaxation, but what do I do now when my body is relaxed but my thoughts are still racing?" For their coping to be effective, participants will require a variety of techniques for a variety of daily hassles.

Nevertheless, for teaching purposes the initial sessions of this program focus exclusively on physical tension and techniques for controlling it. Here we are implicitly trying to teach our participants the process of effective behavior change: one, slow, easy step at a time. Perfectionistic type As are likely to set unrealistic goals and then to give up in frustration when they are unable to meet them. Our aim, instead, is to carefully dose the amount of change required, and to reward participants for any step in the right direction. The message here is that a more relaxed learning pace will, ultimately, be a more effective one. When participants do bring up situations requiring more complex coping than relaxation at this early stage, we can simply ask them to note these situations for future discussions.

A final comment concerns the active role of the therapist in the sessions. In contrast to many forms of group therapy, the therapist does not let group processes emerge but, instead, actively seeks to shape the content of the sessions. Far from remaining silent, the therapist speaks often and forcefully. As the sessions continue and group interactions increase, the therapist will become less dominant, but he or she definitely remains the group leader. In many ways, this leader role defines the distinction between this program and conventional group therapy. Our aim here is not to uncover or to ventilate but, within a limited time period, to impart skills to men and women who have a tendency to try to control their surroundings. Ideally, the leader is warm, accepting, and encouraging. But he or she should also be firmly in control. If not, the anxious type A lions are likely to devour each other, or the therapist, or both!

Program facsimiles

Homework 1; Rationale 2; Homework 2; Homework 9; Homework 13

Homework ①

Stress diary—Skills for detecting stress

What is the goal?

To *learn* to discriminate your physical and emotional signs of tension.

What do I have to do?

1. Fill in the sheet hourly, noting your tension level (low–moderate–high) and physical and emotional signs of tension. (See example sheet.)

2. Use a separate sheet for each day of recording.

Name: Example sheet

Date:

Situation	Time	Tension level			Tension signs	
		Low	Moderate	High	Physical	Emotional
Woke up	a.m. 7:00	X			alert, ready to go	well-being
Arguing with son	8:00			X	knot in stomach	anger, frustration
Working on new project	9:00		X		All systems go	interest, challenge
Phone call – financial data not ready	10:00			X	heart rate up	irritation
Working on project	11:00		X		shoulder muscles tense	Concentration
First draft finished	12:00	X			tired, hungry	satisfied
Lunch with project gang	p.m. 13:00	X			relaxed	friendly
Late for staff meeting	14:00			X	running	hurry
Boring meeting	15:00	X			sleepy	boredom
Meeting real waste of time	16:00			X	tense shoulder muscles	impatience
Desk work	17:00		X		Concentration	resignation
Driving home	18:00	X			winding down	anticipation
Good dinner	evening 19:00	X			comfortable, relaxed	satisfied
Discussion with son re argument	20:00		X		apprehensive, tight	frustration
Discussion with wife re son	21:00			X	stomach getting upset	anger, guilt
Beer – watch ball game	22:00		X		calming down	enjoyment
Ready for bed	23:00	X			tired, little tense	worried
	24:00					

Rationale for managing bodily tension

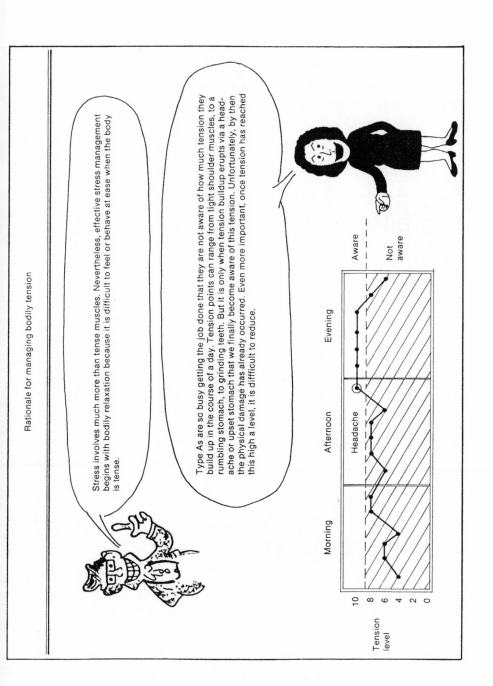

Stress involves much more than tense muscles. Nevertheless, effective stress management begins with bodily relaxation because it is difficult to feel or behave at ease when the body is tense.

Type As are so busy getting the job done that they are not aware of how much tension they build up in the course of a day. Tension points can range from tight shoulder muscles, to a rumbling stomach, to grinding teeth. But it is only when tension buildup erupts via a headache or upset stomach that we finally become aware of this tension. Unfortunately, by then the physical damage has already occurred. Even more important, once tension has reached this high a level, it is difficult to reduce.

Steps involved in learning to manage physical tension

Effective management of physical tension means keeping your bodily tension at a level that is *comfortable* for you and *appropriate* to the situation. To achieve this aim, a number of skills are required:

A. Awareness skills

- Of small variations in bodily tension.
- Of relationships between feeling states (e.g., anger) and bodily states (e.g., pounding heart).
- Of what constitutes a comfortable "cruising speed" for you.

B. Developing new skills

- Learning to discriminate a relaxed muscle from a tense one.
- Learning to lower overall body tension by relaxing muscle groups (e.g., forearm, jaw) one by one.
- Eventually, learning to use a single command to relax your whole body. Take a deep breath and R-E-L-A-X.

C. Applying new skills

- Once you have acquired the ability to relax upon command, this can be used:

- *To monitor and regulate tension during the course of the day:* By checking and reducing tension periodically (e.g., every time you pick up the phone), you can avoid harmful tension buildup.

- *To prepare for a potentially stressful situation* (e.g., an interview, a meeting): By doing so, you will have the advantage of entering the situation in a calm, collected manner.

- *To maintain or regain self-control during crisis:* When you are upset or overwhelmed, management of physical tension is the first step in achieving control over your reactions.

Homework ②

Improving self-awareness + RELAXATION

What is the goal?

To *improve* your ability to discriminate variations in physical and emotional signs of tension.

To *learn* how to relax muscles.

What do I have to do?

1. Fill in stress diary daily, as before.

2. Practice relaxation twice daily, noting tension level before and after each practice. (See example sheet.)

Relaxation practice

Name: Example sheet

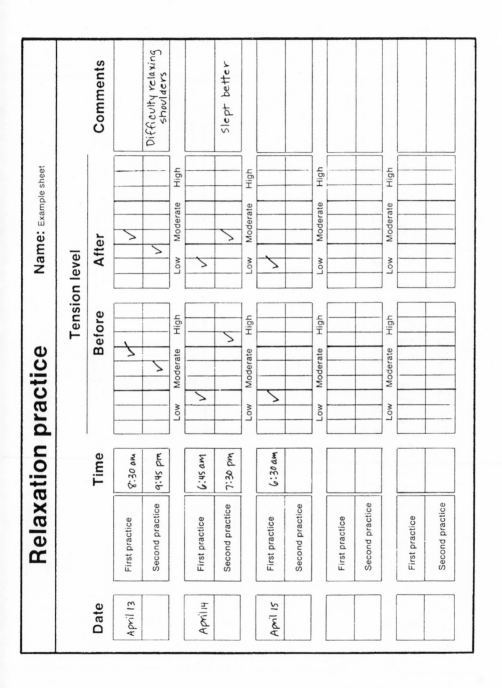

Date		Time	Tension level — Before (Low / Moderate / High)	Tension level — After (Low / Moderate / High)	Comments
April 13	First practice	8:30 am	✓ (Moderate / High)	✓ (After)	Difficulty relaxing shoulders
	Second practice	9:45 pm	✓ (Moderate / High)	✓ (Low / Moderate)	
April 14	First practice	6:45 am	✓ (Low / Moderate)	✓ (Low)	
	Second practice	7:30 pm	✓ (Low / Moderate)	✓ (Low)	Slept better
April 15	First practice	6:30 am	✓ (Low / Moderate)	✓ (Low)	
	Second practice				
	First practice				
	Second practice				
	First practice				
	Second practice				

Homework ⑨

SHORT RELAXATION + Combining change in self-talk and behavior

What is the goal?

To *learn* a *quicker* relaxation procedure.

To *learn* to reduce stress by *combining changes* in self-talk and behavior.

What do I have to do?

1. Practice side B of the relaxation tape twice daily, noting tension before and after.

2. Every time you feel tense, note your nonproductive self-talk and your behavior, then try to reduce stress by changing both. Note new self-talk and behavior. (See example sheet.)

Homework (13)

ONE-STEP RELAXATION + Coping skills for stress emergencies

What is the goal?

To learn one-step relaxation.

To learn to deal effectively with *stress emergencies.*

What do I have to do?

1. Practice one-step relaxation regularly.

2. Everytime you feel signs of rising stress, use an emergency braking signal and institute strategies for regaining self-control. Then note the situation in which you used your emergency braking signal. (See example sheet.)

7. Controlling behavioral responses to stress

Program references: Rationale 3, "Control yourself"; Homework 3–6

The TABP, by definition, refers to an assortment of observable behaviors. These behaviors have been divided into two broad categories, the pressured drive that manifests itself in moving faster and trying harder, and the potential for hostility that refers to an abrasive style of interaction with others. Of these, the first is relatively easy to spot, while the second is far less evident to the casual observer. Thus, someone watching a group of type As interact during the mild stress of an early group session is likely to observe several common characteristics. The participants speak loudly and rapidly, often in a staccato, barking fashion. There is considerable twisting and turning on the chairs, and some participants manifest nervous mannerisms, such as foot tapping or pencil twirling. Watches are frequently consulted, and group members enter and leave the room at a trot, as if perpetually late for an important appointment. However, while they may report an angry exchange with a colleague, or even a dangerous maneuver to cut off an offending driver, their behavior to each other, and to the group leader, is likely to be polite and watchful.

Since aggressive–hostile behavior is often considered the key pathogenic element in the TABP, it is important to understand where and how it is likely to be manifested. In the hundreds of type As with whom I have worked, I have met very few who were aggressive for the sheer joy of hurting other people. On the contrary, for most type As aggressive behavior is a defense, a response to actual or potential threat of harm. Unfortunately, the type A's tolerance for frustration tends to be very low, and consequently, the need for this defense is frequently felt. But even then, the type A is likely to suppress manifestations of aggression that are not socially acceptable. A superior may be nasty or sarcastic, a customer may make unreasonable demands, or the computer may be down just when there is strong pressure to meet a tight deadline. In none of these cases will our white-collar type A use physical violence, and he or she may not even say anything. A few hours later, however, the same type A will become disproportionately angry at a slow waiter, or sarcastic to a colleague who asks for a simple favor. The volcano builds up pressure, erupting whenever the pressure becomes too great and the situation is perceived as relatively safe. Thus, even though our participants initially perceive most of their stress at work, the homework assignments will report most episodes of out-of-control behavior occurring in the home or in interactions with service people who cannot easily retaliate.

To modify the type A's potential for hostility involves far more than simple modification of behavior. The belief system leading to the frequent perception of threat and the low level of frustration tolerance also require modification. One must begin somewhere, however, and it is easiest to begin with the visible tip of the iceberg. Thus, this section deals with helping the type A to become more aware of, and more in control of, his or her behavioral responses to stress.

Awareness of behavioral tension

Behavior is the stock in trade of the psychologist. It was a rude surprise, therefore, to discover in earlier versions of the program that this term had little meaning for group members. I continue to use the word *behavior*, as a form of shorthand, but it is important to provide a definition. One which has proven useful is "what somebody else would see."

The usual procedure in this program is to achieve some consensus on the nature of the problem before introducing techniques to remedy it. The introduction to behavioral stress responses occurs at the end of Session 3, with the presentation of that session's homework assignment. Participants are told that the next topic on which the group will work is methods for controlling behavioral responses to stress. To do so, they must become more aware of when and how these responses occur. Accordingly, the stress diary for this homework assignment has been somewhat modified. Emotional and physical tension signs are combined in a single heading, and a new column is added for behavioral tension signs (Homework 3).

Session 4 begins with a review of this homework assignment, a discussion of what group members have learned about their behavioral signs of tension. Self-disclosure concerning behavioral tension signs is potentially more damaging than that relating to physical tension, and the prudent therapist monitors it carefully. At this point, the group is not yet ready to deal with examples of extreme or aberrant behavior.

Instead, the emphasis should be placed on fast walking, pencil tapping, and other common and relatively innocuous signs. Most of the examples will concern time-pressure behavior, rather than aggressive behavior, and it is advisable to focus initially on these less threatening manifestations of the TABP.

One obvious omission may be remarked on by the attentive reader. Examples of type A behavior abound during group sessions, but at this point no use is made of this material. For group members, to have their behavior observed and commented on by the therapist would be extremely threatening, and this would increase their already high defensiveness. It is far better to wait until the group members feel safe and comfortable enough to comment themselves on behavior manifested during the sessions.

For the same reason of avoiding unnecessary threat, I have abandoned the practice, used in earlier versions of this program, of asking family members and work colleagues to observe participants' behavior. Previously, group members were given copies of the stress diary and asked to have significant others complete these reports. However, this presented two major problems. In many cases, the observer was a type A himself or herself and literally did not see any signs of tension worth recording, thereby reinforcing the member's perception that the behavior in question was normal. In other cases, however, an angry wife or colleague might go to the other extreme and use the recordkeeping as an opportunity to vilify the participant. This would have the undesired effect of making the person attacked defensive, thereby increasing resistance to change.

Rationale for managing behavioral tension

In contrast to the effort to reduce physical tension, the rationale for managing behavioral tension (Rationale 3) requires considerable explanation. For most group members, the voice characteristics and the perpetual hurrying are so common in their environment that these mannerisms are considered normal. Moreover, how would you get your point across at a meeting without jumping in and speaking loudly and quickly? How would you get anything done if you did not move at a rapid pace? Aggressive–hostile behavior may arouse some regrets, but if it is a choice between "keeping it in" and "letting it out," then surely the latter is healthier.

The approach taken by the therapist is that time-urgent or aggressive behaviors are not bad in themselves. On the contrary, there are many situations in which they are appropriate. What is harmful is the automatic, stereotyped fashion in which the behavior is manifested. A fast-food hamburger may be designed to be ingested without tasting, but does it really make sense to wolf down a good dinner in the same fashion? Is it really energy efficient to respond with the same degree of anger to an inattentive salesperson as to a major threat to life? In short, no single behavior is "bad" in itself, but the harm lies in the stereotyped nature of the response pattern, where the only variation is between suppression and eruption, frantic activity and complete exhaustion. The aim of this intervention is to teach the type A how to increase both the range of possible behaviors and self-control in selecting different behaviors for varying situations.

Modifying behavior in one specific situation

If most type As have difficulty is conceptualizing a state of physical relaxation while mentally alert, they have even more difficulty in imagining how one could be effective in the normal, working environment without behaving in a characteristic type A fashion. One useful technique for handling this problem is to find an appropriate model. Before introducing the actual techniques for behavior modification, participants are asked to think of someone with whom they work who is soft-spoken rather than brash, deliberate instead of frantic, but who is both respected and effective. Almost invariably, two or three persons in each group are able to describe such persons, often in high-level positions. To learn how to figuratively speak softly, but still be listened to, becomes the goal of these first efforts of behavior change.

Three basic techniques are suggested for controlling behavior: time-out, focusing on incompatible behavior, and using communication skills to express wishes, opinions, and even negative feelings in a controlled fashion. The first is no more that the old technique of pausing, or counting to 10, in order to interrupt the process and give oneself time to reflect. The second technique involves focusing on a behavior that is incompatible with the undesirable behavior. For instance, slow speech is less likely to be loud speech, the person who focuses on listening carefully is less likely to interrupt, watching the passersby on the street will effectively slow one's hurried pace, and so on. Communications skills—such as focusing on the problem rather than attacking the other person, or beginning sentences with "I" rather than "you"—are more complex (see Roskies & Avard, 1982; Stuart, 1974), but the basic principles of negotiation and communication are familiar to most of our participants from a myriad of business seminars. What is far more difficult is showing them why and how to use these techniques in the interactions of daily life.

The structuring of the first effort to modify behavior in a specific situation (Homework 4) becomes an important vehicle for imparting some basic principles about the general process of behavior change. Many participants try to learn mountain climbing by practicing on Mount Everest. If changing behavior will make them more effective, then they want to change everything, in all situations. When pressed to choose a specific behavior and situation, they will choose a hopelessly difficult and complex one. To counteract these tendencies, about half of Session 4 is spent discussing the choice of a target behavior for change, the situation in which it is likely to occur, and the techniques that can be used to control it. By the questions and comments of the therapist, participants are encouraged to make choices that are both specific and realistic. Although it may be initially disappointing for a participant to realize that one can't cure everything all at once, the group is also learning an important lesson in behavior modification, the importance of "setting oneself up for success." One begins with a greater chance of ultimate success by choosing a realistic goal, and reaching it, than by striving for an unrealistic goal and being forced to abandon it.

The homework assignments of past groups reveals that most members will eventually settle on some aspect of time-hurry behavior. Thus, they seek to eat slower by putting down the fork between mouthfuls, or by concentrating on conversing with a lunch colleague; they try to slow racing speech at a meeting by pausing for a drink of water; and they seek to control impatience in the car by focusing on a favorite musical tape. Most group members attain at least partial success in reaching their goals and are very proud of the resulting feeling of increased control. For many participants, this homework assignment is the first demonstration of the fact that self-control can be as satisfying a goal as control of others.

Obviously, not every group member will report complete success. For some group members, the intention was good but the execution was faulty. Once the therapist has let the "successes" report, it is important that he or she ask for reports of failure, pointing out that we can learn as much from the latter as from the former. In most cases, what the participant calls "failure" is simply a rate of success below 100%; he or she spoke slowly during most of the meeting but at one point got so excited that the homework assignment was completely forgotten. This is an excellent opportunity for the therapist to introduce the notion that success is not an all-or-none phenomenon, but is made up of many gradations. It would be unrealistic to expect to transform overnight behavioral patterns that have served one relatively well for 30 or 40 years. Instead, a 10% reduction in the intensity of a given behavior, if recognized and encouraged, will eventually lead to bigger and better changes. Moreover, just as a small reduction in physical tension level can produce major changes in well-being if repeated often enough, so can small, repeated changes in behavior prove significant.

Controlling behavior in several situations

By the fifth session participants are ready to extend both the number and type of tense behaviors they will seek to modify. Rather than planning a specific behavior modification situation in advance, group members are asked instead to use increases in general tension level as signals to monitor behavior and, if necessary, to introduce corrective action. Obviously, one cannot expect participants to note all occurrences of tense behavior but, as the example sheet of Homework 5 indicates, by now group members could expect to consciously control behavior five or six times during the course of a normal day.

An even more important change occurs at this time, in that participants extend the scope of their behavioral control efforts to include modulation of the abrasiveness of their interactions with others. Paradoxically, assertion training has proven to be very useful for this purpose. In my initial understanding of type A behavior, assertion training seemed the technique least likely to be needed, but experience has shown how often these type As have difficulty in expressing verbally their wants and needs.

For instance, a participant interrupted in a task may tap her foot impatiently, glance repeatedly at her watch, shuffle papers on her desk, and respond in brusque monosyllables. The action that is surprisingly unlikely to occur is a verbal request such as "I'm trying to finish this task now, but could we discuss it in half an hour?" Similarly, a group member may dread a round of family visits on Sunday, and he may eventually blow up at the end of a frustrating day, but this type A would not think of suggesting that the number of visits be limited. When asked why he or she didn't *say* something, rather than behaving aggressively, the participant is likely to respond either that he or she didn't want to hurt the other person or else that the other person should have *known* what he or she was feeling. The lack of appropriate verbal expression of needs and dislikes is a complex issue, impinging as it does on beliefs (e.g., "the other person should know what I want") as well as behavior, but here it is sufficient to reinforce the notion that it is acceptable to want to work undisturbed and acceptable to be frustrated by unmet needs. It is the manner of expressing it, rather than the need itself, that is the goal of change.

This attention to verbal expression of wants and needs helps the therapist to make an important distinction between controlled behavior and repressed behavior. The object of this program is not to eliminate all expressions of anger, but rather to allow the person to consciously choose when and how to become angry. Under certain circumstances, anger is an appropriate emotion; there may even be times when it is very effective to raise one's voice. The difference, however, is between a deliberately chosen course of action and a simple reflex.

A problem likely to surface at this point is the individual who boasts of "giving others stress" rather than experiencing it himself or herself. Thus, this person claims to discharge behavioral tension by unleashing it on someone else, usually someone not in a position to retaliate. It is the hapless airlines reservation clerk, a subordinate, or a family member who bears the brunt of the day's accumulated tension. The individual sees no reason why this behavior should be unhealthy, since obviously it is better to discharge tension than to repress it. In dealing with this attitude, it is useless to appeal to altruistic motives; instead, the emphasis is on how the behavior is hurting the person himself or herself. Thus, the therapist can remark that strong expressions of behavioral tension, be it in the form of yelling or pounding the desk, exact a *physical toll* from the sender as well as the recipient; this type of behavioral display is likely to be accompanied by increases in blood pressure, heart rate, and adrenaline level. Second, *stress carriers*, as we term them, are likely to damage *long-term relationships* and *performance* at work and in the family. The supervisor serves as a model for the subordinate, the parent for the child, and it is very sobering to see one's own behavior reflected in a rude employee or out-of-control child. Showing a hostile type A how his or her hostility is self-injurious is a difficult message to convey; the therapist needs considerable skill in rejecting the behavior, without also appearing to reject the person.

At the other extreme of the continuum from the stress carrier is the *stress victim*. He or she doesn't want to behave in an aggressive fashion, but it is a demanding superior, tardy spouse, or irresponsible child who "makes me mad." The implicit demand to the therapist is that a way be found to change the behavior of the other person. Here one can point out that there is no technique that will magically make the other see the error of his or her ways and transform behavior. However, the participant does have the power to change his or her own response to the provocation, thereby significantly modifying the resulting interaction. For instance, a superior of the stress carrier variety consistently enjoyed baiting his victim, a group participant, and provoking an indignant response. When the participant learned not to rise to the bait, however, but to calmly continue discussing the problem in hand, the supervisor first reacted by repeatedly asking if he were feeling well and then, in a few days, by finding another, more compliant victim. Similarly, when a mother responded to her adolescent's ear-blasting music, not with her usual yelled order to stop, but with a quietly expressed suggestion that they try to work out some kind of compromise, the familiar shouting match remained stillborn. Once again, the message communicated is that one cannot control the other person, but by remaining calm one can influence the interaction.

Sometimes the most powerful motivation for changing aggressive behavior is precisely this goal of increased control. One of the most dramatic reversals in attitude that I have witnessed occurred in a group member who indignantly kept insisting that when he was interrupted during conferences, he would retaliate by shouting. Nothing I or any other group member could say would change his mind about the correctness of this sequence of behavior. Finally, feeling somewhat frustrated myself, I posed the question "Does that mean I can make you shout anytime I want simply by interrupting you? Can someone else really control your behavior to that degree?" There was a startled silence, followed by indignant sputtering. But one of the all-too-rare, sudden transformations in attitude had occurred.

In fact, the connection between controlled behavior and effective behavior is the major focus in reviewing this homework assignment. In asking participants' about their homework, the therapist is interested not only in their changed behavior but also in the impact of this change on the person's effectiveness in handling the situation. The underlying message here is that learning to reduce aggressive outbursts does not make one an ineffectual wimp. On the contrary, the ability to restrain anger and to communicate with a tardy supplier or a recalcitrant employee in a problem-solving manner can increase one's effectiveness, as well as safeguarding personal health.

The content of this module is of a serious nature, but the format in which it is delivered need not be so. Humor is one of the most effective means of conveying potentially threatening messages in a nonthreatening manner. Thus, one of the aims of the therapist is to lighten the sessions by encouraging laughter. Some members begin to enjoy the dramatic opportunities of reporting on stress episodes and will describe them in a fashion likely to elicit laughter. In other cases, the therapist may take the initiative in pointing out the potential humor in a situation by exaggeration or simply by mimicking. The material of these sessions does not dwell on the tragic but on the pratfalls of daily life, and group members are healthy enough to recognize, albeit sometimes ruefully, the humor as well as the stress in the situation. Observers at some of my group sessions are sometimes surprised at the amount of laughter during sessions, but enjoyment does not preclude effective learning.

Controlling time-hurry behavior

The homework assignment devoted to time-hurry behavior (Homework 6) does not introduce any new material, but simply seeks to consolidate previous learning. What is new is that for the first time a label is attached to a group of behaviors; instead of treating fast driving, a barking voice, and foot tapping as independent behaviors, they are now categorized as manifestations of "time-hurry" sickness. By showing the connection between discrete behaviors, we seek to strengthen awareness. Once again, we begin with the less threatening component of the TABP, reserving till much later (Homework 14) any labeling of the aggressive–hostile component.

The review of the homework assignment for time-hurry behavior occurs in Session 7, one third of the way through the program. This is a good time for the therapist to slowly diminish his or her active role and to allow group interactions to become more prominent. By now, members have begun to know each other, as well as some of the significant persons in each other's lives. Thus, the report of a new confrontation with the difficult co-worker and the saga of efforts to have a car satisfactorily repaired begin to resemble episodes in a continuing serial. Members become more active in cheering each other on, or in offering suggestions. This new familiarity may also permit competitiveness and hostility to appear within the group, and it is important to keep a tight reign on these. On the whole, however, the therapist can visibly relax at this session.

One of the benefits of this group discussion of problems is the members' growing awareness of how common their stress problems are. For many of the members, particularly men, these sessions are the first opportunity to unbutton themselves and share some of the daily hassles of their lives. Moreover, it reinforces the message that the existence of stress is not the product of a specific work or family situation, but that regardless of the particular job and marital or parental status, individuals will inevitably confront and have to learn to manage stress.

Concluding comments

The material of this chapter is less structured than that of the previous one. This change is deliberate, reflecting both the difference in what is being taught and the different stage of group process. For control of physical tension, there is a specific technique to be learned—relaxation—which will then be applied to a variety of situations. For control of behavioral tension, in contrast, there is no single control technique, but a variety of possible responses depending on the specific nature of the stress situation. Moreover, most members already have some prior knowledge of the appropriate coping techniques; what they lack is awareness of when to apply them and skill in execution. Thus, in seeking to modify behavioral responses to stress, the therapist changes from a deductive to an inductive process. The basic messages to be communicated will be prepared in advance, but the manner and sequence in which they are presented will depend largely on the specific examples furnished by group members.

The nature of the group process changes, too, as members talk more to each other and to the therapist. Furthermore, the pace tends to quicken. In contrast to the drawn out silences, the sense of heaviness, in some conventional psychotherapy groups, here there is constant, quick repartee. Responding to individual problems while focusing on the underlying theme obviously requires skill and effort. The process of a group session in many ways resembles a tennis match. The conversational ball flies back and forth between therapist and group members, and, while using a variety of maneuvers, one must remember to keep one's eyes on the ball. At the end of a session a therapist may feel as tired as at the end of an active tennis match, but fortunately, at this point in the program the therapist also begins to experience the exhilaration of participating in a quickly moving change process.

Program facsimiles

Homework 3; Rationale 3; Homework 4; Homework 5; Homework 6

Homework ③

RELAXATION + Behavioral stress awareness

What is the goal?

To *improve* your skill in relaxation.

To *improve* your skill in discriminating *physical* and *emotional* signs of stress.

To *learn* to discriminate your *behavioral* signs of stress.

What do I have to do?

1. Practice relaxation twice daily, noting your tension level before and after each practice.

2. Fill in stress diary, adding your behavioral signs. (See example sheet.)

Situation	Time	Tension level			Tension signs	
		Low	Moderate	High	Emotional & physical	Behavioral
Traveling to work - bus slow	a.m. 7h:00		✓		impatience	keep looking at watch
Stress management session	8h:00	✓			interest, apprehension	alert, watch for cue
Correspondence	9h:00			✓	tense shoulders	
Planning session	10h:00		✓			voice rises
Site visit — trouble shooting	11h:00			✓	anger, irritation	walk and talk fast
Lunch	12h:00	✓			relaxed	gobbles food
Office meeting	p.m. 13h:00	✓			none - ordinary meeting	
Coffee break	14h:00	✓				laugh
Office meeting	15h:00				back to business	sit up straight
Answering memos	16h:00				concentration	tap pencil
Squash game	17h:00		✓		effort, competitiveness	play to win
Traveling home	18h:00	✓			tired, relaxed	
Homework with child	evening 19h:00		✓		irritation	edge in voice
Dinner party	20h:00		✓		boredom	drinking too much
Dinner party	21h:00			✓	anger	parties = headache
Time to go home	22h:00			✓	anger	put on coat
Relaxation exercise	23h:00	✓			calming down	relax muscles
	24h:00					

"Control yourself"

③ Rationale for managing behavioral tension

Rationale for managing behavioral tension

When you are feeling overwhelmed by multiple demands and insufficient time, it may seem normal to speak curtly to your secretary, to tap your fingers impatiently during a meeting, and to bark into the interrupting telephone. Unfortunately, such displays of behavioral tension have a double negative effect:

1. The very act of raising your voice or pounding your fist increases the unpleasantness you are already experiencing, creating *within yourself* a negative spiral of escalating tension.

2. Behaving angrily or impatiently toward others leads them to respond in kind, creating *between people* a negative spiral of escalating tension.

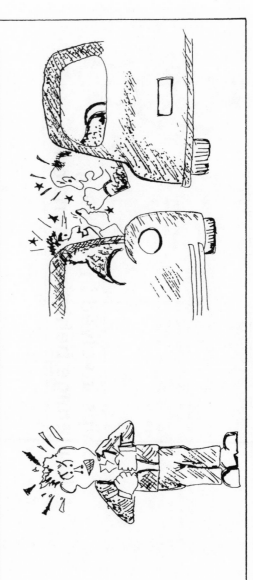

Many people believe that it is necessary to rant and rave when upset in order to "blow off steam." Unfortunately, by the time they have finished their eruption they have created such havoc—within themselves and in their relationship with others—that much time and energy is required to repair the situation. In contrast, the person who can manage his or her behavioral signs of tension expresses needs or complaints verbally, in a forceful but controlled manner. If not always master of the situation, he or she is at least in control of his or her *own behavior*.

Steps involved in learning to manage behavioral tension

Effective management of behavioral tension means that you can move quickly if necessary, express displeasure, and even assert your rights, *all without losing control.*

A.   Awareness skills

- Identify your personal signs of behavioral tension.
- Recognize the relationship between feeling state (e.g., frustration) and tense behavior (e.g., shouting).
- Recognize the situational and interpersonal triggers likely to provoke tense behavior.

B. Developing new skills

- Delay undesirable behavior.

- Engage in behaviors incompatible with the undesirable target behavior; for example, speak slowly to prevent shouting, attentively to prevent impatient tapping of fingers.

- Express needs and complaints verbally, in a nonhostile, controlled manner.

C. Applying new skills

- Express your needs or complaints in a controlled, appropriate fashion. Rather than bottling up anger or losing control, you can use anger purposefully.

- Increase desirable behaviors in the course of the day. The person who speaks in a calm, modulated voice, assumes a relaxed body position, and listens attentively will improve his or her interactions with others, as well as his or her own feelings of well-being.

- Use feelings of emotional upset as a yellow light, warning that special attention is required to monitor and regulate behavior.

Homework ④

RELAXATION + Modifying behavior in one specific situation

What is the goal?

To *improve* your skill in relaxation.

To learn skills for *changing* tense behavior.

What do I have to do?

1. Practice relaxation twice daily, noting tension level before and after each practice.

2. Behavior change
   Step 1: Choose one specific behavior as a change target.
   Step 2: Choose one specific situation in which to implement change.
   Step 3: Prepare strategies for changing the target behavior the next time it occurs.
   Step 4: After the event, evaluate your actions and your feelings.
       (See example sheet.)

Name: Example sheet

Date:

1. Choose one specific *behavior* to change.

My target behavior is: Whenever I get upset, I start to shout.

2. Choose one specific situation in which you want to modify your target behavior.

Target situation:

When: Every week, starting next Friday. Project meeting

Where:

With whom: Joe, Bill, and Dave

3. *Prepare a strategy for modifying your target behavior.*

Incompatible behavior: As soon as I feel my voice rising, I am going to speak as *slowly* as possible.

Delayed behavior: If I shout, I will not say anything else for the next 60 seconds.

4. *Record outcome.*

What happened? I started to shout 3 times during meeting. Once I blocked it completely, the other 2 times it didn't last quite as long as usual.

How do you feel? Well, it's a beginning. Pretty good.

Homework ⑤

RELAXATION + Modifying behavior in several situations

What is the goal?

To *improve* your skills in relaxation.

To learn to *generalize* your behavior change skills to a variety of situations.

What do I have to do?

1. Practice relaxation twice daily, noting tension level before and after each practice)

2. Each time you become aware of tense behavior, introduce strategies to change behavior. Record the tension level and situation associated with the tense behavior, as well as the new behavior. (See example sheet.)

Name: Example sheet

Date:

Situation	Tension level			Tense behavior	New behavior
	Low	Moderate	High		
Anxious to get going		X		Pushed into office	Made a point to smile and say hello to co-workers
Interrupted during presentation			X	Shouted	Spoke more softly
Going to lunch	X			Rushed along street	Concentrated on observing faces of passers-by
Tense meeting			X	Fidgeting in chair	Took deep breaths
Argument with son		X		Raised voice	Took 10-second time-out

RELAXATION + Modifying time-hurry behavior

What is the goal?

To *improve* your skills in relaxation.

To *apply* your skills in behavior change to changing "hurry sickness."

What do I have to do?

1. Practice relaxation twice daily, noting your tension level before and after each practice.

2. Every time you feel hurried, note the situation and your type A reactions. Then change your reactions, noting new behavior. (See example sheet.)

Name: Example sheet **Date:**

Time-hurry level			Situation	Type A behavior	New behavior
No hurry	Moderate	Very hurried			
		X	Driver in front too slow	Honk horn	Switch on radio and practice relaxation.
	X		Interrupted by co-worker while busy	Shuffle papers and wait for him to go	Tell him pleasantly that I am busy; make appointment for later.
X			Eating lunch	Gulping food	Put down fork between mouthfuls.
		X	Co-worker speaks slowly during meeting	Tap foot and wait for chance to interrupt.	Concentrate on what he is saying
X			It's 4 pm and too many items left on agenda	Speed up; try to work faster	Decide to concentrate on most important

145

8. Modifying cognitive responses to stress

Program references: Rationale 4, "Think productively"; Homework 7–9

Many of the stress management skills discussed in previous modules, such as relaxation or time out for tense behavior, are designed primarily to control the damage done by an upset that has already occurred. But type As are characterized not only by exaggerated reactivity to stress but also, and equally as important, by a tendency to *perceive* threat and challenge in situations where type Bs do not. This module of the program, therefore, focuses directly on these stress appraisals, both the initial evaluation of a situation as threatening or challenging and the ongoing assessments of situation and coping efforts throughout the stress episode. Our aim is to make participants aware of how their own expectations and judgments contribute to the intensity and duration of stress experienced, and to demonstrate that modification of these habitual thought patterns can lead to reduced distress.

Because these thought patterns reflect deep-seated values and beliefs, type A clients may strongly resist intervention in this area, perceiving it as a threat to their identity. Therefore, even though our conceptual model places cognitive evaluation first in the temporal sequence of a stress episode (see Lazarus & Folkman, 1984), modification of cognitive responses is placed last in the sequence of basic skills training. It is better to wait until group members have already developed some confidence in the purpose and methods of the program before tackling this sensitive area.

There is now a substantial clinical literature on the nature and treatment of what Ellis has termed "irrational beliefs" (Beck, 1976; Ellis 1962; Meichenbaum, 1977, 1985). The treatment program presented here has borrowed heavily from this work but has also adapted concepts and procedures to better fit the specific problems of the healthy type A. For those familiar with the cognitive behavioral approach, the differences will become apparent in the following description.

146

Awareness of self-talk

Following the usual procedure of this program, the first step in modifying dysfunctional cognitive responses is to increase awareness of when and how they occur. For nonspecialists, the concept of "cognition" is meaningless and, therefore, other terms are needed to describe the phenomena in question. *Self-talk,* defined as the internal dialogue occurring during the course of a stress episode, serves this purpose well. Consequently, the first homework assignment in the cognitive module focuses on monitoring self-talk in moderate to high tension situations.

During the review of this homework assignment (Homework 7) in Session 8, many group members will complain of inability to detect any internal dialogue. These clients can be reassured that this is a very common problem because much of our internal dialogue is so automatic that we are likely to be unaware of it. The analogy here is with other overlearned habits, such as walking, which are exercised without conscious awareness. In fact, learning to bring self-talk back into consciousness can take considerable effort and practice.

As an aid in this learning process, the therapist might ask the individual to relive a particular stress episode in the form of a mentally replayed film. As the participant describes what individuals did and said, he or she can be asked to recall also the internal dialogue that accompanied his or her actions and words. If the participant cannot, then the therapist can supply a possible scenario, perhaps exaggerating for dramatic purposes.

For therapists with an element of ham in them, these sessions can be fun. Usually there is much laughter as members supply additional snatches of preposterous internal dialogue. The underlying message, however, is a very serious one: It is common and normal for our thoughts to race wildly during a stress episode, and sometimes these thoughts can cause as much distress as the actual situation itself.

The rationale for this section (Rationale 4, "Think productively") provides some examples of beliefs and thought processes leading to increased tension and discomfort, such as unrealistic expectations for self and others, making molehills into mountains by catastrophizing, self-denigration, and ignoring the present in favor of bewailing the past or worrying about the future. However, no attempt is made to provide an exhaustive list. Rather than having participants memorize a catechism of erroneous beliefs, it has proven more profitable to proceed inductively, detecting general beliefs from self-talk during specific stress episodes.

There is one belief, however, that is so pervasive among type As that it requires special handling; this is the obligation to be perfect. Because type A clients hold so strongly to the credo that the quest for perfection is what makes the world go round, it helps to have an external authority to support the heretical notion that this fundamental virtue may also lead to discomfort and ineffectiveness. A specific article that I have found useful for this purpose is "The Perfectionist's Script for Self-Defeat" (Burns, 1980).

Rationale for modifying self-talk

The rationale for modifying self-talk is a simple one: We seek to modify our thinking, not because certain thoughts are wrong or irrational, but simply because they are unproductive. By now the notion of efficient use of energy should be well implanted in a group. Unproductive thinking, by definition, is that which leads to inefficient use of energy. Thus, indignation at a tardy subordinate or an ungrateful adolescent child may be well founded; in any case, every individual is free to think whatever thoughts he or she wishes. But if this indignation intensifies the upset, and perhaps even prevents the person from taking effective action, then indulging in uncontrolled self-talk is simply adding to the harm inflicted. For instance, an individual may be angry at the comment of a colleague during a meeting, but if he or she spends the rest of the day brooding about it and regurgitating the incident, then the loss of a day has been added to the initial injury.

As with behavioral management, a major incentive for learning to become aware of and manage self-talk is that it increases the person's control over a situation. Our language implies that our emotions are at the control of others, as in "John made me angry." In fact, an individual has the power to respond even to an apparently provocative act in a variety of ways depending on the manner that he or she *chooses to interpret* that action. Thus, criticism of a design by a supervisor that is interpreted as "just doing his job" will be appraised and reacted to very differently from the same criticism interpreted as "the bastard is out to get me." Effective management of self-talk can also serve the important purpose of enabling the individual to exert control over the *intensity* and *duration* of the emotional upset, even when he or she does experience negative feelings. Few persons are saintly enought to remain completely unmoved by the sarcastic remarks of a colleague, but it is up to the individual to decide if this attack will disturb him or her for a few hours or a few days, or will permanently alter his or her relationship to the offender.

The most common objection to the concept of monitoring and modifying self-talk is that it is analogous to brainwashing, leading to artificial, externally imposed patterns of thought and action. Here the therapist can point out that our current patterns of thought are not innate but were learned at some time or other. They feel natural because they have been repeated thousands of times over a long period of years. Obviously, as in any skill-learning process, the introduction of a new way of reacting will initially feel somewhat artificial. With practice, however, this new pattern will itself become familiar and, hence, natural. Furthermore, the individual is always free to go back to his or her old ways of thinking; alternate ways of viewing a problem will be added, but nothing will be taken away.

Modifying self-talk

There are no general techniques provided for modifying self-talk. Instead, participants proceed on a case-by-case basis, using heightened emotional tension as a signal to examine what they are saying to themselves. The aim is to detect self-talk that aggravates the tension state and to substitute self-talk that will help the person to better manage the emotional disequilibrium. For example, anticipating a difficult sales presentation a person might worry—"It's going to be a mess. Nobody will like it."—thereby intensifying the anxiety, increasing blood pressure, and leading to a nail-biting session. More productive is the following thought: "The presentation will be difficult, but I have done many similar presentations before, and I have prepared carefully for this one. If I concentrate on keeping cool, I should be able to do fairly well."

The major pitfall for novices in modifying self-talk is the tendency to suppress negative emotions completely and adopt an artificial "Pollyanna" attitude. Thus, in the example just cited, the individual might be tempted to completely deny the anxiety, or claim that it didn't really matter if the presentation bombed. Similarly, when a subordinate made a serious error in a job estimate, one of our participants attempted to modify her initial anger and anxiety by saying to herself, "I'm not going to let it bother me." These attempts at denial or suppression of the uncomfortable emotions are not useful in managing stress because they are so divergent from reality that they cannot be maintained for long. To effectively manage negative emotions, one must first recognize that they are present. Thus, the aim for our group member was not to deny the presence of anger and anxiety at a botched job estimate but, instead, to modulate these emotions so that she could focus her energies on repairing the error or, if necessary, cutting her losses.

As participants describe their initial efforts to modify self-talk in Session 9 (Homework 8), the therapist helps them identify and label beliefs that are likely to intensify distress. The specific beliefs and thought patterns to be highlighted will vary from group to group, but based on past experience, three are almost certain to appear: Everybody should be perfect, what is not 100% is therefore 0%, and everybody should think and be like me.

The first of these, the quest for perfection, is probably the single most common belief manifested in the type As I have treated. It is a dearly held belief, for they consider this striving for perfection as a necessary spur for any level of achievement. As one participant expressed it, "If you try for perfection, then you will at least reach mediocrity." Thus, the only way to pass a course at school was to attempt to achieve a perfect mark; now the only way to have an acceptable sales presentation is to attempt to make it a perfect one. It is heresy for the therapist to suggest that by settling for one's best efforts, rather than impossible perfection, one may be less anxious and therefore more effective. Surprisingly, however, this is a heresy that is often welcomed with a collective sigh of relief.

Once participants become more tolerant of their own lack of perfection, they are also likely to tolerate the imperfections of others better. This does not mean that one would not like the salesclerk to be more attentive, other drivers to be more courteous, and our spouse to be more responsive to our needs. In fact, one good safety valve for the annoyance aroused by snafus, be it a traffic jam or a delayed mail delivery, is to fantasize how much better we would arrange the world if we were in charge. But to the degree that one can live with divergence between the real self and the ideal self, it also becomes easier to accept a state of less than perfection in others and in the world at large.

Allied to the concept of perfection is the use of a measuring scale with only two gradations—all and nothing. One of the reasons it is necessary to strive for the perfect sales presentation is that the only alternative envisioned is the completely disastrous one. Similarly, one will have a furious argument with a spouse about the locale of a planned vacation because the situation is perceived in either/or terms; not gaining one's way entirely means losing completely. It is this all-or-nothing way of looking at the world that accounts for the initial efforts to remedy nonproductive self-talk by artificially suppressing it, as if the only alternative to being totally overwhelmed by anger is not to be angry at all.

Sometimes the most effective way of countering this black-and-white view of the world is to exaggerate it until the ridiculousness of the situation becomes obvious to all. For instance, a participant who experienced a state of paralyzing anxiety because his bus was late, making him tardy for a meeting, was encouraged to vividly describe all the negative consequences that could result from such a breach of duty. The therapist and group members helped with speculations about his probable firing, the collapse of the project and the firm, the eventual shame and destitution of his family, and so on. By the time we were ready to declare a national financial emergency, both he and the group had collapsed into laughter, but the point had been made that there are degrees of disaster.

A third strongly held belief among our group members is that everyone should think and be like them. The belief is rarely expressed in such a crude form as this; rather, it is revealed in the surprised indignation manifested by group members every time they encounter opposition, be it in the form of a colleague at a project meeting who questions a design, a child who refuses to eat the good food put on the family table, or a secretary who is more interested in leaving on time than in completing an important manuscript. In their relentless pursuit of perfection, the healthy type As who make up our groups appear to completely ignore the possibility that others might have different models of perfection, and hence different wants and tastes. Once again, humor is the therapist's best aid, as he or she points out that given the number and diversity of people on this earth, the surprise should be reserved for the occasions when two people manage to agree on something.

Moreover, to the degree that the existence of divergent views, interests, and needs is accepted as a normal part of life, then we are less likely to interpret opposition as a personal attack. For instance, many participants view project meetings as battlegrounds in which any disagreement with their point of view constitutes an effort to wound. If, however, the same meeting is perceived as expressly designed for airing differing views, then disagreements are normal and serve a useful purpose. Similarly, the hasty departure of a secretary is less of a defection if one can imagine the competing claims on her time.

It is hardest for our members to accept differences within the family, perhaps because of the wish that the home serve as the refuge from the stresses of the external world. Thus, even an individual whose professional life is devoted to recognizing and negotiating competing interests, such as a lawyer or union negotiator, may be taken aback by the suggestion that conflicting weekend plans in the family could be similarly recognized and negotiated. The fantasy is that the perfect marriage partner will instinctively detect our wants and share our interests. When this fantasy is violated, as it inevitably is, then the all-or-nothing measuring scale intensifies the outrage, since that which is not perfect is terrible. Here the group structure is helpful in injecting a note of rueful realism. The fact that all our participants, single and married, describe these kinds of petty difficulties makes it easier for individual members to grin and bear it.

Because groups are made up of individuals with ongoing lives, occasionally a stress situation will arise of far greater emotional importance than the usual routine of daily hassles. Events of this type include death of a parent, serious illness of a family member, and marriage breakup. Sometimes, the stress will be work related; in one group, a member was fired 10 minutes before the regular group session! Here a participant may attempt to use positive self-talk in an effort to avoid negative feelings. My inclination would be to discourage this. There are times in life when strong anger or sadness is appropriate, and the purpose of a stress management course is not to trivialize all happenings to the lowest common denominator of feeling. On the contrary, we seek to modulate response to minor stresses, to more clearly distinguish them from the major happenings of life that warrant the fullest expression of feelings.

Modifying self-talk and behavior

As good type As, our group members do not wait for instructions before they begin to combine coping techniques. Thus, as early as the section on behavior change, members will report combining a deep breath (physical relaxation) with the effort to speak more slowly or softly. In Homework 9, however, this combination of techniques is made explicit, with group members being asked to reduce tension by changing both self-talk and behavior.

One of the goals of this combination is to demonstrate how greater control of emotions, via more productive self-talk, gives the individual the liberty to initiate more effective action. Rather than stewing in righteous anger at the wrong committed, the person turns his or her energy to problem solving. Thus, instead of crying over milk spilled on a shirt, one can literally change the shirt.

A more complex example of this shift in direction was reported by a group member who was noted for his aggressive outbursts. Even a mild family argument could provoke shouting, followed by an 90 mile an hour car drive. After careful deliberation, this member had ordered a new car, complete with his personal selection of options. When he arrived to take delivery, one of the options was not there. Carefully following the prescriptions of this course, he took a deep breath and asked, in as calm a voice as he could muster, when the missing option would be delivered. The reply was never, since the cost of special ordering the missing part was more than its sale price. As this man graphically described the situation, ordinarily he would have laced into the dealer with his choicest collection of epithets. Instead, he arranged time out for a bathroom visit and rapidly deliberated: He wanted the missing part more than the dealer's hide. Upon his return, he was able to announce, more or less calmly, his regret at not being able to take delivery, since this was not the car ordered. Not surprisingly, the dealer suddenly found that he could special order the missing option. The group cheered this victory, for the basic message was clear: In renouncing the pleasures of uncontrolled anger, this participant had increased his ability to effectively influence his environment.

The carrot versus the whip

As managers of other people, all our participants are at least intellectually aware of the importance of praise for motivation. With themselves and their families, however, they use the whip and engage in self-flagellation to maintain motivation, rather than providing the carrot of positive self-reinforcement. As part of the quest for perfection, a 90% report card is seen mainly in terms of the missing 10%, and even a perfect score would be countered by the fear that it could not be maintained! For the same reason, these extremely hard working individuals will often refer to themselves with perjorative labels, such as "lazy" or "slothful."

If the behavioral changes undertaken in this program are to be durable, then it is essential that group members learn to modify this constant self-denigration and, instead, recognize and reinforce their improved coping efforts. Here therapist modeling can play a crucial role. It is important during sessions not to focus exclusively on the coping problems, but also to emphasize and celebrate even small victories. Thus, every time a group member demonstrates in the homework a change in habitual coping pattern, one takes the time to pause, to congratulate the participant, and, even more important, to encourage the group member to congratulate himself or herself. To the degree that the therapist can emphasize the positive in what the participant is doing, then the group member is implicitly given permission to openly value it himself or herself. Furthermore, this program can then serve as a concrete illustration of how behavioral change is best produced by slow, gradual steps with abundant reinforcement, rather than a hypercritical striving for instant perfection.

A simple but potent example of the value of self-reinforcement was provided by a group member. As many participants were wont to do, he was spending the weekend trying to catch up with the endless list of household chores; the task in hand this particular weekend was painting the house. Usually, he would try to paint as fast as he could, pushing himself on with reminders of how much remained to be done. This time, in contrast, he stopped after finishing each wall, or part of a room, to admire the finished product and congratulate himself on his work. In a surprised but pleased tone, he remarked to the group that this painting session seemed to go much faster and easier than previous ones.

Concluding comments

Although the specific examples are not dramatic, the cumulative impact of small modifications in expectations and judgments is far-reaching. Many of our participants enter into this program with a rather rigid, moralistic view of life: The world should work in a certain way, and if it doesn't, then they are prepared to spend considerable energy in decrying what is wrong. The aim of this program is to substitute a more flexible, tolerant, and pragmatic approach to the stresses of daily life. Both we and the world are imperfect, but we can live with and manage these imperfections, rather than collapsing in helpless rage or depression.

A corollary of this increased pragmatism is the ability to view conflict situations in terms of costs versus benefits as well as right and wrong. The inattentive waiter is obviously in the wrong, but spending the afternoon stewing about it increases the personal cost of the incident without providing any additional benefits. Strong negative emotions, such as anger and depression, use enormous amounts of our valuable, and finite, stores of energy. Thus, in deciding to limit the intensity of one's anger toward the waiter, one is not necessarily conceding defeat and helplessness but, rather, making a conscious decision on how best to spend one's energy. The choice remains of embarking on a lifelong crusade against inattentive waiters, or any other issue the individual deems sufficiently important, but the person is no longer permitting his or her energy to dribble away without awareness or choice.

One of my favorite examples of a client's realization of this cost–benefit balance was provided by a group participant who had asked his 16-year-old son to take out the garbage. The family had recently installed expensive new carpet on the stairs. The son was a star football player on his school team, but instead of exerting himself to lift the bag a few inches above the carpet, he expressed his resentment at the request by bumping the bag down the stairs. Squish, squish went the bag, and the father could feel himself exploding as he visualized the dirt and moisture splattering on the new carpet. Stomach churning, he prepared to raise his voice in a bellow, when suddenly a stop sign flashed before his eyes: "Think of your heart as well as the carpet." Obviously, the son would have to be shown the error of his ways, but there was an advantage for him, as well as his son, in curbing his initial outrage.

The end of this module occurs at the tenth session, halfway through the program. The pace of change tends to quicken perceptibly here, with group members reporting quite dramatic shifts in handling of common stress situations. When I first began working with type As, I was distrustful that anyone could really change that much that quickly, as exemplified by the incident of the very aggressive group member and the missing car part. Here, however, is where the basic healthiness of our clients becomes apparent. These men and women are basically competent copers living in generally favorable circumstances. What has been lacking up to now is a belief in the value of managing personal reactions. Once participants acquire that belief, behavioral change is remarkably quick.

Program facsimiles

Homework 7; Rationale 4; Homework 8; Homework 9

Homework ⑦

RELAXATION + Self-talk awareness

What is the goal?

To learn to *improve* your skills in relaxation.

To learn to *become aware of* what you say to yourself when you are experiencing tension.

What do I have to do?

1. Practice relaxation twice daily, noting your tension level before and after each practice.

2. Every time you feel stressed, note tension level, situation, emotion, and self-talk. (See example sheet.)

Name: Example sheet

Date:

Situation

Tension level

Emotion

Self-talk

Situation	Low	Moderate	High	Emotion	Self-talk
a.m.					
Bob heckles me during weekly project meeting			X	Anger, frustration	I'll never get it right enough to satisfy him.
p.m.					
Incompetent waiter at lunch		X		Impatience, anger	Damn it! I shouldn't have to pay for no service.
Colleague asks me questions I can't answer			X	Discomfort, embarrassment	He must think I'm an idiot.
evening					
Wife complains that I don't pull my weight at home			X	Self-pity, depression	She shouldn't put pressure on me now!

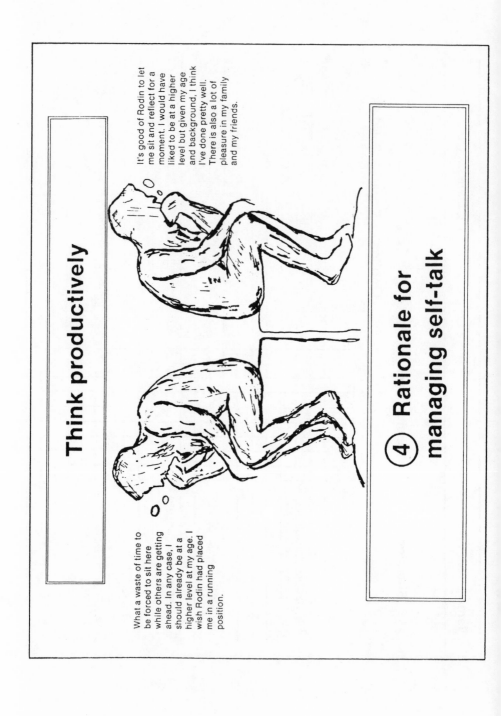

Rationale for managing self-talk

All of us experience frustrations, disappointments, and defeats in the course of our professional and personal lives. How we interpret and react to them, however, depends very much on our individual "internal programs." Two people may be in the same situation of having a pet project turned down by a supervisor:

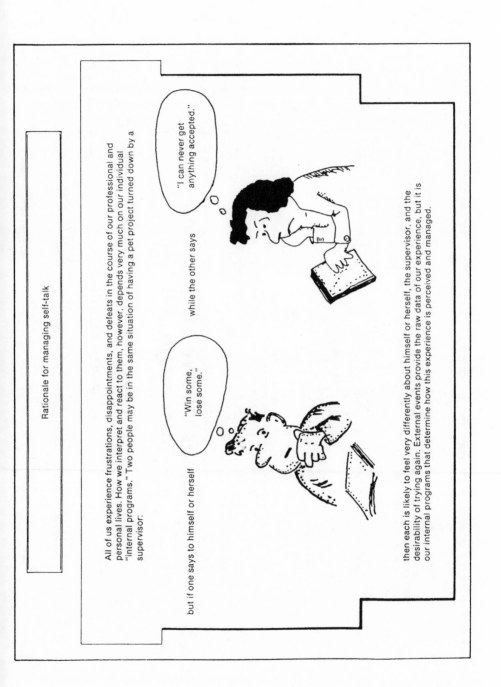

but if one says to himself or herself

"Win some, lose some."

while the other says

"I can never get anything accepted."

then each is likely to feel very differently about himself or herself, the supervisor, and the desirability of trying again. External events provide the raw data of our experience, but it is our internal programs that determine how this experience is perceived and managed.

Many people are afraid that tinkering with thoughts is a form of brainwashing, leading us to react artificially.

On the contrary, more often it is our automatic thought patterns that interfere with our ability to judge each situation realistically and independently.

Learning to critically examine and modify our internal programs (self-talk) increases our ability to react more effectively and appropriately to the events we encounter. Productive thinking means the ability to use self-talk to *reduce*, rather than *increase*, your stress level.

Steps involved in learning to manage self-talk

A. Awareness skills

1. Learn to recognize unproductive self-talk, that is, self-talk that increases tension and discomfort.

A. Awareness skills (continued)

2. Critically examine the beliefs and habits that underlie negative self-talk.

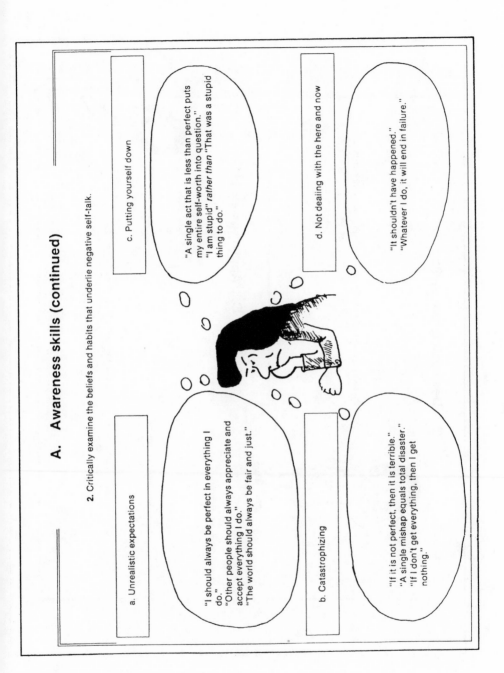

a. Unrealistic expectations

"I should always be perfect in everything I do."
"Other people should always appreciate and accept everything I do."
"The world should always be fair and just."

b. Catastrophizing

"If it is not perfect, then it is terrible."
"A single mishap equals total disaster."
"If I don't get everything, then I get nothing."

c. Putting yourself down

"A single act that is less than perfect puts my entire self-worth into question."
"I am stupid" *rather than* "That was a stupid thing to do."

d. Not dealing with the here and now

"It shouldn't have happened."
"Whatever I do, it will end in failure."

B. Developing new skills

Consciously replace unproductive self-talk with productive self-talk.

C. Applying new skills

1. Develop habits of productive self-talk.

2. When you are upset, examine whether your self-talk is helpful or harmful. If it is harmful, change it.

Homework ⑧

RELAXATION + Changing nonproductive self-talk

What is the goal?

To *improve* your relaxation skills.

To learn to *change* nonproductive self-talk into productive self-talk.

What do I have to do?

1. Practice relaxation twice daily, noting your tension level before and after each practice.

2. Each time you feel stressed, note tension level, situation, emotion, and self-talk. Then change self-talk and note change in emotion. (See example sheet.)

163

Name: Example sheet　　　　　　　　　　　　　　　　　　　　**Date:**

Situation	Tension level	Initial reaction		Modified reaction	
	a.m. Low　Moderate　High	Emotion	Non-productive self-talk	New self-talk	Emotion
Unsuccessful project meeting	X (High)	Despair	This meeting is a disaster.	This meeting not as good as I would like.	Disappointment
	p.m.				
Boss turns down project	X (Moderate)	Frustration Defeat	I never win with him!	Well, this sales talk didn't work. I wonder what I wonder what would.	Disappointment Determination
	evening				
Argument with son	X (Low)	Anger	He doesn't know how to be gyateful!	I wonder what is eating him.	Curiosity

164

Homework ⑨

SHORT RELAXATION + Combining change in self-talk and behavior

What is the goal?

To *learn a quicker* relaxation procedure.

To *learn* to reduce stress by combining *changes* in self-talk and behavior.

What do I have to do?

1. Practice side B of the relaxation tape twice daily, noting tension before and after.

2. Every time you feel tense, note your nonproductive self-talk and your behavior, then try to reduce stress by changing both. Note new self-talk and behavior. (See example sheet.)

Name: Example sheet

Date:

Situation	Tension level				Initial reaction		Modified reaction	
	a.m.	Low	Moderate	High	Stressed behavior	Non-productive self-talk	New self-talk	New behavior
Spilled coffee on shirt during breakfast				X	Clench teeth, swear.	What an idiot! I can't do anything right.	Well, nobody's perfect. How can I remedy this?	Change shirt.
	p.m.							
Went to pick up urgent report and found secretary hadn't typed it			X		Boiling inside. Voice becomes loud and fast.	How inconsiderate! She never cares about my work.	I wonder how quickly I can get this typed.	Ask secretary to type this immediately.
	evening							
Long line at supermarket				X	Mutter, glare at clerk.	Stupid store. They take our money and don't give service.	I don't like it, but there isn't too much I can do about it.	Amuse myself by observing others.

166

9. Applying stress management skills

Program references: Rationale 5, "Be
prepared," and Rationale 6, "Cool it";
Homework 10–14

No matter how proficient a player is in individual tennis strokes—fore-
hand, backhand, or serve—these strokes in isolation do not constitute
a good tennis game. To really play tennis, you must also learn to deliver
the various strokes as required, while keeping your eye on a fast-moving
ball. Analogous to the transition between skill in individual tennis strokes
and actually playing a game of tennis, the content of this chapter is
devoted to integrating the individual coping skills already learned into
a functional coping style. Consequently, the emphasis shifts from the
skills themselves to the situations in which they are to be applied.

For the sake of convenience, stress situations can be divided into
two main categories, those that are predictable, usually because they
are recurrent, and those that appear to occur "out of the blue" and
obviously cannot be predicted. The long line at the supermarket check-
out on a busy day is an example of the former, while losing a crucial
shirt button on the way to work exemplifies the latter. Just as it is easier
to apply relaxation skills when one is not extremely upset, so as it easier
to develop coping strategies when one is not in the heat of battle.
Accordingly, we begin with learning to plan for predictable stress situations.

Awareness of recurrent stress triggers

Homework 10 is straightforward: Every time the participant's tension level becomes high, he or she is asked to identify the stress trigger
and to indicate whether or not it was predictable. The aim here is to
increase awareness that many daily hassles are frequently repeated and
hence predictable. For instance, if one is chronically late for work, or
if every discussion of house repairs results in a quarrel, or if every
meeting with a colleague results in a churning stomach, one may be

anxious, depressed, and angry, but there is no reason to be surprised. In many stress situations a good deal of energy is expended on rhetorical questions: "How could this happen?" For this type of stress situation, we know that "it can happen," because all have occurred many times previously.

The major obstacle to becoming aware of recurrent stress triggers is wishful thinking. This is particularly evident in relation to activities labeled as pleasant. In most people's fantasy, Christmas is a happy occasion when the loving family reunites over a festive meal. Vacations, too, are commonly viewed as a stress-free period when cares and problems are left behind with the job. Even though Christmases past have been marked by the squabbling of family members, or last year's vacation is memorable mainly for the effort to find motels late at night after a too-long drive, we cling stubbornly to our fantasies, convinced that next time it will be different.

Sometimes we refuse to accept potential stress situations because they *should not happen*. If commuter buses did not break down, then we would not be late for work; if spouses were reasonable, then a rational discussion of house repairs would not lead to a quarrel; and so on. Much as we would wish it otherwise, however, balky transit systems and spouses are what they are and neither is likely to undergo sudden, major improvements. To accept the probability that past stresses will reoccur, we must also accept the fact that this world is imperfect and likely to remain so.

This is another occasion where self-revelation by the therapist can be helpful. Fortunately, at least for therapy purposes, I personally have an ample supply of examples of self-delusion from which to choose. Thus, when group members refuse to consider holidays in anything but a positive light, I mention my experience with a ski holiday where, in a fit of enthusiasm, each of the children was allowed to invite a friend. I was dimly aware that we would be in very close quarters, and that the location chosen had no alternate activities, but these mild forebodings were soon stifled by the competing fantasy of a happy family and friends spending all day on the slopes. I reassured myself that there would be no real problems. Eight rainy days later, four caged and disgruntled adolescents had taught me otherwise. The return to work following this "holiday" was welcomed as a parole. I rarely get the opportunity to finish my sad tale, because other members of the group have similar memorable vacations to recount.

One of the disconcerting results of plotting recurrent stress situations is to discover how frequently we "set ourselves up" for pratfalls by ignoring past experience. This is particularly evident in time scheduling. For instance, individuals habitually crowd their daily schedules, making no allowance for the inevitable interruptions, phone calls, and delays, and are then surprised that they spend the day in a state of perpetual tardiness and hurry. Some of the group participants are so tightly scheduled that even a trip to the bathroom is likely to dislocate the day's activities! Similarly, a person will arrive at the bank half an hour before closing on the eve of a major holiday and fume at the length of the line. Or, the person will wait until the eve of the deadline to finish an important report or calculate income taxes, and then will be dismayed to discover that he or she is missing an important piece of data. The usual explanation for this behavior is that the person is trying to be efficient, not to waste time. It comes as quite a shock to discover the waste of energy.

As members recount the stress triggers of their lives, some will be clearly relevant to the purposes of this section, while others will be irrelevant, either because the stress situations were unpredictable or because the problems involved go far beyond the usual daily hassles, revealing a deep-seated, chronic unhappiness with a marital or work situation. For the unpredictable stress triggers, one can simply ask the individual to note these for later discussion in the section of the program on emergency stressors. The problem of real unhappiness with one's life situation is more complex. I feel very strongly that stress management should not be used to trivialize all situations. On the other hand, this program is not appropriate for handling major life crises.

What the therapist actually says or does when confronted with major life problems depends very much on the specific nature of the problem and how it is presented. Often I make the distinction between short-term and long-term solutions; an unsatisfactory work situation may lead to a decision to change jobs, or to pursue further training, or even to shift career directions radically. But such major decisions are rarely made quickly, and in the meantime the individual still has to cope with the day-to-day stresses of the situation. To the degree that he or she can learn to alleviate and manage these minor irritants, then more energy will be available for the major decisions.

Rationale for learning to plan for stress

The advantage in relinquishing fantasy for reality, and thereby learning to plan for recurrent stresses, is increased control over the situation itself and our reactions to it. Many potential stress situations can be avoided entirely by anticipatory planning; in other cases, reactions will be considerably attenuated if the person knows in advance that the stressor is likely to occur, and if he or she has developed strategies for coping with it (Rationale 5).

For most group members, the skills involved in anticipatory planning are far from new. On the contrary, "trouble shooting" is an essential component of every managerial and professional job. What is novel is the application of these skills to the management of personal lives. For individuals who appear resistant to the imagined loss of spontaneity, the therapist can point out instances where they already engage in some forms of anticipatory planning, such as making restaurant reservations to avoid disappointment or "psyching myself up" for the dentist appointment. The program simply seeks to develop and extend already existing skills.

Preparing for one specific stress situation

In Session 11 participants begin the work of planning for an anticipated stress situation by ranking the stress triggers previously identified (Homework 10) in terms of the level of tension generated: high, moderate, and low. The purpose of this exercise is to permit the individual to choose an appropriate stress trigger on which to practice his or her planning skills (see Homework 11 and 12). Here, too, the therapist can use the selection process to impart some basic knowledge about the general process of behavior change. In order to plan successfully for an anticipated stress situation, one must be as specific as possible about its occurrence: when, where, and with whom. Second, since success breeds success, it is important to maximize the chances for success by choosing a target for change that is not too difficult. Better to proceed from the relatively easy to the difficult than to begin too high and have to retreat in failure. In the case of stress triggers, an appropriate goal is one that is likely to occur within the next few days, in clearly identifiable circumstances, and will generate only a low to moderate level of tension.

Once the target stress situation has been selected, the remainder of this session is devoted to helping individuals plan their coping approaches. Stress episodes can be divided into three temporal phases— before, during, and after—and different coping strategies are appropriate for each. To use the relatively simple stressor of the wait at the doctor's office, the participant might prepare for the visit by scheduling it at the end of the afternoon, when a wait would not make her late for other appointments, and by bringing along an interesting article to read. During the wait itself, should she find her irritation rising in spite of these preparations, she might remind herself: "I don't particularly like the wait, but it's not something I have to do very often. This is not personally directed toward me; it is hard to predict how long he will have to spend with each patient. At least I know that if I need more time he will give it to me." Following the visit, she might take pleasure in the reduced irritation experienced and in the fact that even if she did not particularly like the wait, it need not spoil the rest of the day.

More complex are the stress situations involving interpersonal friction, especially with people who, for business or family reasons, one is likely to interact with repeatedly. A common example furnished by participants is the colleague who likes to heckle or make sarcastic remarks. Often the participant cannot easily avoid the agent provocateur, because of weekly staff meetings or a common project. Instead, the group member might prepare for the next encounter by changing both his mental attitude and behavior: "I don't like this guy, but I don't have to let him get my goat. When he starts to bait me, I will not respond in kind but will concentrate on the business at hand and answer as calmly as possible. He may even have some good ideas to offer, and if I focus on what he is saying, I could be less disturbed by his manner."

Even a well-prepared coping plan, however, may be temporarily derailed during the stress episode itself. The colleague may not accept the proferred cease-fire, and may be quite persistent in his sarcasms. Or, one of his remarks may hit a particularly sensitive area. In any case, it is not improbable that the participant may find himself, in spite of his carefully laid plans, drawn into the usual angry exchange. But a rising voice and blood pressure need not signal the complete failure of the coping efforts. On the contrary, they can also serve as the signal to add additional coping measures. The participant may take a deep breath, consciously lower his voice, and declare, "Well, I guess you and I had better agree to disagree on this." Should this be beyond his capabilities at that moment, he can take time out to regain his calm, if necessary using the excuse of a bathroom stop.

A stress episode does not end with the termination of the situation itself but also includes the person's post hoc evaluation of the situation. In the example just cited, the person's usual tendency might be to declare his coping efforts a failure on the basis that the heckling colleague did not change and that he himself had gotten upset. The role of the therapist is to help him to recognize and be proud of even a 10% reduction in intensity and/or duration of irritation. Ingrained behavior patterns are not easily changed, and even a small change represents an important victory.

Most of the discussion will focus on success stories, with individuals reporting better self-control in stress episodes and often, as a result, better control of the external environment. In every group, however, there is at least one person whose coping efforts came to naught. He or she can usually be identified by silence and a glum face. It is important that the therapist recognize and accept these "failures." My habit is to elicit them by asking directly "Does anyone have any failures to report?"

When someone half-heartedly admits to one, this is warmly welcomed on the grounds that unsuccessful efforts can be very instructive. Either the person became so upset during the stress episode that he or she completely abandoned the plan, or else some change in behavior was effected but this was not sufficient to alleviate the distress—physical and emotional—experienced. The focus in dealing with this failure is problem oriented; since the initial plan did not work, how can it be improved for the next try?

Stress preparation as a general coping style

Even though the two conceptual models—that of stress and that of the TABP—on which this intervention program is based are both firmly interactionist in nature, up to now most of the change efforts have been directed toward the person, rather than toward the environment. This is not surprising in short-term intervention with basically healthy people. Practically, too, most of the groups that I have led have been based in the workplace, and it is highly unlikely that the corporate structure would long tolerate a program advocating radical environmental change. Therefore, this program places most of its emphasis on changing individual reactions to daily hassles, assuming that the latter are inevitable in any environment.

As we come to the application of stress preparation skills, however, more attention is given to the possibility of structuring one's environment to reduce stress. This may be as simple as leaving early to avoid the heaviest traffic, or allowing for breathing space between meetings. Sometimes, however, the environmental changes can be quite extensive, as in individuals who arrange the pattern of their working day to permit both noninterrupted time and time for easy access by others. It may also involve taking a close look at the pattern of recreational activities, to distinguish between those that truly refresh and those that create additional stress.

Often, a major obstacle to restructuring the environment is the search for the perfect or no-cost solution. Thus, one cannot refuse the inappropriate request of a co-worker because he or she might be hurt; or one must continue the hated task of driving a child to school, because otherwise the spouse would be forced to take on the task. Instead, one fumes that the colleague "had no right to ask me" and that the spouse has mentally incurred a debt he or she may not even know exists. In the former case it might be better to accept the disappointment of someone else, rather than one's own fury, and even though neither spouse might enjoy the chauffering task, it might be better tolerated by both if it were shared. Once again, by abandoning the fantasy of the perfect solution for the reality of the livable one, the type A considerably increases his or her ability to control the environment.

Inevitably, the question arises as to how much anticipatory planning for daily hassles is desirable. Obviously, if carried to extremes, the cost may outweigh the benefits. For instance, buttons might never fall off shirts if the latter were checked daily, but for most people, preventing this stress would be more energy consuming than experiencing it. The usual rule of thumb is that the higher the stakes, the more anticipatory planning is warranted. For an ordinary business day one would make a reasonable effort to be on time and mentally and physically prepared. For a day on which an important presentation is scheduled, however, the preparations would obviously be more extensive, maybe involving getting to bed earlier, mentally rehearsing behavior, scheduling some open time before the presentation to mentally and physically relax, and so on. One useful technique in stress planning is to scan daily and weekly agendas, highlighting those events that warrant anticipatory trouble shooting.

Coping with stress emergencies

No specific exercise is required to make participants aware of stress emergencies, the unexpected jokers in the day's happenings. Be it the broken shoelace, being cut off in the middle of an important telephone call, or an unexpectedly high bill, everyone has experienced the pounding heart and the tightening muscles that signal attack by a suddenly hostile environment. What most participants do not realize, however, is that the emergency usually does not lie in the situation itself, but in their reactions to it. Situations requiring an immediate response, such as the car speeding toward us in the wrong lane, are relatively rare. For most of the apparent emergencies, taking the time to regain one's self-control will usually lead to more effective action in the long term (Rationale 6).

In order to institute effective braking, participants must first recognize the signs of rising tension and then have available an effective mechanism for stopping. To aid recognition of potential danger, participants can utilize tension in vulnerable body parts, what we have previously termed their *stress signatures*. Behavioral signs can also signal loss of control; a raised voice is an almost infallible signal of a high tension state. Once the individual has recognized the existence of tension, he or she will seek to interrupt the process by braking. Stopping signals can be visual, as in the case of the red traffic light, or auditory, such as the inner voice ordering "STOP." While most group members will rely on these universal signals, a few will develop more personal ones. For example, one of the participants adopted his father's habitual remark, "Wait a minute," as his personal braking signal. The specific nature of the stopping mechanism is unimportant, but if it is to be effective it must be used regularly enough for the procedure to become automatic.

When participants first practice the use of braking signals (Homework 13), there is the tendency to attempt to completely deny the negative aspect of the situation, with declarations such as "I won't let it bother me." This approach is unlikely to prove effective since pounding hearts and raised voices are all too evident witnesses of the contrary. It is unrealistic, too, to assume that reducing the immediate distress will be sufficient in itself to manage the stress episode. In many cases, unless other action is taken, the unpredictable stress episode becomes the recurrent one. What emergency braking is designed to do is to enable the individual to regain control over himself or herself before tackling the situation.

Even after the individual is ready to proceed, caution is indicated. Many participants do not realize that every emotional upheaval leaves an aftermath. Calm may have apparently been restored, but physical and emotional traces of upset can persist for hours. Furthermore, to combat loss of control takes considerable energy, leaving the person temporarily depleted and more vulnerable to the next upset. Using the analogy of a spending spree, this is a time for conservation of energy.

Coping with frustration

For healthy type As, managing frustration (Homework 14) constitutes the crux of stress management. As more than one exasperated group member has exclaimed, "I have no trouble doing my job; it's the people I work with that drive me crazy." When a strong drive for achievement is combined with perfectionism, impatience, and a highly reactive nervous system, then it is almost inevitable that participants will be frequently frustrated, either by the conflicting aims of others or simply by others' indifference to their wishes. It is this frustration that, in my opinion, gives rise to much of the aggressiveness and hostility characteristic of the type A.

Although many of the previous homework assignments dealt indirectly with frustration and its resulting irritation, Homework 14 makes explicit that which has previously been implicit. Stress situations are formally labeled as frustration inducing and the individual is encouraged to utilize all his or her coping skills—physical, behavioral, and cognitive—to manage both the situation and his or her reactions to it.

This homework assignment also serves to consolidate and make explicit the view that the individual is not necessarily the passive victim of the carelessness or malice of others, but has a wide range of coping options in any given situation. Some coping efforts involve restructuring the environment so as to eliminate or alleviate the stress trigger. This can be as simple as avoiding a disliked acquaintance at a cocktail party, or as complex as changing marital partners. In other cases, the focus of coping efforts will be on changing one's reactions to the situation, rather than the situation itself. The latter is not necessarily an admission of weakness or powerlessness but can be a considered decision that the cost of action at this time and in this place is greater than the potential benefits. Thus, the person may decide to tolerate an unpleasant superior, not because he or she is helpless, but because a generally satisfactory job situation makes it worth doing so. Similarly, the individual may choose to dismiss the provocation offered by a rude salesclerk because it is more cost-efficient in terms of the victim's own energy to ignore the wrong, rather than to seek to right it. The example of the angry father who thought of his heart as well as his carpet in deciding how to handle a difficult situation with his son (see Chapter 8) illustrates this point well.

Much as the individual might wish it otherwise, frustration cannot be avoided. Moreover, although there are many ways to manage it, each is likely to incur some costs. But to the degree that the individual is conscious of the choices available, and sufficiently in control of himself or herself to make a considered choice, then this person need no longer feel helplessly angry. Rather than dwelling on the limits of one's resources, the focus, instead, is on how best to manage them.

Concluding comments

Compared to the previous sections of the course, the work of learning to apply coping techniques may appear slow paced. Previously, new techniques and concepts were introduced at each session, while here there is only continued repetition as the group works through literally dozens of specific stress episodes. After a quick climb up a steep slope, there is now only a slow walk along a plateau. In my opinion, however, this period of consolidation is the most essential part of the course. The process of grafting new concepts onto old habits is a slow one, and the time available for this task is all too short.

This plateau period can also be used as a breathing space, allowing the therapist to examine more closely members' behavior and interactions during the sessions. On the whole, these sessions in the middle of the program tend to be looser and more relaxed than the initial ones. By now the group members have at least a nodding acquaintance, not only with each others' spouses, children, and work colleagues, but also with each member's idiosyncratic tender points. For individuals used to relating to others only in a competitive fashion, the implicit learning in sharing human weaknesses without exploiting them can be as important a lesson as the explicit content of the program.

Occasionally, however, aggressive–competitive behavior will surface within the group, for the increased familiarity may also remove the veneer of politeness, and a member may be tempted to pounce on another's weaknesses either by a sarcastic comment or by offering gratuitous advice. After all, the easiest way to demonstrate one's mastery of stress is to highlight others' weaknesses. The therapist should be alert to these manifestations, but it is delicate process to stop the aggression without indulging in similar behavior oneself. Often humor can be used to stop the onslaught, or the therapist may ally himself or herself with the attacked member by revealing a similar personal failing. The group can often be counted on for support, but only if the therapist firmly establishes and enforces the desired norms.

Program facsimiles

Homework 10; Rationale 5; Homework 11; Homework 12; Rationale 6; Homework 13; Homework 14

Homework ⑩

RELAXATION + Awareness
of stress triggers

What is the goal?

To *improve skills* in relaxation.

To learn to *identify situations* that are repeatedly stressful for you.

What do I have to do?

1. Practice the short relaxation exercise twice daily, noting tension before and after each practice.

2. Every time your tension level rises above your cruising speed, note the stress trigger and classify it as "predictable" or "nonpredictable." (See example sheet.)

Name: Example sheet

Date:

Tension level			Stress trigger	Predictable	Non-predictable
Low	Cruising speed	High			
		X	Weekly project meeting	X	
		X	Line up at bank	X	
		X	Phone call from boss		X
		X	Traffic jam driving home	X	
		X	Repair bill for furnace		X

Be prepared

Cafeteria lines

Theater lines

Bank lines

Post office lines

⑤ Rationale for learning to plan for stress

Rationale for learning to plan for stress

When we think of stress, our usual tendency is to equate it with the unexpected and the sudden. But many of the stressful events in our lives result from *repeated reruns of the same situation* (e.g., the monthly project meeting with the hostile co-worker, the time pressure of striving to finish a report the day before deadline, the weekly lineup at the bank). By learning to recognize these chronic sore spots in our lives, we can also learn to take *effective preventive action* to avoid or reduce the stress involved.

Some people might be worried that learning to recognize and prepare for stress would take all the fun out of life. After all, is there not something unnatural in anticipating problems before they occur? But problems are part of life and they are going to happen whether you anticipate them or not. What trouble shooting does is to give you *better control* over problem situations because you are *prepared to meet them.*

Steps involved in learning to prepare for stress

Stress trouble shooting means learning to *identify* potentially stressful situations and to take *preventive action* that will either avoid the trouble spot or reduce its negative impact.

A.   Awareness skills

Identify

Identify situations that are *repeatedly* stressful for you. A good guide to the existence of a chronic stress situation is finding that your tension level *consistently* rises above the comfort zone in that situation, or with that person.

Become aware

Identify what specifically about the situation makes it stressful for you. Here it is important to avoid the booby trap of dwelling on the faulty behavior of someone else, and to focus instead on how this person affects you. After all, you may not be able to directly prevent a colleague from making hostile cracks during a meeting, or even your spouse from being persistently late in getting ready for a social gathering, but by pinpointing how this trigger affects *your thoughts, your feelings, your behavior*, and *your physical functioning*, you will be in a *better position* to take remedial action.

Specify goals

Specify what are the desirable and possible change goals: a changed situation, a changed reaction, or both.

B. Developing new skills

1. *Planning (before)* Make an action plan that will either (a) *prevent* the stressful situation from occurring (e.g., a well-planned schedule can avoid the time pressure of finishing reports at the last minute) or (b) *change your reactions* to it (e.g., "When a colleague starts making hostile remarks during meetings, I will take a deep breath, and then reply in a slow, calm voice, focusing solely on the business at hand"). Be specific: How will you modify self-talk, behavior, and physical reactions?

2. *Stay cool (during)* In the heat of an ongoing stress episode, it is easy to feel overwhelmed and slip into old ways of doing things. But a moment's panic is not necessarily total disaster. *Stop.* Take a deep breath, and *start again.*

3. *Evaluate (after)* Review the stress episode and your behavior during it. Make sure to *give yourself credit* for any positive changes in your own reactions, no matter how *small* and regardless of outcome. Changing long-standing habits is not easy, and success cannot be expected immediately. Moreover, even if you do not always master the situation, success in *controlling yourself* is a praiseworthy achievement in itself. After you have noted your progress compared to past performance, then *plan* for further improvements in future episodes.

C. Applying new skills

Begin small

- In learning to use stress planning skills, tackle one situation at a time. Maximize your chances for success by choosing a situation that is fairly simple and not too tension producing.

- Make a habit of scanning your weekly agenda to pinpoint stress situations that could be planned for.

- Whenever your tension level goes above the comfort level, use this as a signal to explore whether this stress could have been headed off by planning.

"A successful stress manager is an *effective stress planner.*"

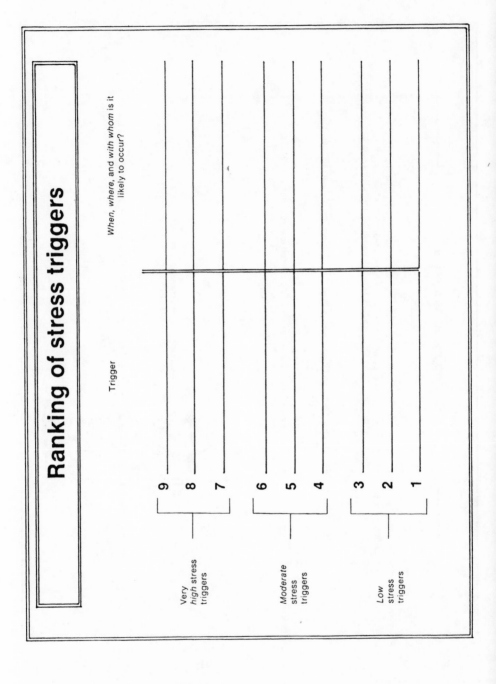

Ranking of stress triggers

Trigger | When, where, and *with whom* is it likely to occur?

Very high stress triggers
9
8
7

Moderate stress triggers
6
5
4

Low stress triggers
3
2
1

Homework ⑪

RELAXATION + Preparing one specific stress situation

What is the goal?

To *improve* skill in relaxation.

To *learn* to prepare for one predictable stress situation.

What do I have to do?

1. Practice short relaxation twice daily, noting tension before and after each practice.

2. Choose one predictable stress situation in the moderate category each day. Plan a coping strategy, detailing what you can do before, during, and after the situation to reduce stress. Afterward, evaluate the effects. (See example sheet.)

Daily stress planner

Name: Example sheet

Date:

Plan
Self-talk strategy

Target situation	Before	During	After
Waiting in the doctor's office.	I know I'll have to wait, so I'll bring something with me to read.	If I start to get upset, remember she's not doing it on purpose.	Even if I don't succeed in staying completely calm, every little bit of progress counts.

Evaluation

What happened?	How did you feel?
Nothing out of the ordinary. Doctor kept me waiting as usual.	I felt pretty good because this time I didn't get upset enough to spoil my whole afternoon.

Homework (12)

RELAXATION + Applying stress preparation skills

What is the goal?

To *improve* skill in relaxation.

To *learn* to apply stress preparation skills to a variety of situations.

What do I have to do?

1. Practice short relaxation twice daily, noting tension before and after each practice.

2. Every day, consult your list of stress triggers and plan a coping strategy for each one that is likely to occur. At the end of the day, evaluate the effects. (See example sheet.)

Name: Example sheet

Date:

Anticipated stress triggers	Coping plan			Evaluation of effects
	Before	During	After	
a.m.				
Traffic driving to work.	Prepare by leaving house in good time and in relaxed frame of mind (practice relaxation, eat breakfast).	If I start getting upset, Remember: "Stewing won't get me there any faster and I'll only be upset all morning."	After the drive, allow myself 5 mins. to unwind before starting workday.	I can't control the traffic, but I can control its negative impact on me. Bravo!
p.m.				
Explaining project to colleagues.	There are always some objections.	Don't jump! Listen to objections, then respond slowly.	A tough meeting deserves a good lunch!	
Secretary gives me messages as I'm ready to leave.	Ask her for messages 1 hr. before			It worked!
evening				
Discussion with daughter re failing mark in math.	Don't rake up all her sins. Concentrate on the problem at hand. Listen to her point of view.	If I get exasperated and shout, STOP, then try again.	After the discussion, try to talk about something pleasant. Mix some good with the bad.	A teenager is not easy, but at least I stayed in control of myself.

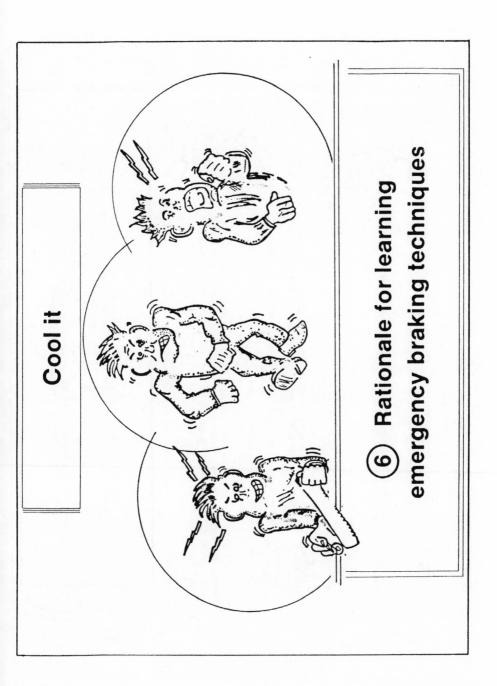

Cool it

⑥ Rationale for learning emergency braking techniques

Rationale for learning emergency braking techniques

The phone rings. Your boss's secretary informs you that the boss wants to see you *immediately*, and the secretary's voice is less than cordial. . . .

You come home at the end of a long, hard day. Sitting in the driveway, *rusting in the rain, is the expensive bicycle* that your son *had* to have and that you haven't even paid for yet. . . .

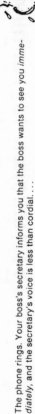

You are driving along to work, feeling good in spite of the traffic. Suddenly, the oil gauge warning light flashes red. For the first few seconds, you ignore it, hoping it is just a momentary aberration. But the light remains stubbornly red. You start *thinking* of the inconvenience of having to take the car to the garage, the cost of a potentially expensive repair. . . .

All these situations are *stress triggers* that cannot be *anticipated and planned for*. Instead, they are the *unexpected jokers* in the day's round of events, happenings that come out of the blue to *bedevil us*. It is unrealistic in this type of situation to try to *avoid anxiety/anger/ frustration completely*. Instead, the aim of a good braking system is to help us *maintain or regain self-control* in spite of our negative feelings. Once we are in control of ourselves, then we can decide how best to deal with the situation. Moreover, by focusing on achieving *self-control first*, we can avoid doing or saying things we are likely to regret later.

Steps involved in learning emergency braking techniques

Effective braking means learning to maintain or regain self-control when confronted by unexpected stress.

A. Awareness skills

Applying the brakes: Each of us has personal signs telling us that we are *out of control* (e.g., flushed face, shouting voice). When these appear, it is important to have a signal telling yourself it is *time to brake.* This can be a simple *verbal command* ("Stop"), a *deep breath,* or a *visual image* such as a red light. Whatever signal you choose, *use it consistently.* It is your personal "code word" for making yourself aware that it is *time to brake.*

B. Developing new skills

1. *Delay*
   There are very *few stress situations* where you have to act *instantly.* If you are so upset that you cannot act in control, don't do or say anything for a few seconds. The *"time-out"* is a pause for you to focus on your primary objective: *self-control.*

B. Developing new skills (continued)

2. *Incompatible behavior*

To counteract signs of disturbance, focus on behavior that is *incompatible* with the behavior you want to avoid. For instance, if you are so upset that your voice automatically rises to a shout, then focus on *speaking slowly*. Similarly, if your usual tendency when upset is to pace up and down, focus on *breathing deeply and slowly* as you do so. As you will soon discover, it is practically impossible to shout slowly, or to pace frenziedly while breathing deeply.

C. Applying new skills

Proceed with caution

Once you feel in *control of yourself*, then you are ready to *deal* with the situation that triggered the disturbance initially. In some situations, you may need only a few minutes before proceeding. In others, a night's sleep or a day's reflection is desirable and possible before proceeding. In each case, however, the fact that you are in *control of yourself* will allow you to deal with the situation with greater *effectiveness and less strain*. Even more important, maintaining self-control allows you to *feel good about yourself* regardless of outcome.

Homework (13)

ONE-STEP RELAXATION + Coping skills for stress emergencies

What is the goal?

To learn one-step relaxation.

To learn to deal effectively with *stress emergencies.*

What do I have to do?

1. Practice one-step relaxation regularly.

2. Everytime you feel signs of rising stress, use an emergency braking signal and institute strategies for regaining self-control. Then note the situation in which you used your emergency braking signal. (See example sheet.)

Name: Example sheet

Date:

Target situation

1. Boss criticizes work — I did the best I could.

2. I get carried away in argument; start to shout.

Signs of a rising stress	Braking signal	Strategies for regaining self-control
1. Tightness in chest and thought, "Boy I'll never satisfy him!"	1. Say "stop."	1. Take deep breath and physically relax chest muscles.
2. Raised voice.	2. Visualize red light.	2. Stop speaking for 10 sec., then resume slowly.

Homework ⑭

ONE-STEP RELAXATION +
Coping with frustration

What is the goal?

To improve your emergency braking techniques.

To learn to recognize frustration as a signal for instituting coping strategies.

What do I have to do?

1. Practice one-step relaxation regularly.

2. Every time you feel frustrated, use coping strategies to regain self-control. Then plan to avoid repetition of same stress. (See example sheet.)

Name: Example sheet

Date:

Signs of frustration	Short-term coping	Long-term coping
I have an agenda planned for the meeting, but others prolong it to talk of other things. Feel impatient; start to interrupt them.	Say "stop." Reduce my physical tension and focus on what they are saying.	Attempt to get agreement before next meeting on length and agreement.
My wife and I repeat the same argument re home improvement costs: "She'll never understand."	Stop the discussion. "I'm too upset to discuss this rationally now. Can we do it tomorrow at 8 pm?"	Schedule planning session in which each expresses needs and fears and try to negotiate compromise on 1 or 2 specific points. Repeat as needed.
Son is late for swimming lesson. "He doesn't know the value of money and my time!"	Try to keep cool. Yelling won't make him move faster.	Set up situation where he pays for missed lesson from his allowance.
Supplier is late with promised shipment.	Grin and bear it.	Decide that the best I can do is grin and bear it.

10. Planning for pleasure

Program references: Rationale 7, "Building stress resistance"; Homework 15–17

It may appear paradoxical to include a section on planning for pleasure in a course devoted to stress management. The basic purpose of this section, however, is not simply to increase the number of pleasant experiences in participants' lives but also, and more important, to teach group members how they themselves can negotiate the round of daily "shoulds" in order to provide for personal "wants."[1] Learning to provide for personal needs is an essential aspect of effective self-management.

Except for a few recent studies on "uplifts" (DeLongis *et al.*, 1982; Kanner *et al.*, 1981), the general stress literature has largely ignored the issue of the degree to which satisfaction in some areas of our lives, or at some periods of time, can reduce the harmful effects of frustration in other areas or at other times. Instead, the impetus for including this section comes mainly from clinical experience with participants in previous programs.

In reading the stress diaries of program participants, I became intensely aware of how little joy most of these individuals described in the course of their very active days. As reported in the stress diaries at least, their entire day, from waking to bedtime, was consumed by striving to fulfill numerous and complex obligations. Even so-called recreational periods, such as weekends and holidays, were frequently dominated by the same type of striving, this time directed toward apparently endless house maintenance tasks, social "obligations," or athletic and cultural "pursuits." Most participants complained somewhat about the absence of free time, but few seemed to be bothered by, or even aware of how rarely feelings of satisfaction and enjoyment figured in the hourly recording. As a therapist, I could not help wondering to what degree the outbursts of aggression and irritation characteristic of these men and

---

1. I am indebted to the writings of G. Alan Marlatt for these felicitous terms (Marlatt, 1985).

women were the results of a deficiency of joy, rather than an excess of stress. Hence, this section on building stress resistance by learning to program pleasures.

This switch in emphasis has an additional advantage in that it provides yet another way of practicing and consolidating the coping skills taught in this program. To make new coping techniques as automatic as old, deeply ingrained habits, extensive repetition is required. By this point, however, impatient type As are likely to exhibit the first signs of boredom with a program that has lasted much longer than the usual business workshop or seminar. The transition to pleasures adds an element of novelty, thus serving to revive flagging interest, while at the same time permitting added time to reinforce concepts and techniques.

Creating a psychological balance sheet

As in previous sections of this program, we begin by charting the behaviors and events that will be the targets for change. As usual, too, this self-monitoring (Homework 15) not only records the frequency of the phenomenon under observation but also serves to define it. Thus, we do not ask individuals to record the number of pleasurable events in their day but, rather, to take their "pleasure temperature" hourly, and only subsequently to describe the activities that produced these feelings of pleasure or displeasure. The focus here is not on events that are conventionally labeled as pleasurable, but on *feelings* of pleasure and on the events associated with these feelings for that *particular individual*. Just as stress is at least partially in the eye of the beholder, so do definitions of pleasure vary widely from individual to individual.

A second implicit definition of pleasure is produced by the request for an hourly record. Most individuals think of pleasure and displeasure as clearly separated in time; there is no overlap between pleasant and unpleasant feelings. In fact, however, the two can exist in close succession during the same activity. During the preparation of a report, for instance, apprehension at beginning the task can be followed by pleasure as the work goes well, only to be followed in turn by fatigue and worry as the individual encounters a new obstacle. Similarly, the feeling of pleasure in watching a TV hockey game can soon be transformed into disappointment and even disgust if the home team appears to be losing. Hourly recording is used to show how the two feelings can quickly alternate, or even coexist.

By now participants in this program are experienced in making discoveries about their own feelings and reactions. Nevertheless, in reviewing this homework assignment in Session 16, group members are surprised to discover how many hourly periods they categorized as pleasurable, compared to those categorized as "displeasures." With very few exceptions, the psychological balance sheet is a favorable one, with pleasures outweighing displeasures. Just as participants initially were unaware of how much tension they actually experienced in the course of the day, so they appear to be equally unaware of the number of times that they experienced pleasure and the variety of situations involved.

Rationale for learning to program pleasures

It is a telling commentary on the type A value system that the rationale for increasing pleasure requires almost as hard a sell as the necessity for reducing physical or behavioral tension. Many participants are worried that enjoyment will interfere with obligations and productivity. Thus, time spent on "want" activities, in contrast to "shoulds," arouses considerable guilt, as if the individual were literally stealing time that legitimately belonged to work and family obligations. Similarly, even the pause to openly enjoy a task well done can be seen as somehow dangerous in that it might make the person too smug and self-satisfied to try harder next time. To spur achievement, the type A typically emphasizes the task remaining to be done, foregoing any pleasure in the task already accomplished or even the task that one is in the process of doing.

The most effective way of countering these deeply held beliefs is not to engage in open confrontation but to focus instead on the link between pleasure and personal effectiveness (Rationale 7). Achievement requires the expenditure of energy, and the wise resource manager must also plan for recuperation and replenishment of this energy. Thus, in permitting ourselves to experience enjoyment, we are not wasting time but, rather, engaging in the crucial task of building stress resistance. The guilt and fears aroused in type As at the prospect of deliberately seeking pleasure can be most effectively alleviated by emphasizing the role of recuperative periods in maintaining health and effectiveness. As one of my relatives justified her trips to southern climates during the cold Canadian winter: "It's not for pleasure; it's for my health."

While feelings of pleasure can occur at any time or during any activity—and it is important to recognize and enjoy these feelings when they do occur—it is also essential to purposefully plan for regular periods of restorative activities. As we all know far too well, savings relegated to money left over at the end of the week are likely to somehow disappear; instead, the wise budgeter allocates his or her savings first. Similarly, unless considerable care and effort are devoted to planning for pleasurable activities, this time is likely to be swallowed up by a host of competing activities.

Building pleasures into the daily routine

The process of planning for pleasure is modeled on the problem-solving skills training developed by D'Zurilla and Nezu (1982). The steps of this procedure are clearly delineated: defining the problem; brainstorming all possible solutions, including preposterous-appearing ones; appraising the positive and negative features of each alternative; choosing a course of action; and establishing when and how the results of this course of action will be evaluated. As with many other of the coping techniques demonstrated in this program, most participants already have considerable familiarity at work with this systematic approach to problem solving. The novelty lies in applying the technique to personal issues, particularly that of increasing pleasurable activities.

In Homework 16 participants are asked to brainstorm activities that they have found pleasant in the past, or that they think might be sources of pleasure. For the time being, the two columns at the right-hand side of the Wish List are to be left blank.

Looking at the homework assignments of previous groups, I am struck by the variety of wishes expressed, both aggregately by the group and by each individual within it. Some are clearly in the realm of fantasy, such as winning a million-dollar lottery, possessing a completely automated house devoid of maintenance chores, being able to speak a dozen languages, spending a wild weekend indulging sexual fantasies with three or four partners, and winning the Nobel prize. Travel to faraway places also figures high on the list: Participants dream of photographing big game in Africa, hearing *Aida* at La Scala, walking the Milford track in New Zealand, visiting China, and cruising in tropical waters.

Most of the wishes expressed, however, are at least partially within the realm of the possible and much closer to home. There is a strong emphasis on hobbies, ranging from computerizing the Bible and learning Japanese to coaching a junior baseball team and setting up a good home workshop for woodwork. A persistent theme throughout these Wish Lists is the desire to improve physical condition, whether by jogging, judo and karate, or unspecified exercise. Good food is a frequently mentioned pleasurable activity, either by dining in a "gourmet" restaurant or, almost as often, by improving one's own cooking skills. Almost all participants mention some form of family activities, but it is perhaps significant that these tend to be rather vague and unspecific; a participant might wish to "spend more time with my family," "play more often with my kids," or achieve "better communication with my spouse."

In spite of the fact that these men and women are heavily involved in work, this area of their lives does not figure heavily in the Wish Lists. Furthermore, when work is mentioned, it is usually in terms of reduced hours; some participants would like to work half time, some wish more flexibility in working hours, and a few dream of a sabbatical year or two away from work. Much more frequent is the wish of time for oneself, to watch the hometown hockey team on TV, to listen to music, to spend a week fishing alone, or simply to have a couple of days at home alone.

It is probable that the Wish Lists submitted by group participants are censored ones, in that they conform to the expectations expressed in the example sheets. Nevertheless, when these lists are shared at Session 17, there is the sensation of a general unbuttoning. Just as members were previously surprised by the resemblances in the daily hassles encountered, so are they surprised, and at the same time reassured, to discover that their wishes are not unique but are shared by many others.

Once the Wish Lists have been discussed, participants are asked to return to them and to complete the two columns on the right-hand side of the page. The first, headed by the initial P, represents a scoring of the amount of pleasure anticipated from that specific wish or activity, with 10 reserved for activities believed to yield the maximum amount of pleasure; and 1, the minimum. The second column, headed by the initial F, is a feasibility scoring, and once again, 10 represents the most feasible activity and 1 the least. The next task for participants is to balance pleasure against ease of implementation and to choose the activity with the highest proportion of pleasure to costs. This activity then becomes the target.

The first step in implementing a pleasurable activity is in making it as specific as possible. "Getting more exercise" is likely to remain in the realm of wishes, but attending an exercise class at the Y three times a week provides a concrete, measurable goal. Similarly, gambling with friends in Atlantic City has a greater chance of realization if the date, the duration, and the individuals involved are all specified. Even "more time for myself" can be specified in terms of where, when, and how often these breaks are to occur.

The major problem here is to help participants set realistic goals, in terms of both what is to be done and how often. With their usual enthusiasm, group members often select targets that are doomed to failure because the change in accustomed habits is too great. Thus, a sedentary individual will not only decide to begin exercising every day, but he or she will schedule the jogging for early morning, even though he or she has never yet found time to do a relaxation exercise at that period of day. Similarly, a person may decide that Sunday will be devoted to family activities, completely ignoring established family habits. I tend to categorize such radical revisions of life-style as "New Year resolutions," with the low chance of success that these resolutions usually have. Instead, once again, I emphasize that we maximize the chances for success in behavioral change when we begin with modest targets.

By the end of Session 17 most participants have selected a suitable target, and Homework 17 is devoted to making a plan for implementing it. To illustrate this process, I have selected two homework assignments completed by actual participants. One concerns a single event, a golf trip to Myrtle Beach with three buddies the following spring, while the other concerns a recurrent activity, monthly serious poker games. As the reader will probably guess, both activities have already undergone considerable specification from the initial wishes expressed "to go on a golfing trip" and "play serious poker." In fact, the second had gone through a further stage of refinement, with the participant reluctantly concluding that his initial goal—to hold weekly games—was probably not realistic.

For each of these activities, participants listed the practical requirements and means of fulfilling them. For the golfing trip, this involved choosing the date, reserving vacation time for that date, putting aside money every payday, assuring oneself that the three partners did the same, and making reservations for car and hotel. The major obstacle foreseen was a failure of one of the partners, either by neglecting to save regularly or by backing out at the last minute. To counteract the former, a list of potential replacements would be formed and anyone who missed two biweekly contributions would be replaced. This replacement list would also be used to substitute for cancellations. The starting date for this plan was set at 6 months before the proposed trip. Progress would be recorded every fortnightly payday, and members' standing would be evaluated once monthly.

For the poker games, the requirements were developing a list of suitable partners, having sufficient money to play, and negotiating for family approval. The first of these could be accomplished by canvassing previous partners and asking friends and acquaintances for suggestions. To allow for sufficient guilt-free money, a regular amount would be set aside each payday. Family approval could be negotiated by offering compensatory family activities. In this case, the participant could foresee a number of reasons why the game schedule would not be maintained, ranging from arguments over rules and losses to simple lack of organization. The former would be countered by obtaining players' agreement on rules and limits, and reviewing them at the beginning of each game. The second would be prevented by appointing a coordinator for the subsequent game at the end of each session. Not all obstacles could be overcome; should he find the family budget short, then this participant would abstain until sufficient money had accumulated. The plan was to be put into action that very lunch hour, when his usual lunch cronies would be sounded out on their interest. To evaluate progress, the participant would record both the frequency of games and the enjoyment derived from each. At the end of 6 months the participant would decide whether he wished to maintain this activity and what modifications, if any, were desirable.

At first sight, such extensive planning for such simple activities might seem to remove the pleasure inherent in them. My experience has been the contrary. For in addition to the activity itself, participants appear to derive considerable satisfaction from the feeling of being in control, of being able to "make things happen." In fact, for the would-be golfer, anticipating and planning the trip appeared to be as important as the golf games themselves! Thus, while I would not realistically expect participants to go through the entire protocol each time, this problem-solving approach to pleasure is likely to significantly alter participants' perspectives both of the importance of satisfying personal needs and of the effective methods for doing so.

Stress and restoration

All of us recognize the desirability of a balanced diet, but few of us manage to achieve it every meal, or even every day. Much as we may bewail it, the fast-food lunch, or even the lunch missed entirely, has become part of the reality of an ever-growing number of North Americans. Similarly, even though the ideal may be a daily balance between "shoulds" and "wants," it is unrealistic to expect the accountant in the days before income tax is due, or the individual on a harried business trip, to maintain the regular rhythm of recreational activities. Instead, the aim is to make participants more aware of the accumulating deficit, and to suggest means of bringing the pleasure budget within a better balance.

One technique for deficit control is to provide for small gratifications even during the stress period itself. For instance, a business trip is likely to obliterate the conventional distinction between working and leisure time, with meetings or business entertainments crammed into all hours of the day. But it is usually possible to find some pleasure sometime in the trip, be it in taking an hour to visit an interesting sight or ordering a food that one usually doesn't get to eat. My personal favorite is the unaccustomed luxury of breakfast in bed with the newspaper; once again, I find that admitting to it in front of the group makes it easier for others to express their wishes. In the same way that one compensates for the stress of a business trip by scheduling some pleasures, a period of intense work pressure at home is also a signal to be extraindulgent to oneself in other areas of one's life; this is when you allow yourself the luxury of mindless TV watching, or buy yourself the expensive record you have been coveting.

Once the acute stress period has passed, it is important to allow for replenishment before hurtling oneself into the next crisis. There is the need, not only for physical rest, but also for mental restoration. The object is not to return to business as usual but to recognize that energy depletion has occurred and that attention must be paid to replenishment before the individual is able to function again at full capacity. Most of our participants are accustomed to coming in early and leaving late during a work crisis; it is more difficult for them to accept the reverse after the crisis has passed.

The carrot versus the whip (continued)

This section on recuperation and restoration, continued from Chapter 8, provides another opportunity to emphasize the importance of self-reinforcement in effective self-management. Just as participants have learned to stop for relaxation breaks, so is it important to allot a few moments to concentrate on the pleasure of the moment at frequent intervals during the day. The "in basket" that is emptied, the difficult phone call completed, or simply a busy morning, all merit self-congratulation. Furthermore, far from detracting from future striving, appreciating what one has already done is likely to provide increased incentive to continue. Equally as important, the ability to dispense adequate amounts of self-praise makes the person less dependent on continuous feeding from others, and hence less vulnerable to frustration.

Concluding comments

In learning to plan for and maximize pleasure, participants in this course have come full circle. Type A individuals usually enter stress management programs seeking greater power in controlling frustrating people and things in their environment. During the course of the program, they are led to accept the reality that the wished-for environmental control is unattainable; daily hassles, in some form or other, are inevitable, and one must learn to cope with them as best we can. Paradoxically, however, the renunciation of the fantasy of magical omnipotence results in the reality of greater environmental control, for by learning both to set more realistic goals and to improve the range and flexibility of coping strategies, group members have significantly increased their chances of impacting on the world around them. One may continue to dream the impossible dream but, in the meantime, one can also learn to achieve and enjoy the art of the possible.

This acceptance of a new reality within the context of a short intervention program is probably possible only with basically healthy individuals living in relatively favorable life circumstances. It would be unrealistic on the part of the therapist to expect this kind of change from individuals stuck in crippling mental illnesses, or from those whose lives are so deprived that reasonable effort is unlikely to produce much tangible improvement. Stress management is not a substitute for other forms of therapy, though it may be useful in screening out those healthy enough to benefit from short-term skills training from those who are not.

Program facsimiles

Homework 15; Rationale 7; Homework 16; Homework 17

Homework (15)

Creating a psychological balance sheet

What is the goal?

To learn to identify pleasant feelings and the situations that produce them.

To become aware of the balance of pleasures versus displeasures in our daily lives.

What do I have to do?

1. Every hour on the hour, note how you feel and classify the feeling as "pleasure" or "displeasure." Then note the activity.

2. At the end of each day, add up the number of pleasures versus displeasures. (See example sheet.)

Name: Example sheet   **Date:**

Time	Feelings	Pleasure	Displeasure	Activity
a.m. 7:00	Boredom		X	Putting on makeup
8h:00	Interest, curiosity	X		Reading mail
9h:00	Challenge, apprehension	X		Preparing report for meeting
10h:00	Tension, frustration			Colleague challenges report
11h:00	Satisfied	X		Meeting over
12h:00	Hunger, good appetite	X		Time for lunch
p.m. 13h:00	Warmth, smiling	X		Walk in sunshine
14h:00	Anxiety		X	Rush job for yesterday!
15h:00	Concentration, working hard	X		Working on rush job
16h:00	Disappointed		X	Results not as good as wanted
17h:00	Rushed, irritable		X	Driving home
18h:00	Rushed, irritable		X	Preparing dinner
evening 19h:00	Enjoying food	X		Eating dinner
20h:00	Relaxed, content	X		Hot bath
21h:00	Excitement, enthusiasm	X		Watching TV
22h:00	Disgust, anger		X	Hockey player given unfair penalty
23h:00	Sleepy, tired	X		Go to bed
24h:00				

Total 10   6

Building stress resistance

"A pleasure a day keeps the stress AWAY."

⑦ Rationale for learning to program pleasures

Rationale for learning to program pleasures

Steps involved in learning to plan for pleasure

Not all pleasures, however, require *inordinate amounts of time and money*. A good dinner, a conversation with a friend, or even a moment's pause to appreciate a job well done can all be sources of pleasure. Even our daydreams can often be realized in part, if not completely. A private yacht and 6 months to sail the Greek Islands may be only a dream for the future, but sailing lessons at the local Y is a present possibility. Like savings, however, pleasures are unlikely to happen if we relegate them to time left over. Instead, a good resource manager *must budget for pleasure* in the same way that he or she *plans for other activities*.

Effective planning for pleasure means learning to *build pleasures into your daily routine.*

A. Scanning possibilities

- Conduct a *brainstorming* session. Sit down for a half hour and list all the activities that have been or might be pleasurable for you. List *everything* you can think of, without stopping to evaluate.

- Observe yourself over the course of a few days. *Note those activities* that make you feel particularly *relaxed, satisfied,* or *replenished.*

B. Choosing an activity

- *Evaluate* each one of the activities you have listed in terms of costs (time, money, special equipment) and benefits.

- *Choose one* activity to begin with. Don't get hung up in searching forever for the "perfect" activity. Alternately, don't undertake too many activities at once.

C. Getting started

- *Develop an action plan.* Specify when, where, with whom, and how you will carry out this activity. Trouble-shoot by identifying possible obstacles and how you can overcome them.

- *Maximize* chance of success by setting realistic goals and arranging circumstances to facilitate reaching them. Enlist the support of your family and friends if this will help.

- *Reward yourself* for any change accomplished. In any new activity, even a potentially pleasurable one, beginnings are hard. Give yourself credit for these first steps.

D. Keeping on

- *Reevaluate regularly.* At regular intervals take an inventory of your pleasurable activities. Is it time to add to the list or to change activities? There is nothing wrong with changing your mind. The criterion is *your* sense of well-being.

- Regularly *monitor* your pleasure level, just as you do your tension level. When your pleasure level drops below the comfort zone, take remedial action.

- During periods of high stress, *pay special attention* to your pleasure level. Even if some reduction is necessary, attempt to maintain at least a minimum level.

- Immediately after a high stress period, allow *extra pleasure time* for rest and replenishment.

And don't forget . . .

A pleasure a day keeps the stress AWAY.

Homework ⑯

Creating a wish list

What is the goal?

To make a list of activities that give you pleasure.

What do I have to do?

1. Equip yourself with paper and pencil, and settle yourself in a quiet spot where you will be undisturbed.

2. Brainstorm activities that you have found pleasant in the past or that you think might give you pleasure. Do *not* judge the practicality of your wishes at this point; just list them. (See example sheet.)

Wish list of
pleasurable activities

	P	F
1. Take a month and travel around world.		
2. Wish I spent more time playing with my children.		
3. Time to just sit quietly and do nothing.		
4. Get to see some hockey games.		
5. Go out to a good restaurant for dinner.		
6. Would really like to improve my swimming stroke.		
7. Buy a boat and go sailing every weekend.		
8. Spend more time in physical exercise.		
9. More and better sex life!		
10. Classify pictures I took during trip last summer.		
11. Buy a new shirt.		

Homework (17)

Making wishes happen

What is the goal?

To *develop* an action plan to increase pleasurable activity.

What do I have to do?

Follow action plan on next page.

Name: Example sheet

Date:

Step 1: Choosing a target wish

Consult your list of wishes. Choose one item that has a favorable cost–benefit ratio.

Target wish: *Get more exercise.*

Step 2: List practical requirements to make this wish happen and how to fulfill them.

Practical requirements

a. Decide what exercise, when, and where.

b. Exercise clothes.

c. Physician's O.K.

d.

e.

How to fulfill them

a. Get list of fitness classes from the local Y. Choose one and enroll.

b. Buy jogging shoes next Saturday.

c. Make appointment with medical dept.

d.

e.

Step 3: Overcoming obstacles

List potential obstacles and how to overcome them.

Potential obstacles

How to overcome them

a. I may do too much at first, get hurt, and quit.

a. Exercise only in supervised class for beginners.

b. Other things might interfere with my schedule.

b. Choose a regular time most likely to be free — e.g., early morning before work or just after work.

c. My husband might object.

c. Explain what you want to do and ask for his help.

d. I have to miss classes because of travel.

d. Ask your instructor for a program to follow while traveling.

e. I don't like the YMCA.

e. Investigate company subsidies for other clubs.

Step 4: *Express your goals in concrete terms (e.g., x times per week). Make sure they are realistic.*

Goals:

Exercise 30 min., 3X per week.

Step 5: Starting date

I shall start my pleasurable activity on   Monday

Step 6: Recording progress

I shall record my progress by   ① Keeping a record of each class attended or exercise session done on my own.   ② Noting how much of the exercises in each class I can comfortably do — e.g., no. of minutes jogging.

Step 7: Evaluation

I shall evaluate my progress on   10 weeks after starting.

How do I feel?

How do I look?

11. Stress management: A lifelong objective

Program references: Rationale 8, "Stress management: A lifelong objective"; Homework 18

This final section of the program deals with some of the issues involved in maintaining behavior change after the end of treatment. There are three main aspects of this effort to make stress management a lifelong objective. The first is to demystify the process of behavior change and have participants attribute correctly the source of change. The second concerns dealing with environmental reactions to participants' changed coping styles. The third, and perhaps most important (Rationale 8, Homework 18), focuses on preparing for lapses in newly acquired habits, or what is termed "relapse prevention" (see Marlatt & Gordon, 1985).

Accepting credit for change

By now most participants in the program will acknowledge that their coping styles have changed, and each session is filled with numerous examples of stress episodes where the participants describe how they reacted differently from their bad, old selves. While these testimonials are gratifying for the therapist, simply acknowledging change is insufficient for continued maintenance postintervention. Unless participants can attribute change to themselves, rather than to the external influence of therapist and program, there is not much likelihood that these changes will be maintained once the external influences are removed.

Essentially, the point I want to make here is that no magical technique or powerful therapist made the participants speak more slowly at a business meeting, or control their temper in arguing with an inefficient employee. Instead, they themselves produced the change, using well-known principles of behavior modification. The underlying components of this program are very similar to the learning of any new skill: clear definition of what is to be learned and why; division of the learning process into sequential, manageable steps; practice of each step with corrective feedback; and, most important of all, reinforcement for each

219

step attempted. All participants have used this process many times previously in acquiring the multiple skills they already possess. The difference this time, to the degree that there is one, is their greater awareness of the skill-building process itself.

It is also worth emphasizing that these changes in coping style do not imply a total refashioning of personality or temperament. These men and women came into the program as active, competent managers and they remain so. What they have done is simply to focus on a new goal: the effective self-management of energy expenditure. This is not a skill that is taught in school, or in the multitude of company-sponsored courses. Once convinced that it was worth learning, however, these men and women have brought the same intelligence and application to bear here that they have used previously to master a host of other skills. Learning occurred quickly because they already possessed many of the component techniques, and because they were used to learning many things quickly.

Discussing the difference between successful and unsuccessful maintenance of weight loss following treatment, Marlatt (1985) makes the distinction between individuals who see themselves as *recipients* of treatment versus those who see themselves as the active *agents* of change. As he describes his observations of clients of a weight loss program attending a postprogram follow-up session, those who were less successful in maintaining weight loss tended to speak in terms of program effects "wearing off" with time; the magic pill of treatment gradually stopped working once it was no longer ingested regularly. One woman who was successful in continuing to lose weight, in contrast, felt that she had mastered the principles of self-control and, therefore, could use a variety of different behaviors to achieve her goals, altering behavior to adapt to the changing circumstances of her daily life. Because the stressors of daily life are even more varied than the temptations to overeat, no coping formula, however well learned, will be sufficiently flexible to cover all situations. Instead, the best hope for durability and generalizability of treatment effects lies in the ability of the participant to understand the principles of behavior change and to believe that he or she can apply them to achieve desired goals.

Coping with an unchanged environment

Most of the individuals who enroll in stress management programs such as this are not only type As themselves but also work and live with other type As. In fact, one of the major ways they justify their perfectionism, frantic striving, and low boiling point is to claim that this coping style is normal because it is shared by so many other people in their immediate environment. Now, however, they are trying to change their behavior, and this places them in the position of the reformed alcoholic condemned to spend his or her days surrounded by old drinking buddies.

For many individuals in the program, co-workers and family members react positively to the change and provide strong support for maintaining it. Thus, a colleague may compliment a participant on his or her coolness during a difficult meeting, or a spouse may be impressed by the participant's ability to discuss a family problem without "flying off the handle." Sometimes, colleagues may even ask about the program that led to these changes; many participants, too, have shown the program rationales and homework assignments to spouses. Occasionally, a spouse will be tempted to try some of the assignments himself or herself, and there are even reports of the whole family listening to the relaxation tapes together.

But change in a work colleague or family member can also disturb existing equilibriums, making others uncomfortable. Thus, one participant's wife had complained about his constant shouting at the children; when he reduced the frequency of his outbursts, his wife starting shouting more. This phenomenon is a familiar one to family therapists, with one family member serving to express other members' needs. When this family member no longer exhibits the "symptom," the other is forced to acknowledge his or her own needs. The challenge here is to help the participant resist the pressures exerted to have him or her resume the old role in the family.

A common family problem of group members is that they are married to spouses who are as type A as they are, or maybe even more so. For this type of spouse, any effort by the participant to modulate his or her behavior can be quite threatening. Thus, the participant may be willing to change his or her schedule to introduce time for relaxation, but the spouse may complain of the participant's laziness and attempt to counteract this change by arranging for long lists of chores or by scheduling multiple social activities. I have even had cases where spouses have complained because participants were driving too slowly or not aggressively enough! Assuming that the basic relationship between the spouses is a good one, then the best way of handling this is to try to make an ally of the opposing spouse by including him or her in the change process. I advise participants to use their communication skills to discuss with spouses what they are trying to change and why, and perhaps enlist the other's aid in monitoring behavior.

Another problem with reformed type As is that their new coping style may run counter to established group norms. This is particularly true in the working environment where the prevailing culture may favor precisely those behaviors we are trying to modify. For instance, one participant reported on a work crisis, the loss of an important order, when all the people in the office "flew around like chickens without heads." He, in contrast, sat at his desk and tried to plan a strategy for compensating for this loss. To his co-workers, however, this lack of frantic though purposeless activity was perceived as indifference, and he was reproached by the question "Don't you care?" It was a test of his new coping style to attempt to respond calmly that indeed he did care, but that he was just trying to figure out what to do about the situation.

Often group members create their own problems with the environment by seeking to convert others. As the old adage would have it, there is nothing worse that the atheist who has found religion. Our members may be reformed type As, but they are still type A enough to attempt to control the world by imparting their newfound wisdom! Here we invoke the principle of individual differences; people are different and they have the right to perceive and handle stress situations as they see fit. Moreover, as the participants themselves know by experience, preaching is not an effective teaching technique; co-workers and family members are far more likely to be convinced of the errors of their ways by behavioral example rather than by verbal assault.

One way of counteracting negative environmental influences is to have participants identify individuals in their immediate environment who do behave the way they would like to. And just as the dieter may choose to dine with persons who do not overeat, so might the type A approach closer to people embodying a behavioral style he or she would like to emulate. Another possibility is for the participant to see himself or herself as an innovator of a coming trend. After all, within the adult lifetime of most participants we have witnessed at least two major transformations of personal habits, smoking and physical exercise, and it is highly possible that stress management will constitute the third.

In spite of the suggestions mentioned here, there is no simple solution to being a reformed type A in a world filled with unreformed and unrepentant ones. It is a difficult task. It may be that to change North American cultural norms significantly, we shall eventually have to go beyond treatment of selected individuals and, instead, use mass marketing techniques to directly influence attitudes in the general public. Or, a simpler alternative to seeking to transform society in general would be to treat a critical mass of people within a specific company in an effort to modify corporate culture. Both are new frontiers waiting to be explored.

Relapse prevention

Theoretical model

Most behavior therapy programs directed to life-style modification (e.g., smoking cessation, weight loss, alcohol abstinence, adoption of a regular exercise program) are short-term ones; the traditional view was that once exposed to new behavioral habits the client would continue to practice them even after the end of formal treatment. The possibility of relapse was not discussed during the course of treatment, and when the therapist was confronted by such a case, this could be treated as a failure of a particular therapist or treatment, or as arising from "lack of motivation" in the client. The accumulating evidence from multiple outcome studies, however, has effectively destroyed this comfortable view of treatment outcome; by now, most therapists are aware that, for life-style modification programs at least, relapse is more likely to be the rule rather than the unhappy exception. Within a few months of ending formal treatment programs, a good number of ex-smokers are smoking again, exercisers are sedentary again, and so on.

The relapse prevention program, developed by Marlatt and Gordon (1985), is an attempt to confront the possibility of relapse during the course of treatment itself and to develop coping techniques for dealing with it. As described by Marlatt (1985), the program has two major goals: (1) to anticipate and prevent the occurrence of a relapse after the initiation of a habit change, and (2) to help the individual recover from a "slip" or lapse before it escalates into a full-blown relapse.

Underlying this program is a radically different conception of the learning curve for new habits; rather than viewing learning as at a maximum during the reinforcement of treatment, with extinction gradually occurring as time away from treatment increases, this conception views the immediate posttreatment period as a "learning trial" in which the individual tests his or her new habit patterns against old temptations. Under these circumstances, "falling off the wagon" is a normal part of the learning process; the challenge for the individual is to climb back on again, having learned how to hold on better. There are a number of specific procedures for incorporating relapse prevention within the treatment process itself: developing awareness of high-risk situations in which lapses are likely to occur, the development of strategies for handling these high-risk situations, and strategies for evaluating and dealing with lapses when they do occur.

Application to type As

The relapse prevention model is not completely applicable to the problem of self-management of energy expenditure, for, unlike other life-style behaviors, here the demarcation between success and failure is far from self-evident. The smoker knows when she is abstinent and when she has lapsed by smoking a cigarette; the would-be exerciser can count the number of sessions he has missed. But the goal of this program is to modulate rather than to eradicate type A behavior; even during the course of the program itself there is no total abstinence from the contraindicated responses, but only a change in degree. Changes in degree of behavior are obviously much harder to evaluate than presence of absence of the behavior, and consequently it is sometimes difficult for participants to recognize that they are reverting to old habits. To make relapse prevention techniques workable for type As, it is first necessary to develop procedures for monitoring and evaluating good performance versus deteriorated performance.

Self-monitoring of stress management performance

A number of techniques can be used to know whether one is staying within acceptable boundaries or is reverting to spinning one's wheels. One way is to utilize stress signatures, the individual's personal signs of physical tension. If one's stomach starts churning again, or one's shoulders start aching, then the individual has clear signals that stress is not being managed adequately. A second is to be sensitive to comments of others. If a spouse or co-worker complains that the former participant appears to be reverting to old ways, or simply remarks that he or she appears harried or irritable, this is a signal of behavior that is off the track. A third way is by maintenance of a stress diary. Using the familiar 1–10 scales, participants are asked to chart pleasure and tension levels at the end of each day. By comparing tension levels to pleasure levels, the individual gains a picture of the current balance in his or her life. Furthermore, by comparing present status to past records, the individual can monitor changes in this balance. Thus, a drop in pleasure level, a rise in tension level, or a change in the pleasure–tension ratio can all signal danger.

In addition to monitoring internal states, the type A can also monitor changes in the external environment; analogous to the high-risk situations of the former alcoholic and smoker, any change in accustomed routine is a signal of potential disruption of the type A's newly established coping patterns. A business trip, involving a change in both routine and locale, can lead to the "forgetting" of regular relaxation breaks. Tired and irritable during a period of heavy work pressure or family crisis, the person may settle for the immediate relief of shouting, rather than consider the longer-term benefits of self-control. During a vacation, the individual may be reluctant to engage in the "spoilsport" activity of anticipating and planning for potential stress episodes. Thus, any time the person is experiencing environmental change, positive as well as negative, it is safe to assume that coping habits may be under pressure.

Rationale for relapse prevention

Nearing the end of the program, most participants appear to attain a state of euphoria about their increased self-control in coping with daily stressors, and almost all are confident that this new coping style will be permanent. Here the therapist is in the reverse position from the beginning of the program when the task was to instill confidence in doubting participants. Now, instead, the therapist's job is to temper the self-congratulations with a dose of realism. These individuals are hyperreactive to stress by temperament, and they live in a world where multiple pressures tend to favor this hyperreactivity. To maintain self-control under these circumstances is not an easy task.

But these individuals have faced many other challenges successfully and there is no reason why they cannot also cope with this one. To do so, however, they must first understand the nature of the challenge. Perhaps the easiest way of doing so is by analogy to another life-style goal that is a challenge to most affluent Americans: weight control. Living in a world where we are constantly bombarded by food advertisements; where business lunches, dinners, and even breakfasts proliferate; where all social gatherings are marked by offerings of food, there are very few of us who are completely immune to the temptation to overeat, or to eat foods best left uneaten. Furthermore, unlike smoking, drugs, or alcohol, here total abstinence is not a feasible method of habit control; we cannot withdraw completely from the temptations of food but must face the issue of what and how much to eat daily.

Nevertheless, the majority of people do manage to keep their weight within acceptable bounds, relying on a process of self-monitoring and corrective feedback. Successful weight maintainers monitor their weight regularly, either by scales or by the tightness of a favorite article of clothing. When weight gain does occur, the individual neither stoops to breast beating in self-flagellation nor uses the gain as an excuse to go on an eating binge, but instead uses the increase in weight as a signal for an adjustment in calorie intake–expenditure ratio, a sign to skip desert the following day or to increase exercise. Weight is not necessarily constant but, because of monitoring and corrective action, fluctuations are kept within 5 to 10 pounds. Thus, we may let ourselves go a little during vacation and holiday periods, only to be more careful during the first week in January. In short, there is no permanent "cure" for the temptation to overeat, nor do most of us manage to exert perfect weight control, but a look around any room will distinguish the more successful from the less successful.

The men and women in this stress management program have invested considerable time and energy in acquiring greater self-control over their reactions to daily hassles. To protect this investment, they can institute techniques of self-monitoring and corrective feedback that will help them maintain and improve this self-control. Obviously, self-control will never be total, and an increase in external pressures, or increased personal vulnerability due to illness, may lead to temporary reversions to older habits. This does not mean that the individual has failed in stress management but simply that it is time to take corrective actions.

Coping with coping disruptions

Where the high-risk situation can be anticipated, the individual can use some of his or her newly acquired coping strategies to take preventive action. For example, before a period of expected work pressure, such as yearly budget planning, the person can make a list of situations and reactions that have led to tension overflow in the past, and then devise strategies for managing them. One might remember that previous work stress periods were particularly difficult, not primarily because of the amount of work involved, but because of feelings of frustration at not being able to do the job as well as one would like to. Knowing this, the person would pay particular attention to self-talk during the crisis and would counter unproductive self-talk with more positive self-statements. To prepare counteracting statements, he or she could reread the program rationale dealing with modifications of cognitions and even review the relevant homework assignments. As a further aid in controlling tension, the person might decide to return to the relaxation tape for a few days, or at least to take one short relaxation break every hour on the hour.

Furthermore, rather than expecting automatic understanding from family members and exhibiting even more irritation when it is not forthcoming, the person might discuss in advance the coming stress period with family members, as well the type of help he or she might like from them. Finally, and perhaps most important, would be the recognition that a period of intense energy expenditure requires both preparation and recuperation. Like the runner preparing for a marathon, one would seek to enter the race in good mental and physical shape. After the race, one would not immediately embark on another marathon but would allow sufficient rest and recreation to replenish depleted stores.

Many times, however, there will be no anticipation of specific problem situations. Only when the former participant finds herself regularly reaching into the medicine chest for the headache analgesic, or finds herself shouting for the fifth time that day, will she recognize that old stress signals have returned. She has fallen off the wagon without knowing exactly when or why. The danger here, of course, is that the person will decide that she is a failure at stress management and might as well not continue to try. The analogy is that of the dieter who, having consumed the first forbidden piece of chocolate cake, decides that he is a failure as a dieter and, therefore, might as well finish the cake. To prevent this slip from becoming total relapse, we should like the former participant to see this instead as a learning experience, one calling on her to use her talents as a stress manager to detect and correct the problem.

Sometimes, a few minutes reflection will provide an obvious stress trigger that is disrupting the existing equilibrium and causing the former participant to "blow her cool." She may be frustrated by an apparent impasse at work, worried about a child's poor school performance, or simply feeling under the weather because of a long, dragging cold. There are seasonal variations in mood state, too, as anyone who has lived through the end of a long Canadian winter will testify. Whatever the reason, once the stress trigger has been identified, the individual can then turn her attention to dealing with it, using the coping techniques learned in the course.

More difficult is the situation of the type A who finds himself reverting to old coping patterns but is unable to identify any specific stress trigger. Before remedial action can be taken, sleuthing is required to help pinpoint what has gone wrong. Here I suggest that the individual return to the stress diary and for a week chart hourly situations and reactions. Rereading the stress manual in conjunction with the diary should provide at least a tentative diagnosis and help the individual chart a course of corrective action. A wide variety of techniques are available for changing the situation or managing the disturbing emotions, or a little of both, and the manual can help the individual select and combine these techniques to develop an appropriate action plan. As with any problem solving, the plan devised should be reviewed and reevaluated after an appropriate interval. Should the individual feel better, then he has strengthened his ability to recognize and correct stress management problems.

Should the malaise persist, however, further sleuthing is required. In some cases the individual may even decide to seek professional help to detect the problem. This is not an admission of failure; on the contrary, it is a sign that the individual is more aware of stress reactions and is better placed to distinguish between those that can be helped by self-treatment and those that may require the intervention of a trained professional.

Concluding comments

The end of the program may leave the therapist with mixed feelings. On the one hand, there is the immense gratification of the healthy type A's quick and positive response to treatment. In 10 short weeks, there are obvious changes in behavior within the group and reports of changed behavior outside. Most participants are eager to tell us how much better they feel, as well as to relate the improvement in their relations with family members and co-workers. Occasionally, a participant will even recount an incident that dramatically illustrates an improved manner of handling a stress episode, further adding to the therapist's sense of satisfaction. Balancing these positive feelings, however, is an anxiety analogous to the parent watching his or her teen-aged child leave home. There was so much to change and so little time in which to do it. Was the preparation adequate? Can short-term intervention of this nature really change deep-seated habits that are so strongly reinforced by the surrounding culture?

There are no simple answers to the problems of habit change and of maintenance of this change posttreatment. We have learned much about this process in recent years, but there is even more left to learn, and programs such as this are obviously open to revision and improvement. Nevertheless, the best antidote to therapist depression and discouragement is to engage in the type of realistic self-talk we advocate for our clients. Neither the program nor the therapist is perfect, and it is probable that not enough has been learned, or that some of what has been learned will soon be forgotten. But in renouncing the fantasy of the total cure, we can also acknowledge the reality of the many positive changes that have occurred. There are many gradations of achievement between success and failure, and while we continue to strive for ever better methods, we can also take pleasure in helping to improve the quality of participants' lives, as well as the lives of the people who live and work with them.

Program facsimiles

Rationale 8; Homework 18

⑧ Rationale for considering stress management as a lifelong objective

Rationale for considering stress management as a lifelong objective

Anyone who has participated in this course has *invested* considerable *time* and *effort* in learning how to manage stress more effectively. You do not have to be reminded of what it took to attend two meetings weekly, practice homework daily, and fill out endless forms. . . . But you stuck to it and for most of you the benefits are obvious. Not only do you *personally feel better*, but in many cases spouses, co-workers, and acquaintances are beginning to *comment favorably* on changes in your behavior. You are now ready to graduate.

Graduation from a course, however, does not in itself guarantee a lifetime of effective stress management. Old harmful habits have a *much longer history* than do your newly developed coping skills, and it is very easy to slip back into old ways. Mark Twain once remarked that it is very easy to stop smoking; in fact, he had done it many times! Learning a new habit is relatively easy; to maintain it is much harder.

Fortunately, there are techniques that you can use to *protect your investment* in good stress management and even make it grow.

Anticipate

The best time to correct slipups is before they happen. To help you *anticipate* potential trouble spots:

- *Make a list* of the events or situations (travel, illness, job crisis) that might cause you to stop using your new stress management skills. Any disruption of the normal routine of life is a *signal* to pay careful attention to your *stress management strategies.*

- *Keep a chart of daily tension and pleasure levels.* A drop in pleasure level and/or a rise in tension level is a *signal* that you are *vulnerable* to stress problems. Try to correct the *imbalance* as soon as you can, either by lowering the tension level or by raising the pleasure level. If no immediate change in either is possible, be aware that you are depleting resistance resources and allow for a period of recovery after the crisis has passed.

Diagnose

- Sometimes, what has gone wrong may be fairly obvious to you. For instance, the announcement of a new boss for your department may create a situation of uncertainty with feelings of physical and mental tension. If the stress trigger is fairly obvious, then turn your attention to dealing with your reactions to it.

- Sometimes, you just don't feel right, but you can't put *your finger on any specific trigger*. Here is a chance to display your *talents as a sleuth.* Start keeping a *stress diary* again, noting hourly: situation, tension level, and signs. Once you have a week's records, sit down and study them. *What times of day, what situations,* and what *signs* correlated with high tension levels? *Read* the stress manual and see if you can pick up any hints as to where the problem lies.

231

Take remedial action

Once you have a tentative *diagnosis*, make a plan for dealing with the problem. During the course of this program you have learned a variety of techniques for controlling *physical*, *behavioral*, and *cognitive* signs of tension, as well as how to increase your pleasure level. Reread the manual and decide how to select and combine strategies so as to develop an *action plan appropriate* to the problem.

Reevaluate

After you have engaged in trouble shooting for a while, *reevaluate*. Has your remedial action improved your *tension–pleasure balance?* Are there any other strategies you might use to improve it still further?

Take credit

- Even constant practice of stress management will not make you *completely* immune to *all the vicissitudes of life*. But if you can keep your head when all about you are losing theirs, if you can learn to roll with the punches, then you will have done a great deal *to improve the quality of your life* and of the lives of people who live and work with you.

- For this, you have *reason to be proud*. You may not be able to *control the world*, but you have learned to *control yourself*.

Homework (18)

Relapse prevention

What is the goal?

To learn to *anticipate* and *deal* with relapses in self-control.

What do I have to do?

1. *List a number* of danger situations that might cause *you* to *stop practicing* good stress management skills. These can be external (traveling) or internal (depressive period).

2. *For each danger* situation, think of *some warning signals* you can use to alert you that your stress management skills are slipping. These signs can be physical, mental, emotional, or behavioral.

3. For each danger situation, *indicate the remedial action* you can take to get on track again.

Name: Example sheet   Date:

Potential danger situation	Potential warning signals	Remedial action
1. Disruption of routine — e.g., going on a trip.	Slipping back to old ways; rushing, shouting.	① Reread section on braking signals. Use them.
2. Period of heavy work pressure.	Arguments with colleagues.	① Increase relaxation practice. ② Examine self-talk. ③ Plan a pleasurable break as soon as possible.
3.		
4. Family crisis	Feel tense and irritable. Headaches; trouble sleeping.	① Insofar as possible, use problem-solving techniques to deal with situation. ② Ask for emotional support from others. ③ Use relaxation and productive thinking to reduce tension.
5.		

References

Ader, R. (1980). Psychosomatic and psychoimmunological research: Presidential address, *Psychosomatic Medicine, 42*, 307–321.

Anderson T. W. (1973). Mortality from ischemic heart disease: Changes in middle aged men since 1900. *Journal of the American Medical Association, 224*, 336–338.

Antonovsky, A., Maoz, B., Dowty, N., & Wijsenbeek, H. (1971). Twenty-five years later. *Social Psychiatry, 6*, 186–193.

Baker, L. J., Dearborn, M., Hastings, J. E., & Hamberger, K. (1984). Type A behavior in women: A review. *Health Psychology, 3*, 477–497.

Bandura, A. (1977a). Self-efficacy: Toward a unifying theory of psychological change. *Psychological Review, 84*, 191–215.

Bandura, A. (1977b). *Social learning theory.* Englewood Cliffs, NJ: Prentice-Hall.

Barefoot, J. C., Dahlstrom, G., & Williams, R. B. (1983). Hostility, CHD incidence and total mortality: A 25-year follow-up study of 255 physicians. *Psychosomatic Medicine, 45*, 59–63.

Beck, A. T. (1976). *Cognitive therapy and the emotional disorders.* New York: International Universities Press.

Belgian–French Pooling Project. (1984). Assessment of Type A behavior by the Bortner scale and ischaemic heart disease. *European Heart Journal, 5*, 440–446.

✓ Bernstein, D. A., & Borkovec, T. D. (1973). *Progressive relaxation training: A manual for the helping professions.* Champaign IL: Research Press.

Blumenthal, J. A., O'Toole, L. C., & Haney, T. (1984). Behavioral assessment of the Type A behavior pattern. *Psychosomatic Medicine, 46*, 415–423.

Blumenthal, J. A., Williams, R. B., Kong, Y., Schanberg, M. D., & Thompson, L. W. (1978). Type A behavior pattern and coronary atherosclerosis. *Circulation, 58*, 634–639.

Bortner, R. W. (1969). A short rating scale as a potential measure of pattern A behavior. *Journal of Chronic Diseases, 22*, 87–91.

Brand, R. J., Rosenman, R. H., Jenkins, C. D., Sholtz, R. I., & Zyzanski, S. J. (1978, March). *Comparison of coronary heart disease prediction in the Western Collaborative Group Study using the Structured Interview and the Jenkins Activity Survey assessment of the coronary-prone Type A behavior pattern.* Paper presented at the Annual Conference on Cardiovascular Disease Epidemiology, American Heart Association, Orlando, Florida.

Burke, R. J., & Weir, T. (1980). The Type A experience: Occupational and life demands, satisfaction and well-being. *Journal of Human Stress, 6*, 28–38.

✓ Burns, D. (1980, November). The perfectionist's script for self-defeat. *Psychology Today*, pp. 34–47.

Byrne, D. (1964). Repression–sensitization as a dimension of personality. In B. A. Maher (Ed.), *Progress in experimental personality research* (Vol. 1, pp. 170–220). New York: Academic Press.

Cannon, W. B. (1939). *The wisdom of the body.* (2nd ed.) New York: Norton.

Carver, C. S., Coleman, A. E., & Glass, D. C. (1976). The coronary-prone behavior pattern and the suppression of fatigue on a treadmill task. *Journal of Personality and Social Psychology, 33,* 460–466.

Chesney, M. A., Black, G. W., Chadwick, J. H., & Rosenman, R. H. (1981). Psychological correlates of the Type A behavior pattern. *Journal of Behavioral Medicine, 4,* 217–229.

Cohen, F., & Lazarus, R. S. (1973). Active coping processes, coping dispositions, and recovery from surgery. *Psychosomatic Medicine, 35,* 375–389.

Cohen, J. B., & Reed, D. (1985). The Type A Behavior Pattern and coronary heart disease among Japanese men in Hawaii. *Journal of Behavioral Medicine, 8,* 343–352.

Cohen, J. B., Syme, S. L., Jenkins, C. D., Kagan, A., & Zyzanski, S. J. (1979). Cultural content of Type A behavior and risk for CHD: A study of Japanese American males. *Journal of Behavioral Medicine, 2,* 375–384.

Davis, F. (1963). *Progress through polio.* Indianapolis: Bobbs-Merrill.

De Berry, S., & Einstein, A. (1981). The effect of progressive muscle relaxation on stress related symptoms in a geriatric population. *Psychosomatic Medicine, 43,* 87–88. (Abstract)

DeLongis, A., Coyne, J. C., Dakof, G., Folkman, S., & Lazarus, R. S. (1982). Relationship of daily hassles, uplifts, and major life events to health status. *Health Psychology, 1,* 119–136.

Dembroski, T. M. (1978). Reliability and validity of methods used to assess coronary-prone behavior. In T. M. Dembroski, S. M. Weiss, J. L. Shields, S. G. Haynes, & M. Feinleib (Eds.), *Coronary-prone behavior* (pp. 95–106). New York: Springer-Verlag.

Dembroski, T. M., & MacDougall, J. M. (1983). Behavioral and psychophysiological perspectives on coronary-prone behavior. In T. M. Dembroski, T. H. Schmidt, & G. Blumchen (Eds.), *Biobehavioral bases of coronary heart disease* (pp. 106–129). Basel: Karger.

Dembroski, T. M., MacDougall, J. M., & Lushene, R. (1979). Interpersonal interaction and cardiovascular response in type A subjects and coronary patients. *Journal of Human Stress, 5,* 28–36.

Dembroski, T. M., MacDougall, J. M., Shields, J. L., Pettito, J., & Lushene, R. (1978). Components of the Type A coronary-prone behavior pattern and cardiovascular responses to psychomotor challenge. *Journal of Behavioral Medicine, 1,* 159–176.

Dembroski, T. M., MacDougall, J. M., Williams, R. B., Haney, T. L., & Blumenthal, J. A. (1985). Components of Type A, hostility and anger-in: Relationship to angiographic findings. *Psychosomatic Medicine, 47,* 219–233.

Derogatis, L. R., Lipman, R. S., Rickels, K., Uhlenhuth, E. H., & Covi, L. (1974). The Hopkins Symptom Checklist (HSCL): A self report symptom inventory. *Behavioral Science, 19,* 1–15.

Dimsdale, J. E., Hackett, T. P., Hutter, A. M., Block, P. C., & Catanzano, D. M. (1978). Type A personality and extent of coronary atherosclerosis. *American Journal of Cardiology, 42,* 583–586.

Dimsdale, J. E., Hackett, T. P., Hutter, A. M., Block, P. C., Catanzano, D. M., & White, P. J. (1979). Type A behavior and angiographic findings. *Journal of Psychosomatic Research, 23,* 273–276.

Dunbar, H. F. (1943). *Psychosomatic diagnosis.* New York: Hoeber.

D'Zurilla, T., & Nezu, A. (1982). Social problem-solving in adults. In P. Kendall (Ed.), *Advances in cognitive-behavior research and therapy* (Vol. 1, pp. 202–274). New York: Academic Press.

Eaker, E. D., Haynes, S. G., & Feinleib, M. (1983). Spouse behavior and coronary heart disease in men: Prospective results from the Framingham Heart Study. *American Journal of Epidemiology, 118,* 23–41.

Elliott, G. R., & Eisdorfer, C. (1982). *Stress and human health.* New York: Springer.

Ellis, A. (1962). *Reason and emotion in psychotherapy.* New York: Lyle Stuart.

Engel, B. T. (1983). Assessment and alteration of physiological reactivity. In T. M. Dembroski, T. H. Schmidt, & G. Blumchen (Eds.), *Biobehavioral bases of coronary heart disease* (pp. 450–458). Basel: Karger.

Folkman, S., & Lazarus, R. S. (1985). If it changes it must be a process: A study of emotion and coping through three stages of a college examination. *Journal of Personality and Social Psychology, 48,* 150–170.

Folsom, A. R., Hughes, J. R., Buehler, J. F., Mittelmark, M. B., Jacobs, D. R., Jr., & Grimm, R. H., Jr. (1985). Do Type A men drink more frequently than Type B men? Findings in the Multiple Risk Factor Intervention Trial. *Journal of Behavioral Medicine, 8,* 227–236.

Forman, S. (1982). Stress management for teachers: A cognitive-behavioral program. *Journal of School Psychology, 20,* 180–187.

Frank, K. A., Heller, S. S., Kornfeld, D. S., Sporn, A. A., & Weiss, M. D. (1978). Behavioral pattern and coronary angiographic findings. *Journal of the American Medical Association, 240,* 761–763.

Frankenhaeuser, M., Lundberg, U., & Forsman, L. (1980). Notes on arousing type A persons by depriving them of work. *Journal of Psychosomatic Research, 24,* 45–47.

Friedman, M. (1977). Type A behavior pattern: Some of its pathophysiological components. *Bulletin of the New York Academy of Medicine, 53,* 593–604.

Friedman, M., & Powell, L. H. (1984). The diagnosis and quantitative assessment of Type A behavior: Introduction and description of the videotaped structured interview. *Integrative Psychiatry, 2,* 123–136.

Friedman, M., & Rosenman, R. H. (1959). Association of specific overt behavior patterns with blood and cardiovascular findings. *Journal of the American Medical Association, 169,* 1286–1296.

Friedman, M., & Rosenman, R. H. (1974). *Type A behavior and your heart.* New York: Knopf.

Friedman, M., Rosenman, R. H., & Byers, S. (1964). Serum lipids and conjunctival circulation after fat ingestion in men exhibiting the Type-A behavior pattern. *Circulation, 29,* 874–886.

Friedman, M., Rosenman, R. H., & Carroll, V. (1958). Changes in the serum cholesterol and blood clotting time in men subjected to cyclic variation of occupational stress. *Circulation, 17,* 852–861.

Friedman, M., St. George, S., Byers, S. O., & Rosenman, R. H. (1960). Excretion of catecholamines, 17 ketosteroids, 17-hydroxycorticoids and 5-hydroxyindole in men exhibiting a particular behavior pattern (A) associated with high incidence of clinical coronary artery disease. *Journal of Clinical Investigation, 39,* 758–764.

Friedman, M., Thoresen, C. E., Gill, J. J., Powell, L., Ulmer D., Thompson, L., Price, V. A., Rabin, D. D., Breall, W. S., Dixon, T., Levy, R. A., & Bourg, E. (1984). Alteration of type A behavior and reduction in cardiac recurrence in post-myocardial infarction patients. *American Heart Journal, 108,* 237–248.

Friedman, S. B., Chodoff, P., Mason, J., & Hamburg, D. A. (1963). Behavioral observations on parents anticipating the death of a child. *Pediatrics, 32,* 610–625.

Garrison, J. (1978). Stress management training for the handicapped. *Archives of Physical Medicine and Rehabilitation, 59,* 580–585.

Gill, J. J., Price, V. A., Friedman, M., Thoresen, C. E., Powell, L. H., Ulmer, D., Thompson, L., Brown, B., & Drews, F. R. (1985). Reduction in type A behavior in healthy middle-aged American military officers. *American Heart Journal, 110,* 503–514.

Glass, D. C. (1977). *Behavior patterns, stress and coronary disease.* Hillsdale, NJ: Erlbaum.

Glass, D. C., Krakoff, L. R., Contrada, R., Hilton, W. F., Kehoe, K., Mannucci, E. G., Collins, C., Snow, B., & Elting, B. (1980). Effect of harassment and competition upon cardiovascular and catecholamine responses in Type A and B individuals. *Psychophysiology, 17,* 453–463.

Goffman, E. (1963). *Notes on the management of spoiled identity.* Englewood Cliffs, NJ: Prentice-Hall.

Goldberg, R., Szklo M., Tonascia, J. A., & Kennedy, H. L. (1979). Time trends in prognosis of patients with myocardial infarction: A population-based study. *The Johns Hopkins Medical Journal, 144,* 73–80.

Goldfried, M. R. (1977). The use of relaxation and cognitive relabeling as coping skills. In R. Stuart (Ed.), *Behavioral self-management: Strategies, techniques and outcomes* (pp. 82–116). New York: Brunner/Mazel.

Goldfried, M. R. (1979). Psychotherapy as coping skills training. In M. J. Mahoney (Ed.), *Psychotherapy process: Current issues and future directions* (pp. 89–119). New York: Plenum.

Goldfried, M. R., & Davison, G. (1976). *Clinical behavior therapy.* New York: Holt, Rinehart & Winston.

Goldstein, M. J. (1959). The relationship between coping and avoiding behavior and response to fear-arousing propaganda. *Journal of Abnormal and Social Psychology, 58,* 247–252.

Goldstein, M. J. (1973). Individual differences in response to stress. *American Journal of Community Psychology, 1,* 113–137.

Hackett, T. P., & Cassem, N. H. (1975). Psychological management of the myocardial infarction patient. *Journal of Human Stress, 1,* 25–38.

Haynes, S. G. (1984). Type A behavior, employment status, and coronary heart disease in women. *Behavioral Medicine Update, 6,* 11–15.

Haynes, S. G., & Feinleib, M. (1980). Women, work and coronary heart disease: Prospective findings from the Framingham Heart Study. *American Journal of Public Health, 70,* 133–141.

Haynes, S. G., Feinleib, M., & Kannel, W. B. (1980). The relationship of psychosocial factors to coronary heart disease of the Framingham study: III. Eight year incidence of coronary heart disease. *American Journal of Epidemiology, 111,* 37–58.

Haynes, S. G., Levine, S., Scotch, N., Feinleib, M., & Kannel, W. B. (1978). The relationship of psychosocial factors to coronary heart disease in the Framingham study: I. Method and risk factors. *American Journal of Epidemiology, 107,* 362–382.

Heberden, W. (1772). Some account of a disorder of the breast. *Medical Transactions of the College of Physicians (London), 2,* 59–67.

Heide, F. J., & Borkovec, T. D. (1984). Relaxation-induced anxiety: Mechanisms and theoretical implications. *Behaviour Research and Therapy, 22,* 1–12.

Herd, J. A. (1978). Physiological correlates of the coronary-prone behavior pattern. In T. M. Dembroski, S. M. Weiss, J. L. Shields, S. G. Haynes, & M. Feinleib (Eds.), *Coronary-prone behavior* (pp. 55–66). New York: Springer-Verlag.

Hillenberg, J. B., & Collins, F. L. Jr. (1982). A procedural analysis and review of relaxation training research. *Behaviour Research and Therapy, 20,* 251–260.

Holmes, D. S. (1984). Meditation and somatic arousal reduction. *American Psychologist, 39,* 1–10.

Holmes, T. H., & Masuda, M. (1974). Life changes and illness susceptibility. In B. S. Dohrenwend & B. P. Dohrenwend (Eds.), *Stressful life events: Their nature and their effects* (pp. 47–52). New York: Wiley.

Holmes, T. H., & Rahe, R. H. (1967). The Social Readjustment Rating Scale. *Journal of Psychosomatic Research, 11,* 213–218.

Howard, J. H., Cunningham, D. A., & Rechnitzer, P. A. (1976). Health patterns associated with type A behavior: A managerial population. *Journal of Human Stress, 2* (1), 24–31.

Howard, J. H., Cunningham, D. A., & Rechnitzer, P. A. (1977). Work patterns associated with type A behavior: A managerial population. *Human Relations, 30,* 825–836.

Jamal, M. (1985). Type A behavior and job performance. *Journal of Human Stress, 11,* 60–68.

Jenkins, C. D. (1971). Psychologic and social precursors of coronary disease (First of two parts). *New England Journal of Medicine, 284* (5) 244–255.

Jenkins, C. D. (1978). A comparative review of the interview and questionnaire methods in the assessment of the coronary-prone behavior pattern. In T. M. Dembroski, S. M. Weiss, J. L. Shields, S. Haynes, & M. Feinleib (Eds.), *Coronary-prone behavior* (pp. 71–88). New York: Springer.

Jenkins, C. D., Rosenman, R. H., & Friedman, M. (1967). Development of an objective psychological test for the determination of the coronary-prone behavior pattern in employed men. *Journal of Chronic Diseases, 20,* 371–379.

Jenkins, C. D., Rosenman, R. H., & Friedman, M. (1968). Replicability of rating the coronary-prone behavior pattern. *British Journal of Preventive Social Medicine, 22,* 16–22.

Jenkins, C. D., Rosenman, R. H., & Zyzanski, S. J. (1974). Prediction of clinical coronary heart disease by a test for the coronary-prone behavior pattern. *New England Journal of Medicine, 290,* 1271–1275.

Jenkins, C. D., Zyzanski, S. J., & Rosenman, R. H. (1971). Progress toward validation of a computer-scored test for the Type A coronary-prone behavior pattern. *Psychosomatic Medicine, 33,* 193–201.

Kannel, W. B., & Gordon, T. (1968). *The Framingham Study.* Washington, DC: U.S. Department of Health, Education, and Welfare.

Kanner, A. D., Coyne, J. C., Schaefer, C., & Lazarus, R. S. (1981). Comparison of two modes of stress measurement: Daily hassles and uplifts versus major life events. *Journal of Behavioral Medicine, 4,* 1–39.

Kasl, S. V. (1978). Epidemiological contributions to the study of work stress. In C. L. Cooper & R. Payne (Eds.), *Stress at work* (pp. 3–48). New York: Wiley.

Kemple, C. (1945). Rorschach method and psychosomatic diagnosis: Personality traits of patients with rheumatic disease, hypertensive cardiovascular disease, coronary occlusion, and fracture. *Psychosomatic Medicine, 7,* 85–89.

Kenigsberg, D., Zyzanski, S. J., Jenkins, C. D., & Licciardello, A. T. (1974). The coronary-prone behavior pattern in patients with and without coronary heart disease. *Psychosomatic Medicine, 36,* 344–351.

Keys, A., Taylor, H. L., Blackburn, H., Brozed, J., Anderson, J. T., & Somonson, E. (1971). Mortality and coronary heart disease among men studied for 23 years. *Archives of Internal Medicine, 128,* 201–214.

Kittel, F., Kornitzer, M., DeBacker, G., & Dramaix, M. (1982). Metrological study of psychological questionnaires with reference to social variables: The Belgian Heart Disease Prevention Project (BHDPP). *Journal of Behavioral Medicine, 5,* 9–35.

Kornitzer, M., Kittel, F., DeBacker, G., & Dramaix, M. (1981). The Belgian Heart Disease Prevention Project: Type A behavior pattern and the prevalence of coronary heart disease. *Psychosomatic Medicine, 43,* 133–145.

Krantz, D. S., Arabian, J. M., Davia, J. E., & Parker, J. S. (1982). Type A behavior and coronary artery bypass surgery: Intraoperative blood pressure and perioperative complications. *Psychosomatic Medicine, 44,* 273–284.

Krantz, D. S., & Durel, L. A. (1983). Psychobiological substrates of the Type A behavior pattern. *Health Psychology, 2,* 393–411.

Krantz, D. S., Glass, D. C., Schaeffer, M. A., & Davia, J. E. (1982). Behavior patterns and coronary disease: A critical evaluation. In J. T. Caccioppo & R. E. Petty (Eds.), *Perspectives in cardiovascular psychophysiology* (pp. 315–346). New York: Guilford Press.

Krantz, D. S., Glass, D. C., & Snyder, M. (1974). Helplessness, stress level, and the coronary-prone behavior pattern. *Journal of Experimental Social Psychology, 10,* 284–300.

Krantz, D. S., & Manuck, S. B. (1984). Acute psychophysiological reactivity and risk of cardiovascular disease: A review and methodologic critique. *Psychological Bulletin, 96,* 435–464.

Krantz, D. S., Schaeffer, M. A., Davia, J. E., Dembroski, T. M., MacDougall, J. M., & Shaffer, R. T. (1981). Extent of coronary atherosclerosis, type A behavior and cardiovascular response to social interaction. *Psychophysiology, 18,* 654–664.

Lalonde, M. (1974). *A new perspective on the health of Canadians.* Ottawa: Department of National Health and Welfare.

Langner, T. S., & Michael, S. T. (1963). *Life stress and mental health: The Midtown Manhattan Study.* New York: Free Press.

Lazarus, R. S. (1966). *Psychological stress and the coping process.* New York: McGraw-Hill.

Lazarus, R. S., Averill, J. R., & Opton, E. M., Jr. (1970). Toward a cognitive theory of emotions. In M. Arnold (Ed.), *Feeling and emotions* (pp. 207–232). New York: Academic Press.

Lazarus, R. S., & Cohen, J. B. (1977). Environmental stress. In I. Altman & J. F. Wohlwill (Eds.), *Human behavior and environment: Advances in theory and practice* (Vol. 2, pp. 89–127). New York: Plenum.

Lazarus, R. S. & Folkman, S. (1984). *Stress, appraisal, and coping.* New York: Springer.

Lazarus, R. S., & Launier, R. (1978). Stress-related transactions between person and environment. In L. A. Pervin & M. Lewis (Eds.), *Perspective in interactional psychology* (pp. 287–327). New York: Plenum.

Lehrer, P. M., Woolfolk, R. L., Rooney, A. J., McCann, B., & Carrington, P. (1983). Progressive relaxation and meditation. *Behaviour Research and Therapy, 21,* 651–662.

MacDougall, J. M., Dembroski, T. M., & Musante, L. (1979). The structured interview and questionnaire methods of assessing coronary-prone behavior in male and female college students. *Journal of Behavioral Medicine, 2,* 71–83.

Magnus, K., Matroos, A. W., & Strackee, J. (1983). The self-employed and self-driven: Two coronary-prone subpopulations from the Zeist study. *American Journal of Epidemiology, 118,* 799–805.

Mahoney, M. J. (Ed.). (1980). *Psychotherapy process: Current issues and future directions.* New York: Plenum.

Manuck, S. B., Craft, S. A., & Gold, K. J. (1978). Coronary-prone behavior pattern and cardiovascular response. *Psychophysiology, 15,* 403–411.

Manuck, S. B., & Krantz, D. S. (1984). Psychophysiologic reactivity in coronary heart disease. *Behavioral Medicine Update, 6,* 11–15.

Marlatt, G. A. (1985). Lifestyle modification. In G. A. Marlatt & J. R. Gordon (Eds.), *Relapse prevention: Maintenance strategies in the treatment of addictive behaviors* (pp. 280–348). New York: Guilford Press.

Marlatt, G. A., & Gordon, J. R. (Eds.). (1985). *Relapse prevention: Maintenance strategies in the treatment of addictive behaviors.* New York: Guilford Press.

Marx, J. L., & Kolata, G. B. (1978). *Combatting the #1 killer.* Washington, DC: American Association for the Advancement of Science.

Mason, J. W. (1975). Emotion as reflected in patterns of endocrine integration. In L. Levi (Ed.), *Emotions: Their parameters and measurement* (pp. 143–181). New York: Raven Press.

Matteson, M., & Ivancevich, J. M. (1980). The coronary-prone behavior pattern: A review and appraisal. *Social Science and Medicine, 14A,* 337–351.

Matthews, K. A. (1982). Psychological perspectives on the type A behavior pattern. *Psychological Bulletin, 91,* 293–323.

Matthews, K. A. (1985). Assessment of type A behavior, anger and hostility in epidemiological studies of cardiovascular diseases. In A. M. Ostfeld & E. D. Eaker (Eds.), *Measuring psychosocial variables in epidemiologic studies of cardiovascular disease: Proceedings of the NHLBI workshop* (NIH Publication No. 85-2270, pp. 153–183). Washington, DC: U.S. Government Printing Office.

Matthews, K. A., & Carra, J. (1982). Suppression of menstrual distress symptoms: A study of type A behavior. *Personality and Social Psychology Bulletin, 8,* 146–151.

Matthews, K. A., Glass D. C., Rosenman, R. H., & Bortner, R. W. (1977). Competitive drive, pattern A and coronary heart disease: A further analysis of some data from the Western Collaborative Group Study. *Journal of Chronic Diseases, 30,* 489–498.

Matthews, K. A., Helmreich, R. L., Beane, W. E., & Lucker, G. W. (1980). Pattern A, achievement striving, and scientific merit: Does pattern A help or hinder? *Journal of Personality and Social Psychology, 39,* 962–967.

Matthews, K. A., Krantz, D. S., Dembroski, T. M., & MacDougall, J. M. (1982). Unique and common variance in Structured Interview and Jenkins Activity Survey measures of the Type A Behavior pattern. *Journal of Personality and Social Psychology, 42,* 303–313.

Matthews, K. A., & Siegel, J. M. (1982). The Type A behavior pattern in children and adolescents: Assessment, development and associated coronary-risk. In A. Baum & J. E. Singer (Eds.), *Handbook of psychology and health* (Vol. 2, pp. 99–116). Hillsdale, NJ: Erlbaum.

Meichenbaum, D. (1977). *Cognitive-behavior modification: An integrative approach.* New York: Plenum.

Meichenbaum, D. (1985). *Stress inoculation training.* New York: Pergamon.

Meichenbaum, D., & Jaremko, M. (Eds.). (1983). *Stress reduction and prevention.* New York: Plenum.

Menninger, K. A., & Menninger, W. C. (1936). Psychoanalytic observations in cardiac disorders. *American Heart Journal, 11,* 10–21.

Mettlin, C. (1976). Occupational careers and the prevention of coronary-prone behavior. *Social Science and Medicine, 10,* 367–372.

Murphy, L. R. (1984). Occupational stress management: A review and appraisal. *Journal of Occupational Psychology, 57,* 1–15.

National Center for Health Statistics, (1982). *Monthly vital statistics report* (Vol. 33). Hyattsville, MD: U.S. Government Printing Office.

Novaco, R. (1975). *Anger control: The development and evaluation of an experimental treatment.* Lexington, MA: D. C. Heath.

Obrist, P. A. (1981). *Cardiovascular psychophysiology.* New York: Plenum.

Osler, W. (1892). *Lecture on angina pectoris and allied states.* New York: Appleton.

Osler, W. (1910). The Lumleian lectures on angina pectoris. *Lancet, 1,* 839–844.

Pearlin, L. I., & Schooler, C. (1978). The structure of coping. *Journal of Health and Social Science, 19,* 2–21.

Price, V. A. (1982). *Type A behavior pattern: A model for research and practice.* New York: Academic Press.

Rabkin, J. G., & Struening, E. L. (1976). Life events, stress and illness. *Science, 194,* 1013–1020.

Rahe, R. H. (1975). Life changes and near-future illness reports. In L. Levi (Ed.), *Emotions: Their parameters and measurements* (pp. 511–529). New York: Raven Press.

Report of the Joint Working Party of the Royal College of Physicians of London and the British Cardiac Society. (1976). *Journal of the Royal College of Physicians of London, 10.*

Review Panel on Coronary-Prone Behavior and Coronary Heart Disease. (1981). Coronary-prone behavior and coronary heart disease: A critical review. *Circulation, 63,* 1199–1215.

Rose, R. J., Grim, C. E., & Miller, J. Z. (1984). Familial influences on cardiovascular stress reactivity: Studies of normontensive twins. *Behavioral Medicine Update, 6,* 21–24.

Rosenman, R. H. (1978). The interview method of assessment of the coronary-prone behavior pattern. In T. M. Dembroski, S. M. Weiss, J. Shields, S. G. Haynes, & M. Feinleib (Eds.), *Coronary-prone behavior* (pp. 55–70). New York: Springer-Verlag.

Rosenman, R. H., Brand, R. J., Jenkins, D., Friedman, M., Straus, R., & Wurm, M. (1975). Coronary heart disease in the Western Collaborative Group Study: Final follow-up experience of 8½ years. *Journal of the American Medical Association, 233,* 872–877.

Rosenman, R. H., Brand, R. J., Sholtz, R. I., & Friedman, M. (1976). Multivariate prediction of coronary heart disease during 8.5 year follow-up period in the Western Collaborative Group Study. *American Journal of Cardiology, 37,* 903–910.

Roskies, E. (1981, August). *Reducing coronary risk in occupationally successful type A men.* Paper presented at the NATO Advanced Study Institute: Work, Stress and Health. Château de Bonas, France.

Roskies, E. (1982). Type A intervention: Finding the disease to fit the cures. In R. Surwit, R. B. Williams, A. Steptoe, & R. Biersner (Eds.), *Behavioral treatment of disease* (pp. 71–86). New York: Plenum.

Roskies, E. (1983a). Stress management: Averting the evil eye. *Contemporary Psychology, 28,* 542–544.

Roskies, E. (1983b). Stress management for type A individuals. In D. Meichenbaum & M. Jaremko (Eds.), *Stress reduction and prevention* (pp. 261–285). New York: Plenum.

Roskies, E., & Avard, J. (1982). Teaching healthy managers to control their coronary-prone (type A) behavior. In K. R. Blankstein & J. Polivy (Eds.), *Self-control and self-modification of emotional behavior: Advances in the study of communication and affect* (pp. 161–183). New York: Plenum.

Roskies, E., Kearney, H., Spevack, M., Surkis, A., Cohen, C., & Gilman, S. (1979). Generalizability and durability of treatment effects in an intervention program for coronary-prone type A managers. *Journal of Behavioral Medicine, 2,* 195–207.

Roskies, E., & Lazarus, R. S. (1980). Coping theory and the teaching of coping skills. In P. O. Davidson & S. M. Davidson (Eds.), *Behavioral medicine: Changing health lifestyles* (pp. 38–69). New York: Brunner/Mazel.

Roskies, E., Seraganian, P., Oseasohn, R., Hanley, J. A., Collu, R., Martin, N., & Smilga, C. (1986). The Montreal Type A Intervention Project: Major findings. *Health Psychology, 5,* 45–69.

Roskies, E., Spevack, M., Surkis, A., Cohen, C., & Gilman, S. (1978). Changing the coronary-prone type A behavior pattern in a non-clinical population. *Journal of Behavioral Medicine, 1,* 201–216.

Ruberman, W., Weinblatt, E., Goldberg, J. D., & Chaudbury, B. (1984). Psychosocial influence on mortality after myocardial infarction. *New England Journal of Medicine, 311,* 552–559.

Rustin, R. M., Dramaix, M., Kittel, F., Degre, C., Kornitzer, M., Thilly, C., & DeBacker, G.

(1976). Validation des techniques d'evaluation du profil comportementale "A" utilisées dans le "Project Belge de Prévention des affections cardiovasculaires." *Revue Epidémiologie et Santé Publique, 24,* 497–507.

Scherwitz, L., Berton, K., & Leventhal, H. (1977). Type A assessment and interaction in the behavior pattern interview. *Psychosomatic Medicine, 39,* 229–240.

Scherwitz, L., Berton, K., & Leventhal, H. (1978). Type A behavior, self-involvement, and cardiovascular response. *Psychosomatic Medicine, 40,* 593–609.

Scherwitz, L., McKelvain, R., Laman, C., Patterson, J., Dutton, L., Yusim, S., Lester, J., Kraft, I., Rochelle, D., & Leachman, R. (1983). Type A behavior, self-involvement, and coronary atherosclerosis. *Psychosomatic Medicine, 45,* 47–58.

Schlegel, R. P., Wellwood, J. K., Copps, B. E., Gruchow, W. H., & Sharratt, M. T. (1980). The relationship between perceived challenge and daily symptom reporting in type A vs. type B postinfarct subjects. *Journal of Behavioral Medicine, 3,* 191–204.

Schmale, A. H., Jr. (1972). Giving up as a final common pathway to changes in health. *Advances in Psychosomatic Medicine, 8,* 20–40.

Schuker, B., & Jacobs, D. R., Jr. (1977). Assessment of behavioral risk for coronary disease by voice characteristics. *Psychosomatic Medicine, 39,* 219–228.

Schwartz, G. E., & Weiss, S. M. (1978). Yale Conference on Behavioral Medicine: A proposed definition and statement of goals. *Journal of Behavioral Medicine, 1,* 3–12.

Selye, H. (1956). *The stress of life.* New York: McGraw-Hill.

Shekelle, R. B., Gayle, M., Ostfeld, A. M., & Paul, O. (1983). Hostility, risk of coronary heart disease and mortality. *Psychosomatic Medicine, 45,* 109–114.

Shekelle, R. B., Hulley, S., Neaton, J., Borhani, N., Lasser, N., Mittlemark, M., & Stamler, J. (1983, March). *Type A behavior and risk of coronary death in MRFIT.* Paper presented at the annual meeting of the American Heart Association Council on Epidemiology, San Diego, CA.

Shekelle, R. B., Schoenberger, J. A., & Stamler, J. (1976). Correlates of the J.A.S. Type A behavior pattern score. *Journal of Chronic Diseases, 29,* 381–394.

Siegel, J. M. (1984). Type A behavior: Epidemiologic foundations and public health implications. *Annual Review of Public Health, 5,* 343–367.

Silber, E., Coelho, G. V., Murphy, E. B., Hamburg, D. A., Pearlin, L. I., & Rosenberg, E. B. (1961a). Competent adolescents coping with college decision. *Archives of General Psychiatry, 5,* 517–527.

Silber, E., Hamburg, D. A., Coelho, G. V., Murphy, E. B., Rosenberg, E. B., & Pearlin, L. I. (1961b). Adaptive behavior in competent adolescents. *Archives of General Psychiatry, 5,* 354–365.

Silver, B. V., & Blanchard, E. B. (1978). Biofeedback and relaxation training in the treatment of psychophysiological disorders: Or are the machines really necessary? *Journal of Behavioral Medicine, 1,* 217–239.

Smith, T. W., & Sanders, J. D. (1986). Type A behavior, marriage, and the heart: Person-by-situation interactions and the risk of coronary disease. *Behavioral Medicine Abstracts, 7,* 59–62.

Stamler, J., Berkson, D. M., & Lindberg, H. A. (1972). Risk factors: Their role in the etiology and pathogenesis of the atherosclerotic diseases. In R. W. Wissler & J. C. Geer (Eds.), *Pathogenesis of atherosclerosis* (pp. 41–119). Baltimore: Williams & Wilkins.

Storment, C. T. (1951). Personality and heart disease. *Psychosomatic Medicine, 13,* 304–313.

Stuart, R. B. (1974, June). *Communication skills.* Paper presented at the annual meeting of the Association des spécialistes en modification du comportement, Moncton, New Brunswick, Canada.

Theorell, T., Lind, E., & Floderus, B. (1975). The relationship of disturbing life-changes and emotions to the early development of myocardial infarction and other serious illnesses. *International Journal of Epidemiology, 41,* 281–293.

Thoits, P. A. (1983). Dimensions of life events as influences upon the genesis of psychological distress and associated conditions: An evaluation and synthesis of the literature. In H. B. Kaplan (Ed.), *Psychological stress: Trends in theory and research* (pp. 33–103). New York: Academic Press.

Thoresen, C. A., & Ohman, A. (in press). The Type A behavior pattern: A person–environment interaction perspective. In D. Magnusson & A. Ohman (Eds.), *Psychopathology: An interaction perspective.* New York: Academic Press.

Ursin, A., Baude, E., & Levine, S. (Eds.). (1978). *Psychobiology of stress: A study of coping men.* New York: Academic Press.

U.S. Department of Health and Human Services, Public Health Service. (1979). *Healthy people: The surgeon-general's report on health promotion and disease prevention.* Washington, DC: U.S. Government Printing Office.

Waldron, I. (1978). The coronary-prone behavior pattern, blood pressure, employment, and socio-economic status in women. *Journal of Psychosomatic Research, 22,* 79–87.

Waldron, I., Zyzanski, S., Shekelle, R. B., Jenkins, C. D., & Tannenbaum, S. (1977). The coronary-prone behavior pattern in employed men and women. *Journal of Human Stress, 3,* 2–18.

Waterhouse, G., & Strupp, H. (1984). The patient–therapist relationship: Research from the psychodynamic perspective. *Clinical Psychology Review, 4,* 77–92.

Weiss, E., Dlin, B., Rollin, H. R., Fischer, H. K., & Bepler, C. R. (1957). Emotional factors in coronary occlusion. *Archives of Internal Medicine, 99,* 628–641.

Welsh, G. S. (1956). Factor dimensions A and R. In G. S. Welsh & W. G. Dahlstrom (Eds.), *Basic reading on the MMPI in psychology and medicine* (pp. 264–281). Minneapolis: University of Minnesota Press.

Williams, R. B., Barefoot, J. C., & Shekelle, R. B. (1985). The health consequences of hostility. In M. A. Chesney & R. H. Rosenman (Eds.), *Anger, hostility and behavioral medicine* (pp. 173–185). New York: Hemisphere/McGraw-Hill.

Williams, R. B., Haney, T. L., Lee, K. L., Kong, Y., Blumenthal, J. A., & Whalen, R. E. (1980). Type A behavior, hostility, and coronary atherosclerosis. *Psychosomatic Medicine, 42,* 529–550.

Williams, R. B., Lane, J. D., Kuhn, C. M., Melosh, W., White, A. D., & Schanberg, S. M. (1982). Type A behavior and elevated physiological and neuroendocrine responses to cognitive tasks. *Science, 218,* 483–495.

Zyzanski, S. J., & Jenkins, C. D. (1970). Basic dimensions within the coronary-prone behavior pattern. *Journal of Chronic Diseases, 22,* 781–795.

Zyzanski, S. J., Jenkins, C. D., Ryan, T. J., Flessas, A., & Everist, M. (1976). Psychological correlates of coronary angiographic findings. *Archives of Internal Medicine, 136,* 1234–1237.

Index

Aerobic exercise (*see* Physical exercise)

Age, 5, 9, 14, 22, 67

Alcohol ingestion, 36, 44, 48, 75, 222

Anger–hostility (*see* Healthy type A; Type A behavior pattern [TABP]; Type A program)

Anger–hostility control, 42, 53, 56, 70, 125, 126, 129–131, 149–154, 170, 171, 174–176, 197, 198, 204, 226

Anger-in, 17

Angina pectoris, 4, 6, 14, 17

Anxiety, 41, 44, 57, 64, 68, 81, 107, 108, 149, 150, 228

Application of coping skills, 41, 42, 52, 53, 56, 70, 106, 107, 111, 112, 127, 152–154, 167–176, 198, 200, 221, 222

Aspirin Myocardial Infarction Study (AMIS), 15

Assertion training, 129 (*see also* Communication skills; Social skill training)

Attendance at treatment sessions, 69, 71, 74–77

Attribution of treatment benefits, 39, 219, 220

Autogenic training, 40

B

Bandura, A., 38, 237

Beck, A. T., 37, 53, 146, 237

Behavior, definition of, 125

Behavioral engineer, 51, 64

Behavioral medicine, 11

Behavioral responses to stress control of, 49, 52–54, 56, 70, 124–133, 152, 153, 171, 174, 175

measurement of, 125, 126

Belgian–French Pooling Project, 13, 14

Bernstein, D. A., 53, 107, 237

Bibliography, use in treatment, 71, 148

Biofeedback, 27, 40, 106, 107

Blood pressure, 5, 10, 15, 16, 20, 22, 26, 130, 149, 171

Borkovec, T. D., 53, 107, 108, 237

Bortner Short Rating Scale, 13, 14, 18

Brainwashing, 148, 149

Braking signal, 173, 174

Business travel, 74, 76, 203, 224

C

Cannon, W. B., 30, 237

Catastrophizing, 147, 150, 151

Catecholamine excretion, 5, 19, 20, 30, 130

Chicago Detection in Industry Study, 23

Cholesterol (*see* Serum cholesterol)

Cognitive behavior therapy, 28, 37–43, 78

Cognitive responses to stress, control of, 40–42, 49, 52, 53, 56, 70, 146–155, 168, 170–175, 226

Combination of coping skills, 56, 152

Communication skills, 40–42, 52, 53, 56, 70, 127, 129, 221, 226

Cook–Medley Scale, 17

Coping (*see also* Healthy type A;
    Stress; Stress management;
    Type A behavior pattern
    [TABP]; Type A program)
    costs, 48, 49, 130, 172, 175
    cost–benefit analysis, 130, 154,
        175
    resources, 29, 34, 35, 52
    role of, 29, 34, 35
    stability over time, 33, 35, 41
    styles of, 33, 35, 38, 40
    treatment of, 36–45
Coping formula, 51
Coronary angiography, 15, 17
Coronary heart disease
    consequences, 4
    etiology, 4, 5, 17
    incidence, 4
Coronary personality (*see* Type A
    behavior pattern [TABP])
Coronary-prone behavior (*see* Type
    A behavior pattern [TABP])
Cortisol, 20, 30

D

Daily hassles, 31, 32, 48, 49, 52, 77,
    154, 167, 169, 201, 204, 220
Davison, G., 53, 240
Delay (*see* Time-out)
Dembroski, T. M., 11–13, 16, 17,
    58, 238
Denial versus control, 129, 149, 150,
    174
Diabetes mellitus, 5
Dunbar, H. F., 6, 7, 238
D'Zurilla, T., 53, 200, 238

E

Ellis, A., 37, 146, 239
Emergency braking, 53, 54, 56, 70,
    112, 173, 174
Energy management, 25, 26, 29,
    48–51, 82, 148, 154, 199, 204,
    220, 223 (*see also* Self-
    management)

Environment, management of, 37,
    44, 50, 110, 130, 169, 204, 222
Environmental restructuring, 34, 36,
    110, 152, 172, 175, 222
Exercise (*see* Physical exercise)

F

Fantasy (*see* Wishful thinking)
Fatigue, 48 (*see also* Stress
    recuperation)
Feedback, 81, 82, 106
Fight or flight syndrome, 30
Framingham Heart Study, 5, 12, 14,
    18
Framingham Type A Scale, 12–14,
    18, 73
Friedman, M., 6–10, 13, 14, 20, 23,
    58, 239
Frustration, 53, 56, 70, 82, 124, 125,
    129, 174, 175, 204, 206, 226
Future, worrying about, 147, 153,
    199

G

General adaptation syndrome, 29, 30
Glass, D. C., 20–22, 240
Goal setting, 75, 76, 79, 81, 108–110,
    113, 128, 149, 153, 201, 225,
    228
Goldfried, M. R., 37, 53, 107, 240
Gordon, J. R., 53, 242
Group treatment, 42, 63–65, 68, 72,
    73, 75, 77, 132, 151, 152, 176
    (*see also* Type A program)

H

Harold Brunn Institute, 11
Healthy type A (*see also* Type A
    behavior pattern [TABP];
    Type A program)
    appropriate treatment for, 1, 19,
        26, 44, 45, 47, 49–57, 63–65,
        68
    characteristics of, 3, 8, 9, 47–49,
        52, 82, 83, 113, 124, 125, 128,

150, 151, 153–155, 168, 172, 174, 197–200, 204, 205
resistance to change, 23, 48, 49, 50, 51, 54, 55, 57, 59, 64, 69–72, 74–77, 79, 81–84, 102, 105–107, 109, 146, 204
Heart disease (see Coronary heart disease)
High-risk situations, 223, 226
Homework, use in treatment, 41, 55–57, 68, 70–73, 78, 84, 104–106, 108–111, 125, 128, 129, 131, 132, 147, 149, 170, 174, 198, 200–203, 226
Humor, use in treatment, 73, 131, 147, 151, 176
Hyperreactivity (see Stress, reactivity to)
Hypertension (see Blood pressure)

I

Incompatible behavior, 53, 54, 56, 70, 127, 128
Internal dialogue (see Self-talk)
Intolerance of divergent views, 150, 151, 154
Irrational beliefs, 146 (see also Catastrophizing; Intolerance of divergent views; Perfectionism)

J

Jenkins, C. D., 5, 10–12, 24, 241
Jenkins Activity Survey (JAS), 11–13, 15, 18, 20, 21, 24, 73
Joy, absence of, 197, 198 (see also Pleasure)

K

Kemple, C., 6, 7, 241
Krantz, D. S., 12, 20–22, 241

L

Lazarus, R. S., 28, 31, 33–36, 40, 146, 242

Life crises, 59, 66, 77, 78, 152, 169

M

Mahoney, M. J., 37, 242
Marital problems, 39, 41, 78, 151, 169, 175, 221 (see also Spouses)
Marital status, 67, 68
Marital therapy, 78
Marlatt, G. A., 53, 197, 220, 242
Massage, 27
Matthews, K. A., 12, 16–18, 20–25, 243
Meditation, 27, 40, 106
Meichenbaum, D., 36, 37, 39–43, 47, 53, 78, 146, 243
Menninger, K. A., 6, 243
Menninger, W. C., 6, 243
Missed sessions, 69, 76, 77
Modeling, 43, 78, 79, 127, 153, 222
Montreal Type A Intervention Project (MTAIP), 58
Motivation for treatment, manipulation of, 23–26, 43, 44, 50, 51, 53, 55, 57, 59, 63–77, 79, 81, 82, 102, 105–111, 126, 128, 131, 148, 149, 152, 153, 170, 198
Multimodal therapy, 41, 113
Multiple Risk Factor Intervention Trial (MRFIT), 14, 15
Myocardial infarction, 4, 14–17

N

National Heart, Lung, and Blood Institute, 15
Negative treatment effects 59
Nezu, A., 53, 200, 238
No-cost solution, 172, 175
Novaco, R., 53, 243
Nutrition, 27

O

One-step relaxation, 56, 70, 111, 112
Osler, W., 6, 243

P

Parent–child relationship, 73, 130, 148, 154, 168, 227
Past, dwelling on the, 147, 154
Perfectionism, 79, 113, 147, 148, 150, 151, 153, 172–174, 220, 228
Personal control, 21, 22, 49, 82, 83, 112, 128, 130, 131, 148, 154, 169, 173–175, 203, 204
Personal effectiveness, 48, 49, 83, 109, 112, 131, 152, 153, 173, 199, 204
Personal relationships, 50, 51, 125, 129, 130, 148, 171–174, 226–228
Physical exercise, 5, 27, 58, 75, 76, 106, 107, 200, 201, 222, 223
Pituitary–adrenocortical system, 30
Pleasure
  definition of, 198
  planning for, 53, 54, 56, 72, 199–205
  measurement of, 198, 201, 224
Positive reinforcement, 74, 79, 81, 102, 106, 108, 109, 113, 128, 153, 171, 219, 220
Problem solving, 41, 52, 53, 110, 200, 226, 227
Professional consultation, 227
Program facsimiles, 86–101, 114–123, 134–145, 156–166, 178–196, 206–218, 229–235
Progressive relaxation (*see* Relaxation)
Psychoimmunology, 30
Psychological balance sheet, 56, 198, 199, 203, 224
Psychopathology, 3, 48, 50, 52, 66, 82, 155, 204, 205
Psychotherapy, 28, 37–39, 42, 78, 113, 133

R

Rahe, R. H., 31, 32, 245
Recreation, 129, 168, 172, 197, 198, 200–204, 221
Recurrent stress triggers (*see* Stress preparation)

Relapse prevention, 42, 43, 53, 54, 56, 220–228
Relaxation
  choice of technique, 40, 106, 107
  tape, 41, 71, 107, 109, 111, 226
  training, 40, 41, 52, 53, 55, 56, 70, 72, 77, 78, 102, 106–113, 226
  use as coping skill, 42, 49, 50, 53, 56, 70, 107, 111–113, 152, 171, 174, 226
Relaxation breaks, 112, 204, 226
Resource management (*see* Energy management)
Response cost, 57, 69
Rosenman, R., 6–10, 20, 23, 244
Roskies, E., 16, 19, 21, 25, 27, 28, 58, 59, 244

S

Scherwitz, L., 22, 245
Schmale, A. H., Jr., 32, 245
Self-denigration, 147, 153
Self-exposure, 67, 77, 78, 84, 125, 126
Self-indulgence, 199, 203
Self-management, 25, 26, 28, 34–38, 42, 48–53, 56, 70, 82, 111, 112, 128, 131, 152, 153, 174, 175, 197, 204, 219, 220, 225
Self-monitoring, 41, 43, 48, 49, 51, 53, 56, 70, 103–105, 110–112, 125, 126, 147, 149, 173, 198, 223–227
Self-reinforcement, 153, 171, 199, 204, 225
Self-talk, 56, 70, 147–153, 226, 228
Selye, H., 28–30, 245
Serum cholesterol, 5, 8, 16, 20
Shaping desired behavior, 74, 75, 79, 104
Shoulds versus wants, 197, 199, 203
Sick role, 44, 45, 48, 50
Skill practice (*see also* Homework, use in treatment), 41, 52, 55, 84, 104
Smoking, 5, 6, 26, 75, 76, 222–225
Social Readjustment Rating Scale (SRRS), 32

Social skill training, 27, 40, 41
Social support, 35, 40, 41, 48, 63, 64,
    67, 221 (see also Type A
    program)
Spouses, 30, 35, 48, 51, 58, 64, 74,
    126, 130, 151, 200, 221, 224,
    226 (see also Marital
    problems)
Stress (see also Coping)
    client definitions of, 82, 104
    cognitive appraisal of, 33–35
    environmental triggers of, 29–32,
        34, 47, 167–169, 173–175,
        224, 227
    health consequences of, 28–33,
        35–37
    individual variations in response
        to, 29, 31–33, 35
    levels of analysis of, 29, 33, 34
    models of, 28–36
    reactivity to, 9, 13, 19–21, 34
Stress carrier, 130
Stress diary, 56, 70, 72, 73, 104, 110,
    125, 197, 198, 224, 227
Stress emergencies, 173, 174 (see also
    Emergency braking)
Stress inoculation training, 27, 36,
    40, 42, 44, 53
Stress management (see also Type A
    program)
    characteristics of, 38–46
    client role in, 40, 41, 43
    clientele for, 1, 27, 36, 37, 44, 45
    definition of, 27, 28, 45, 46
    goals of, 36–39, 43–45
    limits of, 1, 36–38
    manuals for, 29, 32
    popularity of, 27, 44
    techniques, 1, 27, 40, 41, 52
    therapist role in, 37, 39–45
Stress preparation, 53, 56, 70, 72, 79,
    149, 167–173, 199, 226
Stress recuperation, 48, 54, 79, 174,
    199, 203, 204, 226
Stress resistance, 56, 198, 199
Stress signatures, 105, 111, 173
Stress triggers (see Stress,
    environmental triggers of)
Stress victim, 130

Structured Interview (SI), 9, 11–15,
    17, 20, 58, 59, 66, 70, 73
Stuart, R. B., 53, 127, 245
Sympathetic–adrenomedullary
    system, 19, 20, 29, 30

T

Tension thermometer, 103, 104, 108,
    110, 112, 224
Therapist (see also Stress
    management; Type A
    program)
    self-disclosure, 43, 103, 104, 168,
        203
    skills, 42, 43, 72–79, 81, 82
    number of, 65
    language, 44, 103, 106
    values, 36–39, 50, 51
Time-hurry behavior, 17, 54, 56,
    126–128, 131, 132
Time management, 40, 49, 52,
    107–109, 168–170, 172, 197–
    199
Time-out, 53, 54, 127, 152
Treatment contract, 37, 39, 40, 76,
    81–84, 102
Treatment manual, 54, 55, 57, 61,
    72, 80, 227
Treatment rationale, 37, 39–41, 47,
    49, 50, 54, 81–84, 106, 126,
    127, 130, 147–149, 169, 199,
    224, 225 (see also Type A
    program)
Trouble shooting, 53, 170
Type A behavior pattern (TABP)
    alcohol ingestion and, 48
    anger–hostility in, 9, 12, 14,
        17–20, 124, 125, 197
    as coping response, 19, 21, 22,
        47–49
    components of, 9, 12–14, 16–19, 25
    contribution of Friedman and
        Rosenman, 7–10
    controversial nature of 5–8
    coronary risk of, 7–10, 12–21, 26,
        29, 58, 59
    definition of, 8, 18

Type A behavior pattern (continued)
  etiology of, 21–23
  history of, 6, 7
  literature about, 1, 3, 4, 11
  marriage and, 18, 19, 24
  measurement of, 7, 9, 11–14,
     16–18, 68, 73
  naming of, 7
  occupational achievement and,
     23–25
  occupational status and, 9, 12, 14,
     16, 18, 23–25
  personality tests and, 13, 73
  physiological manifestations of, 8,
     9, 12, 13, 19–22, 25, 26, 29,
     58, 59
  prevalance of, 16
  reactivity to stress, 9, 13, 19–22,
     29, 58, 59
  situational variations in, 9, 18–20
  stability over time, 11, 12
  standard risk factors, and, 5, 10,
     15, 17
  women and, 14, 18, 23–25
  work habits and, 24, 25
Type A program (see also Coping;
     Healthy type A; Stress
     management)
  aims, 26, 47, 49–52, 81–83, 111,
     112, 127, 129, 131, 146, 149,
     154, 174, 175, 204
  distinctive characteristics, 55–57
  evaluation of, 13, 58, 59, 73, 74,
     227, 228
  group interaction in, 63, 64,
     66–68, 72, 73, 81, 82, 105,
     106, 113, 124, 125, 132, 133,
     150, 151, 175, 176, 201
  identification of coping problems;
     1, 47–49, 52, 55, 82, 103–107,
     110, 124–127, 131, 132, 146,
     149, 168, 169, 173, 197, 198
  limits of, 50, 51, 59, 66, 75–78,
     151, 152, 169, 205, 220, 227
  physical setting for, 69, 71, 80, 108
  problem situations, 74–77, 80, 82,
     83, 103–105, 107–110, 126,
     128, 130, 147, 149, 171, 172,
     174, 176, 198

recruitment and selection, 65–68,
     76, 81
  shorter version, 70, 71
  structure, 51–55, 61, 63–65,
     70–73, 80–84, 125, 131–133,
     147, 198, 219, 220
  therapist fees, 63, 65
  therapist role in, 50, 51, 64, 71–73,
     78, 79, 84, 106, 109–111, 113,
     125, 126, 128, 130–133, 147,
     153, 169, 170, 171, 176, 225
  timing, 52, 53, 68–71, 84, 85, 102,
     113, 125, 126, 132, 146, 175,
     227, 228
Type B, 9, 16, 25, 68, 83 (see also
     Type A behavior pattern
     [TABP])

U

Unproductive thinking (see Self-talk)
Unrealistic expectations, 147 (see
     also Wishful thinking)
Unsuccessful treatment strategies,
     77, 111, 112, 126

V

Vacation planning, 150, 168, 224

W

Weight control, 5, 75, 76, 220, 222,
     225, 226
Weight training (see Physical
     exercise)
Western Collaborative Group Study
     (WCGS), 9–12, 14, 16, 17, 23
Wish lists, 56, 200, 201
Wishful thinking, 35, 151, 168, 169,
     172, 173, 200, 204, 228
Work
  co-workers, 58, 67, 132, 148, 171,
     221, 222, 224, 228
  environment, 24, 35, 50, 77, 78,
     151, 169, 220–222
  pressure, 30, 48, 64, 67, 69, 105,
     152, 200, 201, 224, 226, 227